THEOLOGY *THAT* MATTERS

THEOLOGY *THAT* MATTERS

ECOLOGY, ECONOMY, AND GOD

Darby Kathleen Ray, Editor

FORTRESS PRESS
Minneapolis

THEOLOGY THAT MATTERS
Ecology, Economy, and God

Cover design: The Designworks, Inc.
Book design: James Korsmo

Library of Congress Cataloging-in-Publication Data

Theology that matters : ecology, economy, and God / Darby Kathleen Ray, editor.
    p. cm.
  Includes bibliographical references and index.
  ISBN-13: 978-0-8006-3794-1 (alk. paper)
  ISBN-10: 0-8006-3794-1 (alk. paper)
  1. Christianity and culture. 2. Stewardship, Christian. 3. Human ecology—
Religious aspects—Christianity. 4. Globalization—Religious aspects—
Christianity. 5. Money—Religious aspects—Christianity. 6. Wealth—Religious
aspects—Christianity. I. Ray, Darby Kathleen, 1964-
  BR115.C8T474 2006
  261—dc22
                          2006017917

The paper used in this publication meets the minimum requirements of
American National Standard for Information Sciences — Permanence of Paper
for Printed Library Materials, ANSI Z329.48-1984.

Manufactured in the U.S.A.

10   09   08   07   06   1   2   3   4   5   6   7   8   9   10

Contents

PART THREE: ECONOMY

Contributors

ELLEN T. ARMOUR is E. Rhodes and Leona B. Carpenter Associate Professor of Feminist Theology at Vanderbilt Divinity School. She is the author of *Deconstruction, Feminist Theology and the Problem of Difference: Subverting the Race/Gender Divide* (1999) and co-editor of *Bodily Citations: Religion and Judith Butler* (forthcoming).

ELEAZAR S. FERNANDEZ is Professor of Constructive Theology, United Theological Seminary of the Twin Cities, Minnesota. Among his most recent works are *Reimagining the Human: Theological Anthropology in Response to Systemic Evil, Realizing the America of Our Hearts: Theological Voices from Asian Americans* (co-edited with Fumitaka Matsuoka), and *A Dream Unfinished: Theological Reflections on America from the Margins* (co-edited with Fernando Segovia).

DAVID H. JENSEN is Associate Professor of Constructive Theology at Austin Presbyterian Theological Seminary. He is the author of *In the Company of Others: A Dialogical Christology* (2001) and *Graced Vulnerability: A Theology of Childhood* (2005) and is currently writing a book on theology, work, and vocation.

GORDON D. KAUFMAN is Edward Mallinckrodt Professor of Divinity *Emeritus* at Harvard University Divinity School. As a Christian theologian, he has been principally occupied with the question whether and in what respects Christian faiths, symbols, and doctrines can continue to be significantly relevant in today's modern/postmodern world. He understands theology to be an activity of fresh imaginative construction of our understanding of humanity, the world, and God, in ways that will provide meaningful and fruitful orientation for human life today. His most recent works are *In the Beginning. . . Creativity* (2004) and *Jesus and Creativity* (2006).

CATHERINE KELLER is Professor of Constructive Theology at the Theological School and Caspersen Graduate School of Drew University. Her publications include *From a Broken Web: Separation, Sexism and Self* (1988), *Apocalypse Now & Then: A Feminist Guide to the End of the World* (1996), *Face of the Deep: A Theology of Becoming* (2003), and *God & Power: Counterapocalyptic Journeys* (2005).

JAY MCDANIEL is Director of the Steel Center for the Study of Religion and Philosophy and Professor of Religion at Hendrix College in Conway, Arkansas. His books include *Gandhi's Hope* (2005), *Living from the Center* (2000), *With Roots and Wings* (1995), *Of God and Pelicans* (1989) and, with Donna Bowman, *A Handbook of Process Theology* (2006). As an active member of the United Methodist Church and an oblate in a Benedictine community, Jay has been actively involved in Buddhist-Christian dialogue for many years.

SALLIE MCFAGUE is Distinguished Theologian in Residence at the Vancouver School of Theology and Carpenter Professor of Theology, Emerita, Vanderbilt University. Among others, her books include *Models of God* (1987), *The Body of God* (1993), *Super, Natural Christians* (1997), and *Life Abundant: Rethinking Theology and Ecology for a Planet in Peril* (2001).

DARBY KATHLEEN RAY is Associate Professor of Religious Studies and Director of the Faith & Work Initiative at Millsaps College in Jackson, Mississippi. She is author of *Deceiving the Devil: Atonement, Abuse, and Ransom* (1998) and *Christic Imagination: An Ethic of Incarnation and Ingenuity* (forthcoming).

JOERG RIEGER is Professor of Systematic Theology at Perkins School of Theology, Southern Methodist University in Dallas, TX. His publications include *God and the Excluded: Visions and Blindspots in Contemporary Theology* (2001), *Remember the Poor: The Challenge to Theology in the Twenty-First Century* (1998), *Opting for the Margins: Postmodernity and Liberation in Christian Theology* (2003), and *Methodist and Radical: Rejuvenating a Tradition* (2003). He is currently working on a book on christology and empire.

MARCIA Y. RIGGS is the J. Erskine Love Professor of Christian Ethics at Columbia Theological Seminary in Decatur, Georgia. Her publications include *Aware, Arise & Act: A Womanist Call for Black Liberation* (1994); *Can I Get a Witness? Prophetic Religious Voices of African American Women: An Anthology* (1997); and *Plenty Good Room: Women vs. Male Power in the Black Church* (2003). She is currently writing a book on ethics as cross-cultural encounter.

NANCY M. VICTORIN-VANGERUD is Visiting Women's Studies Professor at United Theological Seminaries of the Twin Cities and pastor of Prospect

Park United Methodist Church, a reconciling congregation in Minneapolis, Minnesota. From 1997 to 2003, she was Lecturer in Systematic Theology at Murdoch University, Perth, Western Australia, and served for two years as the Principal of the Perth Theological Hall (Uniting Church). Nancy is author of *The Raging Hearth: Spirit in the Household of God* (2000).

MARK I. WALLACE is Associate Professor in the Department of Religion and member of the Interpretation Theory Committee and the Environmental Studies Committee at Swarthmore College, Pennsylvania. His teaching and research interests focus on the intersections between Christian theology, critical theory, environmental studies, and postmodernism. His publications include *Finding God in the Singing River: Christianity, Spirit, Nature* (2005), *Fragments of the Spirit: Nature, Violence, and the Renewal of Creation* (1996), and *The Second Naïveté: Barth, Ricoeur, and the New Yale Theology* (1990). He edited Paul Ricoeur's *Figuring the Sacred: Religion, Narrative, and Imagination* (1995), and co-edited *Curing Violence: Essays on René Girard* (1994). He is a member of the Constructive Theology Workgroup, active in the environmental justice movement in the Philadelphia area, and recently received an Andrew W. Mellon New Directions Fellowship for a research sabbatical in Costa Rica.

SHARON D. WELCH is Professor and Chair of Religious Studies, and Professor of Women's and Gender Studies at the University of Missouri-Columbia. A graduate of Vanderbilt Divinity School, she is the author of four books including *After Empire: The Art and Ethos of Enduring Peace* (2004).

PROLOGUE

Darby Kathleen Ray

We live in extreme times—times of unprecedented abundance and prosperity, times of unparalleled difference between rich and poor, times of war and terror. In such times, we might wonder: Why bother with Christian theology? Why engage in disciplined religious reflection at all? One wonders whether Christians and the wider world might be better off without theology, without its tiresome attempts to connect religious wisdoms and practices with the challenges, questions, and sensibilities of the contemporary world.

The question is not partial to ideology. To some Christians, theology looks like a diversion, a siphoning of precious energies away from biblical truths and living. To conservative Christians, God's revelation in Jesus Christ and in Holy Scripture is eternal and complete; no updating for new cultural moments or political contexts is necessary. From this perspective, theology properly understood is God's (*theos*) word (*logos*) as revealed in Jesus Christ (the eternal *logos*) and the Bible (the literal *logos*). On this account, the intent and content of God's *logos* are assumed to be either utterly self-evident and hence inimical to human interpretation or elaboration, or else subtle and complex enough to warrant prayerful study and, eventually, submission to the meanings God will graciously reveal during such study. In both cases, theology is defined as the faithful handmaid of Scripture, and it is assumed that theological imagination and construction are the prerogative of God and God alone. From this standpoint, what mainline, liberal, or progressive Christians tend to think of as theology is highly problematic—even dangerous—because it appears to privilege human reason and experience as sources of knowledge and arbiters of truth. As such, theology is the enemy of revelation—a sign of human confusion, arrogation, and sin.

For many mainline, liberal, and progressive Christians, on the other hand, theology is troubling for quite different reasons. For some, its tendency to rely on specialized language and concepts marks it as an exclusivist discourse—well suited for the ivory towers of the academy but not for the pews and parish halls of the church, much less the streets and airwaves of the real world. For others, it is theology's apologetic intention—its desire to partner faithfully with the texts and traditions of the Christian past—that is worrisome. Rather than

1

look backward and be constrained by the past, it is thought that theology must untether itself and move boldly into the future. Commitment to tradition can stifle the imagination and create barriers to genuine dialogue and mutual transformation with those from other traditions or no tradition at all. For still others in the Christian center or left, the problem with theology is its essentially reflective mode. Theology is "God-talk" instead of "God-action," and the last thing needed in challenging times is more talk.

The contributors to this volume are resolute in their contention that theology matters for today's world—today's churches, living rooms, boardrooms, ghettos, and wetlands. It matters that those of us who would call ourselves Christian take time to reflect on what we mean by that identity claim, what difference it makes in our thinking and living, our worship and our politics. Clearly, if theology makes no difference, then it matters not. But as this book's authors demonstrate with vitality and persuasion, theology can and does make a difference. For them, theology is by no means a passive parroting of biblical truisms or ecclesial authority, though it takes both Scripture and church seriously. Theology is neither tethered slavishly to tradition nor absolutely free from indebtedness to and responsibility for it. Theology's task is not merely to listen to God's talk, to divine revelation, but also to talk about—and even to—God. In this volume, some of today's most promising and accomplished theologians engage in this passive-active work, this listening-to and talking-about process. And in every case, their listening and speaking inspire and guide specific modes and aims of acting; for them, God-talk is not divorced from God-action but is rather codetermined by and generative of it.

This book is a symposium on three themes, or loci, critical to Christian thought and practice in the twenty-first century: God, ecology, and economics. While ecology and economics have not always been viewed as theological loci, today's situation demands that they be recognized as crucial partners in any theological conversation or construction.

Economics is, quite simply, the world's common and primary language. Global capitalism touches every shore, influences every value system, and increasingly produces the desires and self-understanding of every individual. It is the master narrative of today's world, the taken-for-granted story of how things work. Religious people and institutions and the God-talk we affirm and produce cannot ignore this reality, this context within which all contemporary theology necessarily takes place. Even if we admit that religion has always been shaped by and has in turn also shaped economic realities, we cannot ignore the fact that never before has economics loomed so large and wielded so much authority as it does today. In our contemporary world, God-talk must engage economics, recognizing it not merely as a fellow or rival discourse but, moreover, as that which has become the universal language of our era. Theology must ask about its own identity, intentions, and effects in relation to this master narrative. Like a mother tongue being heedlessly abandoned by the new generation, theology must fight for its life or accept its lot as a dead language.

The contributors to this book are keenly aware of the power and scope of economics in today's world. They know full well that theology cannot sidestep, deny, or otherwise avoid economics. On the contrary, if theology is to matter, it must be explicit, even bold, in its engagement of economics. It cannot pretend to exist in a vacuum or live in fear of defilement by "secular" discourses. Indeed, a key challenge Christianity must address in our day is the increasing privatization and consumerization of religion—the subtle but definite remaking of religion in the image of neoliberal economics. Evidence of this transformation can be seen in the notable shift in popular discourse and practice from "religion" to "spirituality." What may appear to many of us as a mere change in semantics is likely a much more substantive transition. If Richard King and Jeremy Carrette, authors of *Selling Spirituality*, are right, then we need to consider that spirituality's steady displacement of religion is resulting in the devaluation of long-term connections, communal values, and commitment to social justice traditionally associated with "religion" in favor of consumerist values like individualism, self-interest, and short-term gratification. Far from leveling a prophetic critique of consumer culture, spirituality may function to reiterate and strengthen it.[1]

This book resolutely opposes the community-diminishing values and aims of neoliberal economics. It embraces, instead, "old-fashioned" priorities like intergenerational wisdom, communal values, social justice, care for the earth, and long-term flourishing. Contributors to this volume such as Filipino theologian Eleazar Fernandez know that theology that matters is theology that is not afraid to oppose an unjust status quo. It is theology that dares to question the privatization of religion and the sacralizing of consumerism. It articulates a bold and imaginative counternarrative to the reigning economic paradigm of our day. If nonmarket values such as compassion, mutuality, the common good, and the integrity of creation are to stay alive in today's world, then religious people must contest the false gods of consumerism with courage, creativity, and stubborn persistence. For this task, theology is critically important. Theology gathers the resources of the past; envisions a more humane and faithful future; and develops language, marshals arguments, and inspires convictions that motivate transformation in the present.

Unlike economics, ecology is by no means a master narrative in our world. Still, its importance would be difficult to overestimate. We might say that while economics is the universal language of our time, ecology is the physiology of sound itself. Without the material bases for existence—the elemental forces of earth, air, water, and fire—there would be no economics, no religion, no anything at all. Christian tradition has long recognized "creation" as a foundational reality, and yet it has struggled to acknowledge humanity's dependence upon this foundation. Whether motivated by fear and loathing, arrogance, greed, or mere indifference, Christian thought and practice have by and large turned a deaf ear to the cries of the Earth.

Thanks to the fortuitous ecologies of Europe and North America, which have played host to so much of Christian theology, it has been relatively easy for Christians to ignore the ecological substratum on which human civilization depends. Today, however, as fossil fuels wane, climates warm, and sea levels rise, even those long insulated from the worst environmental dangers face an ecologically precarious future. Our God-talk cannot afford to ignore the elemental forces upon which we all depend for our very life.

A major premise of this book is the recognition that theology and ecology are necessarily related. If theology is to be responsible, then it must be framed within an ecological context. Theology must account for humanity's and religion's negligence of Earth and its nonhuman inhabitants, and it must actively foster a relationship of care and authentic connection. Likewise, if Earth is to continue to support life as we know it, then it needs theology. Earth needs theology's imaginative capacities, its conceptual and rhetorical power, and its insights into and access to the hearts and minds of humanity. As this book demonstrates, theology that matters is theology that makes ecology a primary partner.

This book takes up the three loci of God, ecology, and economics in three parts of four chapters each. Part one begins with a kind of preamble: David Jensen's critical reflection on the discipline of theology itself—its intended audience, method, and aims. Jensen's apparently modest typology of theology's primary conversation partners turns out to be a surprisingly comprehensive and compelling entrée into contemporary theology itself. To avoid "muttering to themselves," says Jensen, theologians have always sought other voices for dialogue. Interestingly, one's choice of conversation partner or audience determines in large part the character and content of one's theological project. Thus, where Karl Barth chooses the church as his primary conversation partner, Paul Tillich selects culture, and Sallie McFague looks to the vulnerable other. Not surprisingly, different theological conversations and projects ensue, each of which represents one of contemporary theology's definitive modes: theology as proclamation or dogmatics, theology as correlation, and theology as advocacy. Without rejecting church and culture as key contexts for theologizing, Jensen and the other contributors to this volume gravitate toward the model of theology as advocacy—theology as the active listening to the concrete voices of the vulnerable and the suffering and, in response to that listening, the speaking *with* those voices to affirm and express God's liberating Word for all creation. As the essays in this book demonstrate, church, culture, Scripture, and tradition continue as vital conversation partners for Christian theology—not as theology's endpoints or limits, however, but as vital means toward life abundant for all.

The opening chapter of each of the book's three parts raises questions of method, among other things. At the beginning of part one, Jensen ponders the relationship between theology's audience and its construal of the theological task. Nancy Victorin-Vangerud inaugurates part two, on theology and ecology, by considering the usefulness of maps, mapping, and a maritime framework for rethinking the God-world relationship. The focus in part three on theology and economy begins with Marcia Riggs's enactment of a method she names "mediating theological ethical reflection." This method, which involves a creative bringing together of diverse and sometimes tensive voices, genres, and perspectives, becomes a catalyst for the cultivation of responsive moral agency in the face of the dehumanizing dynamics of global capitalism.

In all three parts of the book, the theological virtue of imagination is impressively practiced. Limitations of space demand the selection of only three examples, but they are plenty compelling. In Nancy Victorin-Vangerud's essay, maritime cartography charts a theological journey of stunning creativity and depth. Having herself been transformed by learning to "see the sea," Victorin-Vangerud invites her readers to unmoor themselves from "grounded images of God" in order to "imagine [them]selves as islands within the ocean of God"—"diving deep into the multipolar, maritime Mystery we all share." In the wake of this essay, it is difficult to ignore the promise of an archipelagic imagination for a culturally diverse, ecologically and socially just Christianity. Mark Wallace's bold interpretation of the Holy Spirit as "the green face of God in the world"—an "earthen reality" that in our time of widespread ecological devastation must be recognized as "the wounded sacred"—is no less creative or compelling. Integrating insights from Scripture, Hildegard of Bingen, and the Crum Creek watershed near his Pennsylvania home, Wallace breathes fresh air into Christian pneumatology. Gordon Kaufman extends his recent work on creativity by exploring the particular place of humanity within the larger web of life. Pressing boldly beyond theism, Kaufman nevertheless contends that the natural order exhibits a set of serendipitous creative intentions and trajectories that evoke "awe and gratitude" and that are strongly suggestive of a unique "human niche"—a niche we ignore at our collective peril. In Kaufman's project, imagination or creativity is a primary, even metaphysical, virtue. Along with Victorin-Vangerud and Wallace, he joins the other contributors to this book in making imagination a priority for contemporary theology. If theology is to matter in today's world, it must be creative, resourceful, flexible, visionary. It cannot be content with the way things are but must yearn for the *basileia,* the reign, of God. Theology that matters imagines life abundant and enacts its grace-filled in-breaking.

In addition to an emphasis on theological imagination, a notable point of convergence for many of the volume's authors is the issue of how best to figure divinity given the complex character and challenges of today's world. One particular point of interest for several writers are impersonal or nonanthropomorphic images of divinity. Christian tradition is saturated with personal images of the Divine: father, son, advocate, teacher, rabbi, shepherd, mother, lover, friend. Is the framework of personal relationship the only suitable one for conceptualizing divinity? Might there be compelling reasons for exploring impersonal images as well? This book's intriguing proposals about the character of divinity stretch and enrich our notions of ultimate reality. Whether it is Ellen Armour's elemental transcendentals, Catherine Keller's "inconceivable edge," Gordon Kaufman's "serendipitous creativity," or Nancy Victorin-Vangerud's "sacred archipelago," readers will find themselves newly appreciative of the potential of impersonal images to express key dimensions of divine reality.

Another challenge taken up by several contributors is how precisely to understand the relationship between God and world. What, for instance, is meant by the suggestion that God is in the world or the world is in God? When theologians use this kind of language, as many certainly do, are they sufficiently aware of the risk they take—the risk of dissolving the distinction between Creator and Creation? Is Christianity to become a kind of monism? Several of our authors ponder these important questions and offer thoughtful, clarifying, and sometimes provocative proposals for how God and world are related. Jay McDaniel's meditation on God as a kind of "Deep Listening," for example, takes up the issue, suggesting that the world is to God as our bodies are to our conscious minds, or as a developing embryo is to its mother's womb: "just as what happens in the womb of a mother happens inside of her, even as she is more than the embryo, so what happens in the universe happens inside God even as God is more than the universe." Catherine Keller's provocative probing of the issue takes her from pneumatological considerations to the biblical book of Job, where she sees "the whirlwind poetry" effecting an "eye-opening dis/closure," according to which God is at one and the same time "the invisible, the unspeakable," the "bottomless mystery," *and* the earthy specificity of "the untamed creatures": "What Job 'sees' in the vision is only the untamed creatures. To 'see' God, then, means to see the creation. But to see with new eyes."

Several of the book's authors encourage us to see the mundane challenges of everyday living with new eyes. If theology is susceptible to esotericism and a lack of interest in quotidian matters, then this book is refreshingly practical. Theology that matters, its authors know, makes a difference in the real-life experiences and everyday practices of regular people. Theology that matters is theology that informs daily living, nurtures life-giving habits, and breeds courage and hope in relation to life's inevitable struggles and disappointments. For Sharon Welch, it is the "sound bite political culture" with which we contend today that begs for attention. She reflects on the challenge of devising alternative cultural practices (for example, new metaphors, stories, and forms of music) to help us engage in "self-critical reflection—affirming, and not denying, [our] capacities as moral agents." For Joerg Rieger and Eleazar Fernandez, it is the church's daily self-understanding and practices that beg for fresh evaluation. Reflecting on the biblical story of Naboth's vineyard, Rieger challenges the church not to identify too readily with the prophet Elijah but to recognize in King Ahab's grasping for power and property a reflection of its own pretensions. If the church is to be a "household of life abundant," says Fernandez, then it must reconceive practices such as the eucharist and Christian formation in order to create an effective counternarrative to the life-diminishing dynamics of "the god of mammon." Ellen Armour takes up the weighty and yet eminently practical question of how our conceptions of the divine and our religious practices are related to the tangible elements of everyday existence: earth, fire, air, and water. My own essay considers the obstacles to humane and sustainable living posed by our culture's 24/7 temporality and *ex nihilo* economics and advocates for a countercultural theology of rest.

The book concludes with an essay by Sallie McFague, whose own theological commitments, style, and vision inspired the collection. McFague's Christian theology has through the years been ahead of its time in its recognition of the interpenetration of God, ecology, and economics. Her current work, as evidenced by her contribution to this book, continues to hold these three crucial dimensions together in thoughtful and persuasive ways. It also reminds us that the energizing and sustaining impulse for all our theological work is our life in God: "The only reason we dare to imagine a different world is because God is before us, God is there already."

In the final analysis, this book suggests that theology that matters is theology that is rooted in tradition; responsive to the concrete sufferings and possibilities of today's world; and inspired by a vision of God's *basileia*, of life abundant for all. Theology that matters is in active conversation not only with sacred texts, with church, and with God, but also with the other vital discourses of this or any other age. In our time, this means that theology engages economics and ecology, the two key frameworks of twenty-first-century existence. Theology encounters these and other discourses with imagination, critical reason, and faith seeking understanding and transformation. In so doing, it demonstrates that theology does, indeed, matter.

PART ONE

GOD

WHOSE CONVERSATION?
Theology and Its Audience

David H. Jensen

Too often theologians do not capture much of the public's imagination. The-ology, the discipline of reflecting on God-talk, can seem rather far-removed from daily concerns that occupy the attention of ordinary people. Because of their supposed distance from the everyday, theologians are particularly ripe for caricature. For many, the very term invokes academic eccentricities of a bygone era: dusty tomes, cultivated isolation, abstruse musings, and knowledge rarely placed in service of the world. Small wonder that the audience for theology is rather limited. The persistence of such caricatures raises an important question: For whom, and with whom, do theologians speak? In North America, theology does not have a wide audience outside seminary and college students and their professors. Adult education classes in most North American churches tend to avoid reading theology. As a result, contemporary theologians write and talk primarily with other theologians. Yet if theology involves reflection on God-talk, faith seeking understanding, the liberation of the oppressed, and hope for the world, its audience—and conversation partners—needs to be wider than those who practice its art.

To counteract the danger of theologians muttering to themselves, theology must seek *other* voices, listen to them, and respond to them. For whom and with whom do theologians speak? For some contemporary theologians, that audience is the church; for others, that audience is culture; and, for yet others, theology does not speak *for* others so much as it strives to speak *with* others, particularly the vulnerable and marginalized. Classic instances of each vision of theological conversation exist in the contemporary church. The first—theology as a church discipline—is epitomized by Karl Barth; the second—theology as critical correlation with culture—by Paul Tillich; and the third—theology as advocacy with others—by the more recent work of Sallie McFague. Each offers a viable approach to theology as a conversation that involves more than the voice of the theologian.

THEOLOGY FOR THE CHURCH

Much of Karl Barth's work sounds as a warning against the kinds of speech that theology should *not* employ. Before theologians can ask for whom they speak, they have to wrestle with the co-optation of theological speech by alien tongues. Writing in the wake of a theological liberalism that seemed incapable of resisting extremes of nationalism, Barth noted the ease with which many theologians related God's revelation to movements in human history. Some of his theology teachers also wrote speeches for the Kaiser, boasted of German culture, and embraced the ascendance of the German state. By the time of the Third Reich, the correlation between revelation and nation had reached blasphemous proportions. A Christian theological vocabulary supplied the veneer for demonic assertions of power and hatred, as Hitler cited the "resurrection of the German Volk" and God's blessing as he assembled the machinery of death. Barth wrote in the midst of these cataclysms, uttering an emphatic "no!" to any movement that would correlate God's revelation in Jesus Christ with other movements and powers in human history. Before theologians can speak for others, they must be careful that others do not speak for them. If theology allows other voices to dictate the terms of conversation, or if it opens the door to a correlational conversation (theology *and* politics, theology *and* culture), it compromises its witness to God's revelation. Barth begins theological conversation by restricting the subject of theology proper: theology is about God's purposes, not ours.

Yet theology proceeds not out of fear of co-optation but in thanksgiving to what God has already done in Jesus Christ. To speak of God in human words is not an impossible burden but a joy: "Human knowledge of God is an act of gratitude and therefore partakes of the veracity of the revelation of God."[1] Theology, in this sense, comes after the fact; it is the human exposition and response to what God has already initiated. Because theology involves our words and reflections, though, Barth considers theology a "broken thought . . . to the extent that it can progress only in isolated thoughts."[2] A grand system of theology, despite Barth's prodigious *Church Dogmatics*, is impossible—and were one to attempt it, it would give the false impression that God is a subject for examination alongside other subjects. True theological speech, by contrast, is ever-partial, ever-feeble in responding to the Word that God has already spoken.

Who is the audience of this conversation? Barth responds in no uncertain terms: the Christian church. Theology has its meaning and mooring in the community of faith. Barth's preferred mode of doing theology is dogmatics, "the scientific self-examination of the Christian Church with respect to the content of its distinctive utterance concerning God."[3] Theologians speak *to the church* not because they have privileged access to God's revelation, but because they have been trained in the discipline of the church's own mode of storytelling. Theologians reflect on what God is doing in the world not by accommodating church-talk to world-talk, but by telling the distinctive stories of Christian faith—God's covenantal embrace of the world that is consistently shown in particular shape: Israel, Jesus Christ, the church. The task of theology is not to communicate these stories to the world by transposing them to other keys, but by clarifying and reflecting on them for the sake of the church. Only by living in light of these stories can theologians speak for the church. The audience and purpose of theology, thus, is well defined: not a well-meaning crusade for the world, but clarification of the church's own self-understanding in light of God's grace. Theology is for the world insofar as it is for the church. Theologians do not mutter to themselves, but converse with the church, responding to and being corrected by the telling of those stories in community. Theology, for Barth, is *faith seeking understanding*, the church's continued search for clarity in its belief as it stands under the judgment and grace of God's Word.

One might suppose that for Barth, the church is defined as the community gathered around the story of God's revelation, made up of those who respond to what God has already done. Voluntaristic understandings of church, however, are alien to Barth's method. The church that is "called out" of the world is nothing less than the "earthly historical form of existence of Jesus Christ himself . . . The Church is His body, created and continually renewed by the awakening power of the Holy Spirit."[4] The church is that sinful, huddling, feebly responsive gathering of people who are *also* the body of Christ for the world. The audience for theology, then, is not a special group set apart from the world, but a body claimed by God in its brokenness, distinguished from the world in its own recognition of its brokenness. As theology is a broken thought, the body of Christ takes shape in a broken body, the church.

Yet the church is also marked by holiness. It is called "out" of the world as holy. Its holiness, however, is not a mark of its moral life or its privileged status in receiving God's revelation, but of its belonging to the crucified and risen Savior. The holiness of the church is derivative: it is holy "because and as Jesus Christ is holy."[5] Holiness is not the church's gift to the world, but Christ's gift to the church: "Jesus Christ is not the Holy One for Himself, but for the world and in the first instance for His community in the world."[6] Barth's refrains here echo themes of election. Behind the supposition that theology is for the church, beneath the ground that affirms the church as the body of Christ, is God's sovereign, electing grace. The ultimately hopeful chord of Barth's theological symphony is that Jesus Christ is *for us,* regardless of merit, regardless of our response. Theology comes after this action of the Word, for those caught up in its movement. One does not make sense of that music by jumping in mid-measure, but by listening from the outset, being transfixed by its grace. Like all great music, moreover, it cannot be transposed at will to alien keys.

On the question of theology's audience, Barth is clear: theology is for the church, for understanding its life in light of the story of God's grace. Only by restricting the scope of theology in this way are we opened to its supreme harmony. Otherwise, theology is bound to meet dissonant chords amid competing movements. This refusal of theology to conform to other modes of speech is one of Barth's lasting legacies. Indeed, it is worth hearing his voice again amid the multiple chords that compete for Christian allegiance. When the president of the United States invokes God's blessing in the crusade against terror, when the Stars and Stripes are offered as a Christian symbol, when the Prince of Peace becomes the legitimator for wars of national "self-interest," Christians have to ask themselves whether their stories and speech are being co-opted for other purposes. Barth's mode of speech for the church alerts us to theology's failings.

This capacity for saying no, however, hampers Barth's project in other ways. One of the weaknesses of his model of theological speech is that it restricts one's conversation partners. Barth's ecclesiology tends to minimize the world's witness to the church and implies that the church is shaped by its own unique stories that are free from the influence of other stories. In construing theology *for* the church, Barth supposes that the church's story is monolingual rather than polyglot. In an age when the church's story has claimed many victims—witness the narratives of Native Americans, African slaves in the New World, and gay persons who experience the church's venom—it is critical that theologians adopt some form of correlational method, of hearing the voices in culture beyond the church that the church's story has suppressed and ignored. The danger of dogmatics alone is that theologians again wind up talking only with themselves.

THEOLOGY FOR CULTURE

Paul Tillich could hardly be described as a theologian trapped in self-muttering. The trajectory of his life, some have said, was "conversation seeking understanding," a life in search of discussion partners.[7] That search proved fruitful: other than Reinhold Niebuhr, no American theologian has commanded such vast attention, especially outside the church. As a public intellectual, Tillich consulted with psychologists and novelists as well as philosophers and clergy.

Like Barth, Tillich initially formed theology for the church, but unlike his Swiss contemporary, Tillich operated with a broader understanding of the *ecclesia*. The opening lines of his magnum opus reflect this emphasis: "Theology, as a function of the Christian church, must serve the needs of the church."[8] The church never exists as an entity to itself in Tillich's imagination. As Christian faith seeks truth, it expresses truth anew in each generation, attending to the particular and ever-changing circumstances in which seekers of truth live. As the church seeks understanding, it also seeks a world and bleeds into the world. Though the Word encounters persons in Christ throughout every age, the reception of that Word takes on varied hues, themes, and responses as Word becomes flesh and dwells among us. Tillich claims his theological method differs from orthodoxy and fundamentalism by its careful attention to the present: "The 'situation' to which theology must respond is the totality of man's creative self-interpretation in a special period."[9] If Barth's attempt at dogmatics emphasizes the *otherness* of the Word, Tillich's stresses the *incarnation* of the Word. As Word takes flesh, all flesh has a stake in responding to that Word.

Tillich has no qualms about calling his theology a form of apologetics. His correlational method assumes that the present cultural situation supplies questions that theology answers by lingering in the questions themselves. Questions of meaning, purpose, and value are not unique to Christian faith: apologetic theology takes these questions seriously, regardless of whether they're asked inside the church. Presupposing common ground between the "situation" and the gospel, "however vague it may be," does not compromise the church's message, but confirms and enriches it.[10] Were there no common ground between gospel and culture, people simply could not hear the answers of Christian faith. "Religious symbols are not stones falling from heaven. They have their roots in the totality of human experience, including local surroundings in all their ramifications, both political and economic."[11] We encounter the gospel's answers as they respond to our search for meaning and purpose in God's world. Indeed, Tillich suggests that Christian theology has *always* engaged in dialogue with strands of culture that do not find the gospel self-evident: Augustine and Plato; Thomas Aquinas and Aristotle; Friedrich Schleiermacher and Enlightenment critics.

If Barth's vision for theology is faith seeking understanding, or of the church seeking clarity in its confession as it stands under God's judgment and grace, for Tillich theology is *faith seeking intelligibility* in a pluralistic world. The Christian theologian lives and breathes in a world where the questions of faith are often more keenly asked by those who do *not* claim Christ as Savior. Tillich's method begins by listening to those questions, regardless of their origin. He was one of the first theologians of his time to pursue these questions *across* religious traditions. Through the encounter with other religious traditions, Christianity learns from other traditions even as it judges them and judges itself. This cross-religious dialogue confirms that the movement of God's Spirit is not the property of any one tradition: "Christianity will be a bearer of the religious answer as long as it breaks through its own particularity."[12] Theology, then, does not simply bolster the church's confidence in its own proclamation, but engages in ecclesial criticism of that proclamation, as it encounters the questions and traditions of others. Dialogue deepens rather than dilutes Christian confession; it results not in the relinquishing of a particular confession "for the sake of a universal concept," but the penetration of one's own tradition "in devotion, thought, and action."[13] Christian confession does not occur in a language unintelligible to others, but relies on a reservoir of shared meanings accessible to many that criticize both church *and* culture.

Like few theologians of his time, Tillich was able to blur the lines between the sacred and secular, because such separation implies there are areas of life that do not stand under God's claim. "The sacred does not lie beside the secular, but it is its depths. The sacred is the creative ground and at the same time a critical judgment of the secular."[14] Theology, properly speaking, speaks to what concerns us "ultimately," that which determines our being or nonbeing.[15] The depths of these questions and answers are accessible to all but come into particular focus in the incarnation, where God's Son takes flesh and dwells among us. One senses that, for Tillich, all Christian claims—about revelation, incarnation, creation, eschatology—become accessible as they take shape in the world. Christian claims do not so much overturn world and self, as they confirm the depths of world and self. Inasmuch as theology whispers the intimacy of the gospel with the depth of human being, the Christian theologian speaks to the world, and not only to the church.

Though Tillich dubs his work a systematic theology, he is as aware as Barth of the ever-fragmentary character of theological claims. This is the case because it is God who "answers man's questions, and under the impact of God's answers [that] man asks them."[16] Theology, as God-talk, is modest, and it speaks in the language of symbol. One cannot comprehend God, as if God were a subject alongside other subjects. If Barth's theology is a "no" to any attempt to compromise the Christian message through alien speech, Tillich's theology is a "no" to the domestication of God with wooden or dead symbols. Any word for God, no matter how anchored in the tradition, can lose its essential qualities as symbol—to point beyond itself and to participate in the reality to which it points—and become an idol. Symbols for God live and die in communities of faith. Theology becomes idolatry if it claims that some names for God are sufficient and beyond change. In this respect, Tillich anticipated contemporary debates over gender and God-talk; even if his conversations with feminism were indirect, his theological method would acknowledge that the word *Father* can die if it is spoken as an exhaustive name rather than a symbol for God. Theology, then, both *responds* to God's initiating action in the world and *constructs* models that describe that activity. For Tillich, theology relies on revelation *and* imagination.

As theologians discern the use of theological symbols, they are both committed to and alienated from the theological tradition.[17] Sustained engagement of the symbolics of religious speech requires a high level of investment and a healthy dose of skepticism, lest one substitute a particular symbol for God, the Ground of Being: "That symbol is most adequate which expresses not only the ultimate but also its own lack of ultimacy."[18] This capacity for self-criticism—of the church, of theological claims, of religious symbols—makes Christianity "capable of universality."[19] In Tillich's dialogical imagination, theology is aware of its own limitations and the limitations of human creaturehood itself. The theologian converses with culture because culture seeks grounding in the ultimate. Human finitude does not absolve us from the theological task, but frames it with modesty and urgency.

One strength of Tillich's theology is its insistence on the interface between gospel and culture. Persons hear the Christian message, the answer of theology, as persons shaped and formed by culture. Christian faith does not hover above experience, but immerses itself within experience. Word becomes flesh and dwells among us; we do not ascend from our lives to dwell with the Word. Tillich's approach, as a result, may call for renewed attention to the body and cultural analysis; it may also account for the stunning diversity of Christian piety and practice among Christians worldwide. The Word, for Tillich, is hardly monosyllabic. Because Tillich consistently engages culture, his approach to theology avoids the trap of making theology a language game accessible only to those who know its distinct vocabulary. Theological claims have to be *translated*; otherwise, Christian confession does not seek the world.

Tillich assumes a coherence between culture and the Christian story that enables the translation of Christian claims into culturally accessible idioms. Creation does not represent an odd sojourn for Christians, but the place where we meet God. Cultures, as they take shape in history, are expressions of human persons in creation and can manifest divine immanence. In most cases, this robust doctrine of creation enhances our understanding of the God who dwells with us in creation, in culture. But what of those cases when the gospel offers an alternative read of "the way things are," particularly as it names the violence of culture? Many have probed the deep roots of violence in Western modes of thought; some have implicated Christian theology in this deadly cycle.[20] But what if the Christian story offers another perspective: that the heart of the universe is not violence, tooth and nail, but vulnerability—not the assertion of power, but letting go of it for the sake of life itself?[21] Can the nonviolence of the

Christian gospel be translated into speech that assumes violence as part of the natural order? Sometimes, it seems, theological claims cannot be translated, but must stand on their own, regardless of how well culture receives them.

THEOLOGICAL ADVOCACY

Contemporary theologian Sallie McFague offers an alternative model of theological conversation that draws on Tillich's dialogue and Barth's prophetic edge while pushing theology toward greater advocacy for the threatened planet. Readers discern in her multiple works a deep appreciation of classical traditions, attention to their blind spots and horrific undertones, and an eagerness to reconstruct those traditions out of the ashes of (post)modernity. In her writing and teaching, McFague invites others to lend a voice. Her patience for those who would enter this conversation as dilettantes, however, is thin. Theology, for McFague, is not a luxury for a privileged few, but an act of advocacy: to seek abundant life in God's world, especially for marginalized peoples, in the face of death-dealing forces that endanger the life of Earth itself.

The urgency of theology's task, however, does not mean the theologian becomes a crusader for those who live in the dark. McFague claims that the theologian cannot speak *for* anyone. Theologians neither speak for the church nor the world. Speaking for others implies that the theologian stands at the center of conversation and dictates the terms of speech. If Barth's approach tends toward overwrought confidence in the church's story, and Tillich's a conclusion that the story of culture is also the church's story, McFague suggests that the theologian must not speak for others, but *seek* others. The conversation of theology always implies a speaking *with*. Christian theology must take shape not as a quasi-independent conversation with a grammar solely its own (Barth), or as a coherent apologetics on behalf of the world (Tillich), but as concretely located, critically engaged speech that seeks others to express God's liberating Word. Between the Scylla of sectarianism and the Charybdis of universalism weaves her attempt to draw *others* into theological conversation—not as pupils, not as mere "sources" for theology, but as conversation partners that correct and give new shape to Christian life.

The sequence of McFague's books reveals a decidedly eclectic conversation: in her first several volumes, literature and literary theory figured prominently; in works such as *The Body of God* and *Super, Natural Christians,* the natural sciences emerge as distinct voices; and, in *Life Abundant,* even the dismal science of economics appears as a voice in its own right. McFague's use of these rarely employed resources, and willingness to be corrected by them, suggests at least two things for the task of Christian theology. First, theology is not a privileged discourse. It cannot expect to make claims that are immune from scrutiny by other forms of speech. When Christians pray, in the Lord's Prayer, "forgive us our debts, as we forgive our debtors," they are making economic claims as well as faith claims; Christian spirituality and economics are inextricably intertwined. Because theology seeks to express the fullness of life in God's world, it expects to be informed and criticized by other voices. Second, McFague's use of broad and surprising conversation partners invokes the wind of Pentecost rather than the confusion of Babel. Hearing each other into speech enables life to flourish. If all speech has its origin in the divine Word that speaks creation into being, in the Word that becomes flesh, then the speech of many has a claim to God's future. Theology that listens only to one voice invariably suffers, because it reduces the splendor of Pentecost to one human voice.

An acknowledgment of multiple conversations also means the theologian cannot speak for all voices in all places. Theology is concretely located. Each of McFague's books begins by locating herself and her audience. She makes no pretense to speak the universal Christian message, but as a middle-class North American to other middle-class North Americans: "We middle-class North American Christians are destroying nature, not because we do not love it, but because of the way we live."[22] As Word becomes flesh and dwells among us, so too does theological speech. The theologian speaks with others not to offer the triumph of that speech, but to add a voice, that one might listen to the still, small voice that is God's alone.

In McFague's analysis, faith seeks. But instead of seeking understanding or intelligibility, *faith seeks others*. If faith does not exhibit this shift outward, it becomes an evasion of the Jesus-story. The restlessness of Christian faith is both a journey into God and a journey into the world, into others. This itinerary takes its shape in the story of Jesus, a story that claims, "The shape of God's body includes all, especially the needy and outcast."[23] This movement toward others is why theology is in the business of advocacy. Theology seeks neither an objective assessment of the present state of creation, nor an authoritarian prescription for the world's ills; rather, it speaks as a passionately involved participant in the movement of God's Spirit, who is already advocating for creation, especially among the humiliated, despised, and oppressed of the earth. Theology is in the business of advocacy because the Spirit is already our Advocate as the enlivening, quickening power of life itself. It is no coincidence that the title of McFague's latest book, *Life Abundant,* draws on a Johannine theme ("I came that they may have life and have it abundantly," John 10:10); John is alone in describing the Spirit as Advocate (John 14:16, 26; 15:26). Theologians who write in advocacy participate in nothing less than the life of the Spirit.

This conception of life in the Spirit and the task of theology yields a surprising recovery of classical themes for church. For McFague, church takes shape

in the lives of ordinary people whose walk becomes extraordinary as they journey toward others. In books that span more than twenty-five years, McFague
hearkens the communion of saints, figures such as John Woolman, Dorothy
Day, and Augustine, who are "walking parables of a new way of life."[24] These
figures, as they reappear in McFague's texts, cause us to see particular shapes of
new life in Christ. "The value of attending to the 'lives of the saints' is not to
mimic them but to pass back to one's own life and read it from a new and different perspective—the perspective of God's abundant life for all—and then to
implement that new reading in concrete, mundane, practical ways."[25] Church
is the People of God; the lives of the saints, accordingly, suggest the life of the
church is restless until it rests in God. McFague's implicit ecclesiology is *ec-
centric*. Just as theology seeks others, the church (to paraphrase Bonhoeffer) is
only the church when it exists for others.[26] The church's center is outside itself:
in the reign of God where there is always room for one more.

If church is only the church when it exists for others, when it is drawn out
of itself, this momentum is drawn from the life of Christ, who makes room in
the Body for the whole world. Jesus Christ is *with others*, especially the despised
of the earth. Christ's body extends to all creation, as well as it reveals the scars
of suffering creation.[27] The Body bears fullness in becoming incarnate and brokenness in its agony on the cross. For McFague, the cross exposes the wounds
we have inflicted on creation and ourselves: "In our time, the natural world
is joined in its oppression with Christ: it too is being crucified. Just as in the
face of a suffering child, woman, or man, Christians see the face of Christ, so
also there is a trace of that face in a clear-cut forest, an inner-city landfill, or a
polluted river."[28] The cross reveals the way things are; writing to North Americans, McFague claims that the material abundance of our life—its consumer
gadgets, its superfluous acquisition—is connected directly to crosses that others
bear. Recalling Luther, McFague reminds us that the cross convicts us of sin: as
Americans devour cheap goods produced in sweatshops staffed by women and
children, as consumer mobility feeds on predations of the planet's resources,
"Jesus turns up in bodies other than his own."[29]

As it convicts us of sin, the cross also frees humanity to live differently:
abundance *with* others rather than consumer abundance built on mammon.
McFague notes, "I believe Christian discipleship for twenty-first-century North
American Christians means 'cruciform living,' an alternative notion of the abundant life, which will involve a philosophy of 'enoughness,' limitations on energy
use, and sacrifice for the sake of others."[30] The cross symbolizes the abundance
of voluntary self-limitation, not in order to mortify the flesh, but so that others may live. In a North American context, McFague claims, we simply cannot
claim to extend that life to others, we cannot love our neighbors, without at

the same time paring down our voracious consumer appetites.[31] As Jesus Christ makes room for others, particularly the vulnerable and oppressed, those who follow Christ are called to be with others. If consumerism insulates North Americans from others, cruciform discipleship strips away the barriers of comfort so that we might not only love our neighbors more fully, but live differently with them, that we might be poorer in things and richer in communion with God, the earth, and each other.

McFague's approach to theology, as it speaks with others, is an invitation to view self, world, and others differently—as living not to themselves, but out of God toward others: "We (the universe) come from God and return to God, and in the 'interim' we live in the presence of God—even when we do not know or acknowledge it."[32] Our own stories are found within the story of God's embrace of creation. Theology, therefore, involves autobiography—a claim that has been present in McFague's work since its earliest days. The autobiographical self is a resource for theology because it is a self claimed by God and others. McFague calls this the "vocational" self—the self drawn toward others, where there is no separation between faith and life.[33] The Christian theologian seeks others because there is no isolated self, because "the story of each and every Christian is formed by the story of another, Jesus of Nazareth."[34] To consider autobiography as a resource for theology is to pay attention to the everyday. Theology—as it speaks with others, as it gives voice to a God who covenants with others, as it witnesses to a Savior who makes room for others—attends to everyday realities and autobiographies. Theology is not a privileged discourse reserved only for the church or only for those who seek intelligibility in the Christian faith, but an eccentric conversation that invites others to lend a voice. When theology attends to the ordinary, it recognizes that "human life in all its complex everydayness will not be discarded, but that it is precisely the familiar world we love and despair of saving that is on the way to being redeemed."[35] When theologians converse with others as advocates, their ordinary words bear witness to the extraordinary claim that God has taken the life of this planet as God's own.

FRAGMENTS OF CHRISTIAN SPEECH IN A BROKEN WORLD

As Christian theology enters its twenty-first century, each of the approaches to theology that I have sketched is viable, addressing different concerns and dangers in a North American context. Perhaps, if theology really is a dialogical discipline, the insights of each attempt might inform the others as Christian theologians face new challenges and opportunities in the years ahead. I conclude, then, with four observations on the current state of theology in the church and wider public, and what they might bode for future theological conversation.

The disestablishment of the Christian church is an opportunity for faithfulness and fuller dialogue.

Disestablishment has a lengthy history in Europe: it was incipient in the Germany that Tillich fled and full blown in the Basel of Barth's later career. Whereas in Europe disestablishment has become an accepted fact of Christian life, in North America many Christians long for reestablishment. For many, the demise of the self-evidence of Christian commitment is something to be lamented. The "good old days" when the church had the willing ear of civic leaders were to the glory of church and world. Nostalgia of this sort, however, invariably obscures the church's own participation in struggles for power that trampled over others—African slaves, Native Americans, or laborers in the *maquiladoras* that line the U.S.-Mexican border.

But what if the disestablishment of the church were seen not as a lamentable demise, but as an opportunity for faithfulness with others? On this read, disestablishment means the decentering of the church and the self, and a recentering of Christian life on the reign of God with others. The risk of an establishment church is that it collapses its proclamation of God's reign into the reign of whatever empire from which it seeks establishment. By empire, I mean the systematic extension of power at the expense of otherness: the power of a nation that regards other nations as satellites for its own benefit; the power of global capitalism that squashes local, alternative economies; the power of Hollywood that minimizes the reach of other film industries. Empires—whether political, economic, or cultural—suppress dialogue. They assume that the good lies within themselves rather than in encounter with others. Empires tend to construe "otherness" as a threat to their long-term viability; they work best when they homogenize or commodify difference.

A disestablishment church, by contrast, welcomes difference and shuns the center so that it may make God's reign known: a reign that sees difference not as a threat but as a prerequisite for life abundant. A disestablishment church makes room for others so that they, too, may give voice to the abundant life. McFague's hearkening of the pre-Constantinian church is not a call for Christian sectarianism: to withdraw from culture in the name of its own purity or to proclaim its story as if no other story mattered. Rather, it is a call for Christian participation in society in a more robust way. When the church is freed from its status as establishment, it can speak to culture without being a cultural mouthpiece. Establishment breeds monologue—the church talking to itself without "needing" others; disestablishment situates the church in the company of others and impels the church to be attentive to those others, in dialogue, and to listen through dialogue for the whispered presence of God. Freed from Christendom, the church might finally become the *ec-clesia*, those called out from the world, to the world, to live into God's reign.

The co-optation of Christian speech by empire is a clear and present danger.

Karl Barth's warning against equating God's purposes with any one nation, people, or worldview is as germane today as it was in the 1930s. For North Americans, moreover, this warning often falls on deaf ears because the United States is the empire of our time. Those who inhabit an empire and "benefit" from it rarely acknowledge its idolatry. American mythology is steeped in a story of a "chosen people," a "good" nation with a godly mission to the world: to bring democracy and freedom to benighted peoples. Political leaders have often invoked the mantle of divine blessing on the American experiment: from pilgrims who claimed it their divine prerogative to uproot Native peoples and plant holy cities on hills, to restless explorers who moved westward in the name of Manifest Destiny, to current struggles against terror that invoke God's blessing and promise to "rid the world of evil."[36]

It is tempting to think that the only danger to the integrity of theological speech comes in the form of nationalism and jingoism. Perhaps an even greater danger, however, is the commodification of religious language by American consumer culture. The logic of the marketplace betrays its own logic that draws on theological language—of redemption through money, of "saving" by hanging on to what's mine, of abundance of things and scarcity of spirit, of communion through virtual means. Even church life itself falls captive to consumerism—when "church shopping" becomes the norm, where worship serves as entertainment, when spirituality simply meets people's needs and cravings. Theological language, obviously, can be twisted toward ends other than the reign of God. Amid these chords, Barth's stubborn "no" to the commodification of religious speech is worth hearing again. One question that theologians of every generation must ask is this: What is the ultimate referent and purpose of theological speech? Is it to glorify God and God's creation? Or is it to glorify my empire, myself, and those like me?

Modesty, reverence, and imagination are theological virtues.

If Thomas Aquinas envisioned theology as the "queen of the sciences," contemporary North Americans might view it as a partner discipline that is inconceivable without other partners. Theology is modest, first, because it makes claims about God in human speech. Theology uses our words to bespeak the infinite, and because theology does this, it always falls short. Reverence, therefore, is a prerequisite for speaking about God truthfully. Theologians always stand in awe of the subject of their discourse, a subject that involves the strange claim that

God has taken the life of the world—my life, your life, the life of the Mississippi River—as God's own. Reverence begets modesty because our language can never encompass the grandness of God's movement in the world. At the center of Christian faith is the claim that the Word becomes flesh and dwells among us. The Word speaks through our words. These words are but fragments of the Word that speaks through them and will always fail to encompass that Word, but the Word can speak truthfully through our words.

If we recognize the modesty of Christian theology, we will—like Tillich—reclaim the pivotal role of the *imagination* in its work. Christian theology summons the imagination for at least two reasons. First, its subject, God, does not exist alongside other subjects in the world. God can neither be reduced to the commonplace nor proven as a fact of pure reason. The God that human beings commodify or prove invariably becomes a god of their own making. Because God is always more than our experience, reason, or traditions, God invites us to imagine as we respond to the divine: God cannot be comprehended, but God stretches the imagination beyond expectation. Second, at the heart of Jesus' proclamation is the reign of God—an invitation to imagine and envision the world differently—where swords are beaten into plowshares, where all have a place at the banqueting table, where strangers to the covenant are brought within the fold. Jesus' proclamation calls us to live into that imagination as reality, as we move and have our being within God.

Our words, as they imagine God, can be bearers of the abundant life of God's reign or harbingers of death. Words about God can be twisted into self-interest perhaps more readily than any other form of speech.[37] Theologians must therefore be careful about what they say and modest about how they say it. It is God's Word, after all, not ours, that is the ultimate source of life in the cosmos. And, because theologians must be modest, they must seek out conversation partners in disciplines heretofore ignored by the church: economics, critical social theory, and gender studies, as well as philosophy, literature, and history. Theology cannot conduct itself as an "in-house" conversation, for such insularity runs contrary to the ec-centric life of the church. Theology seeks the company of others, other languages, other insights. It offers one small piece in the much larger—and never-ending—business of planetary flourishing and glorifying God. Because no one can attempt that task alone, theology seeks other voices.

The centrality of others is indispensable to Christian confession of Christ as Savior.

Some might claim that envisioning Christian theology as dialogical in a disestablishment age amounts to watering down Christian belief—that openness to others comes only at the expense of sacrificing the confession of Christ as Savior.

Yet others are central to the ministry of Jesus of Nazareth; he is the Savior who proclaims little on behalf of himself and much on behalf of others. Throughout his ministry, Jesus seeks, heals, welcomes, confronts, and breaks bread with others. His encounters—proclaiming the reign of God, healing the sick, dining with sinners and outcasts—are not for *his sake*, but for *others'* sake. Jesus seeks others and recognizes their claim upon him, not because he wants to show himself through them (other miracle workers in the ancient world "proved" their divinity through acts of healing and wonder), but because he recognizes others as children of God. He is revealed as God's Son because he embodies the *basileia,* the reign, he proclaims—a "kingdom of nuisances and nobodies," where the sick are healed, sinners made whole, children made welcome, and Samaritans are good.[38] His transgression of boundaries shows that the barriers we create between "insiders" and "outsiders" are not significant in God's sight. To follow Jesus Christ is to be caught up in this eccentric, itinerant dynamic of faith seeking others. At the center of Christian proclamation is not a personal relationship with Jesus, but the Christ who is continually summoning us toward others, not for our behalf, but for *theirs*.

In the Gospel of John, during the Last Supper, Jesus tells his disciples, "It is to your advantage that I go away, for if I do not go away, the Advocate will not come to you; but if I go, I will send him to you" (John 16:7). Christians follow one who is no longer with us in the flesh, yet encounter him whenever we seek out and are claimed by the others whom Jesus blessed in his ministry. Though Jesus has gone away, we are still with him. It is to our advantage that he has gone away so that we may be claimed by others—and Christ in others—as we stake our lives with them. Life in the Spirit is a life shaped by the Advocate, who convicts us when we turn from others and empowers us to live more fully with others. Theological advocacy, as a model for contemporary theology, seeks nothing less than a vision of planetary flourishing: because God takes the world as God's own, we, too, might live abundantly.

IN THE BEGINNING IS THE LISTENING

2

Jay McDaniel

Benedictine spirituality is the spirituality of an open heart. A willingness to be touched. A sense of otherness. There is no room for isolated splendor or self-sufficiency. Here all of life becomes a teacher and we its students. The listener can always learn and turn and begin again. The open can always be filled. The real discipline can always be surprised by God.
—JOAN CHITTISTER[1]

The best nature writers understand their objects as subjects. They know that genuine knowledge of these others demands not only textbook information about them but empathy, patience, delight, openness, and a willingness to be surprised.
—SALLIE MCFAGUE[2]

We Christians are a gregarious people. When presented with problems of injustice and oppression, we like to solve them. When presented with questions of meaning and values, we like to answer them. Many of us feel commissioned by God to preach the Word, to proclaim the gospel, to be a light unto the nations, to change the world. Often we are guided and even driven by a sense of purpose.

One expression of our gregarious spirit is evangelism. Armed with the idea that we have a unique revelation that is the salvation of the world, we have transformed the world in ways both healthy and unhealthy. Today more than a third of the world is Christian, and more converts are in the making. An observer from a less populous and proselytizing tradition—Judaism, for example—can only marvel that a social movement that began as a reform movement within Judaism itself has now grown so large. She might also marvel that in our sharing of the good news it has rarely occurred to us that some people might be happier without our intervention; or that the living spirit of God might work in their lives without our mediation; or that, even as we might have good news for them, they might also have good news for us. She would note that our evangelism, like our image of love, has focused on unilateral action: on giving without expecting anything in return, save the conversion of the other.

Amid our gregariousness, then, there is a problem. We have too often forgotten that there is a receptive side of love: a side that listens to others on their own terms and for their own sakes and that is transformed in the listening without trying to change them according to preconceived purposes. We have also forgotten that the hills and rivers, animals and plants need to be appreciated on their own terms and for their own sakes—that is, listened to—so they can have the space to be themselves. If the Christian life is a walk in love, then this walk should include, and must include, a walk in listening, which is then understood as part of a walk with God.

Of course, everything hinges on what is meant by love. In what follows, I follow the definition of love offered by a fellow process theologian, Thomas Oord. Oord is familiar with traditional distinctions between *agape* and *eros* and *philia* but does not want to define love in such sharply contrasting terms. Accordingly, he does not reduce love to self-sacrificial love or other-regarding love, or, for that matter, to friendship or to *eros*. He proposes instead that authentic love can be expressed in all of these forms. "To love," he says, "is to act intentionally, in sympathetic response to others (including God), to promote overall well-being."[3] If this definition is adequate, then the kind of listening I have in mind, which I will describe more carefully in a moment, is loving in two important ways. First, the listening side of love is the very heart of sympathetic response. By sympathetic response Oord means empathy or compassion. We sympathize or empathize with others by listening *to* them and *with* them, such that their lives become part of our own. Second, the listening side of love is loving because, under certain circumstances, it can be a form of intentional action, something we consciously choose to do when we could do otherwise. As most caregivers know, the decision to listen is itself one of the most loving acts a person can undergo. So often, when people in need seek our help, they do not necessarily want us to solve their problems, but they want us to share in their suffering. Even when problems cannot be solved, this sharing is an act of love.

Of course, for many of us, listening does not come easily. We must learn to listen even when it goes against the grain of our own inner impulses to assert ourselves and be heard by others. An interesting feature of this learning is that it requires education in the art of vulnerability. In the words of Joan Chittister, it involves a "sense of otherness" and a "willingness to be touched," such that the listener himself or herself is willing to be changed by others. "The listener can learn and turn and begin again."

I suspect that, even as we might not be good listeners ourselves, many Christians might applaud this willingness to "learn and turn and begin again" as an essential feature of healthy Christian living. We might rightly envision the Christian life as a process of ongoing conversion into ever-widening patterns of love. The founder of the tradition to which I belong, John Wesley, envisioned the Christian life in just this way. He thought that the Christian life necessarily involves a desire to grow toward perfect, unbounded love in which our hearts are in accord with the spirit of love itself, which is God. Indeed, many Christians will join Wesley in saying that God is love. But this raises a question. If, as I suggest, love involves learning and turning and beginning anew, must God do the same?

Given that we often conceive of the divine reality in static terms, we might understandably balk at this idea. We ourselves might begin anew, but in God there are no new beginnings. Shortly, however, I will propose that even the divine reality, even God, must "learn and turn and begin again" if God is worthy of trust. My point is not that God learns to become more loving. As a process theologian, I believe that the love of God is steadfast and everlasting. No matter what happens, God will be lovingly present until the end of time, if ever there is such an end. But the universe itself constantly presents new happenings, some happy and some sad, to which God must sympathetically respond. Flowers bloom and children are murdered; people love one another and tsunamis kill thousands. Many traditional Christians believe these new happenings are known by God in advance, even as God might not cause them. I propose, by contrast, that even God must wait and see what happens and that this flexibility—this capacity for creative adaptation to each new situation—is part of what makes God "God." God is not divine because God is less adaptive than us but because God is more adaptive. God is a Deep Listening who begins anew at every moment, and this freshness, this capacity to begin anew, is an essential dimension of the divine life.

My aim in the remainder of this chapter, then, is to offer a further meditation on listening and the role it can play in the life of love—human and divine. The essay is intended as an essay in constructive Christian theology in the process tradition, and it builds upon ideas that have been developed earlier in several books in ecological theology, interreligious dialogue, and spirituality in the age of consumerism. It also builds upon the work of Sallie McFague. Given the necessary and perhaps inevitable dominance of visual experience in human life, and given the role that images increasingly play in an age of electronic globalization, I cannot be content with emphasizing listening alone. Rather, I want to suggest along with McFague that a listening heart as well as gentle touch can rightly inform the way we *see* the world with our physical eyes, and that it is seeing that is critical to life, if only because seeing plays such a dominant role in life. The chapter is divided into three sections: The Listening Heart, God as Deep Listening, and The Loving Eye.

THE LISTENING HEART

In the beginning is the listening. Neighbors cannot live peacefully as neighbors, or nations as nations, unless first they listen to one another. Friends cannot be good friends and lovers cannot be good lovers unless they hear one another's needs. Indeed, listening is essential to healthy relationships with the natural world. Farmers cannot be effective farmers and poets cannot be effective poets unless they listen to the rhythms of the seasons, the songs of the birds, the howling of the wolves, the music of the spheres.

Even God must begin with listening. After all, God cannot respond to the cries of the world or share in its joys unless God first hears those cries and feels those joys. And if there was once a time when God existed all alone—when there was no universe as we know it but only the potential in God's mind for there being a universe—then God had to listen to the potentialities. In the beginning, even for God, there had to be a listening.

This suggests that we humans are called to listen, not only by our own innermost needs for peace in the world, but also by the very heart of the universe. We follow God's guidance by listening to others, trustful that in our finite ways we are participating in a deeper Listening, which is everywhere at once: equally present to the most distant of galaxies, the smallest of sparrows, the most vulnerable of children, and, yes, the most violent of sinners. This listening emerges as a diagnostic test of authentic spirituality.

Where there is no listening, God is absent. Of course, God may be present to the lives of those who live and dwell on earth: to the children and the murderers, and to the nonlisteners. God may know what they feel and why they feel as they do. God may be shaped by them, just as we are shaped by those to whom we listen. But in our moments of nonlistening, we ourselves are not present to God. At least this is the case if being present to God means walking with God and sharing in the divine life. If God is a Deep Listening and we ourselves do not walk in listening, we are absent from God even as God is present to us.

Of course, there are many kinds of listening. An advertising executive will listen to other people in order to manipulate their desires; a celebrity will listen to others in order to receive flattery; a torturer will listen to others in order to intensify their suffering. This is not what I have in mind when I speak of divine Listening, and it is not the kind of listening I recommend to us. I have in mind what a Buddhist might call wise and compassionate listening. I mean listening that is guided, not by the aim of conquering or controlling, but by the aim of being *with* another in a sensitive way and of responding with wisdom and compassion. We might call it *deep listening*.

Deep listening is not simply a psychological state, but also in its own quiet way an ontological realization. In moments when we truly listen to others, the sharp dichotomy between subject and object falls away, and we realize that we are more connected to others than we might otherwise have imagined. They are outside our bodies but inside our experience, which means that our own lives are composed of them in some way. Buddhists speak of this presence of others in our own lives as interconnectedness or interbeing. Christians call it communion. The Catholic writer Thomas Berry speaks of the universe as a communion of subjects, not a collection of objects. If this is true, then deep listening is an implicit awakening to this communion. It is communion lived from the inside out: that is, from the heart.

This communion is not simply a matter of the ears. It can occur through touch, sight, smell, and sound; it can be guided by intuition, imagination, and reason; and it can set the stage for more assertive and intervening kinds of love when they are necessary. When a nurse gently binds the wound of a person who is injured, she is listening with her hands; when a naturalist walks through the forest and sees a new bird on a spring morning, he is listening with his eyes; and when a businesswoman calculates the possible outcomes of a business decision with an eye to serving the poor, she is listening with her imagination. There are many ways to listen and there are many kinds of listeners. People who do not hear very well can listen very deeply—and people with perfect hearing can fail to listen.

Indeed, most of us, at least some of the time, fail in just this way. When people talk to us, we aren't really listening at all. We may hear them speaking and look them in the eye. We may nod our heads in encouragement. But inwardly we are hurried and impatient because we have places to go and things to do. Even if we are not especially hurried, we may still be distracted by our own private concerns and want to turn the conversation in our own direction. Before they complete their sentence, we are busy composing our own responses.

And sometimes, of course, when we begin to talk with them, they, too, are not listening. We may be sharing ideas and feelings that are very important to us; we may want to be heard and taken seriously. But inwardly they are distracted by their own private agendas. They, too, are composing their responses to our sentences before we have finished uttering them. An observer might say that the two of us are having a conversation, but in fact we are having two monologues simultaneously. Two people are talking, but no one is listening.

In order for genuine communication to occur, at least one person in the discussion has to set aside his or her agenda and simply be present to the other. This "being present" is no small accomplishment. But the difficulty does not always lie in selfishness or self-absorption. Rather, it lies in the restlessness and impatience of our own minds. The religions of the world—Buddhism and Christianity, for example—offer various antidotes to this restlessness.

Buddhists typically approach it directly and in psychological terms. They compare our minds to drunken monkeys that are flitting from one branch of a tree to another, such that for most of us, having a calm and undistracted mind— a mind of presence—is very difficult. We think that we control our thoughts, say the Buddhists, but in fact our thoughts control us. Accordingly, many Buddhists recommend a daily practice of meditation as one way of developing a calm mind, so that we can then bring into our daily activities a less-distracted presence. With practice, they say, we can gradually find ourselves more centered and more available to the call of each present moment.

Similarly, some Christians who are influenced by the contemplative traditions within Christianity recommend a daily practice of centering prayer. If we learn to "center down" even for a brief time every morning, say these Christians, we slowly understand that we can live from the center in our daily lives. We realize that each present moment is a sacrament of sorts and that the very light of God shines through the face of the other people who need our listening ear. Some, such as the Benedictines, go further and say that we meet Christ in the other person, whether stranger or friend, attractive or frightening. "When I was hungry you gave me food, and when I was in prison you visited me," says Jesus in the Gospel of Matthew. "And when I needed someone to talk to," the Benedictines add, "you listened to me." In the Christian tradition, this listening is the inner dimension of the practice of hospitality.

Of course, as we enter into a life of hospitality, we will not always like what we hear. We can listen to a person's sadness and wish that person were not so sad; we can listen to a person's anger and wish that person were not so angry; we can listen to our own compulsions and wish they would go away. In relation to the rest of creation, we can listen to the wanton destruction of forests and wish it would cease; we can listen to the abuse of individual animals and wish it were not occurring; we can listen to the pollution of rivers and lament their demise. But listening—while including an acceptance of things as they are, even if very sad—can always be combined with a hope for healing and growth.

In short, a life of listening—of hospitality—includes attunement to actuality and possibility: to *the way things are* and to *the way things can be in the future*, given the way things are. The first aspect of listening is essential, and without it the second easily becomes misdirected. If we are trying to help others and we do not listen to them first, we project onto them possibilities for growth that are irrelevant to their lives. Typically these hopes pertain more to our own hopes for growth, or to our own sense of what would be "right" in the future, than to their actual needs and objective conditions. We do unto them what we wish were done unto us, forgetting that they are different from us.

The corrective to this oversight is patient attention to what is happening as it happens, which Buddhism calls being mindful in the present moment. The most relevant and hopeful of possibilities become apparent to us, not by projecting our values onto a situation, but from listening to the situation itself with an eye toward those hopeful possibilities that emerge from it. These hopeful possibilities are, as it were, the open spaces within a situation. A life of listening includes this hopeful eye, this attention to open spaces. These open spaces are how God is present and influential in human life, and part of what Christians call discernment lies in feeling the presence of, in listening to, these spaces. In order to be attentive to them, it can help if we have times in our lives when there is silence, or at least a sabbath from busyness. There must be times when we don't talk at all, not even to ourselves, and instead just listen. This, say the Buddhists, is one of the primary values of Buddhist meditation. It is an opportunity to just sit, just breathe, just listen.

This does not mean, though, that listening and talking are incompatible. When people talk too much, it is not simply because they are using too many words in a continuous way without giving another person a chance to speak; it is because they are not listening as they talk. Consider a lively worship service in which the minister is preaching but the congregants are simultaneously responding with "amen" and "yes" and "tell us more." Amid it all there is a reciprocity, a give-and-take, a communion. The minister's words are like the words of a poet, emerging organically in sympathetic response to how the congregation has responded to him—and their responses are similarly organic in nature. Indeed, the service itself is like an improvisational jazz concert: an ongoing and reciprocal relationship between all the players, each responding to the other in a spirit of call and response.

In our daily lives, most of us are almost always in the situation of the minister or the jazz musician. We are all composing our lives, moment by moment, by responding to the circumstances of our lives, visible and invisible, real and imagined. Listening, then, is a form of self-composition that can occur in, and as, we communicate with others in various ways. It is the social glue by which societies and families and neighborhoods and nations are held together, and it is a creative act by which individual human beings become fully alive. If, as Christians say, we humans are made in the image of God, and if even God is listening, then we are made in the image of divine Listening. Our task is to grow into the likeness of the image in which we are made. It is to become good listeners.

GOD AS DEEP LISTENING

Of course, everything hinges on what is meant by God, and there are many ways to envision the divine reality. Some conceive God as a feeling, some as a cosmic person, some as the interconnectedness of it all, and some as the creative abyss of which all things are manifestations. In different contexts the word *God* can be used in all of these ways, plus more. It is simply a name for something ultimate. This chapter is shaped by process theology and its distinctive way of understanding God as Deep Listening.

Process theologians envision God panentheistically: as One-embracing-many rather than One-over-many. Indeed, they—we—are especially interested not simply in how God is in the universe as an embracing and compassionate presence, but also how the universe is in God and partially composes God. Of course, everything hinges on what it means to say that the universe is in God. Theologians influenced by philosopher Alfred North Whitehead do not propose that the universe is in God in the same way, for example, that a piece of paper might be in a trash can or a body is in space. God is not an empty container or a vacuum. Rather, it suggests that the universe is in God in much the same way that our own bodies are inside our conscious minds, or a developing embryo is inside the womb of her mother. Just as what happens inside our bodies happens inside us, even as we are more than our bodies—and just as what happens in the womb of a mother happens inside her, even as she is more than the embryo—so what happens in the universe happens inside God even as God is more than the universe. God is the unifying consciousness or living mind of the universe, which means that God is everywhere at once: equally intimate to the most distant stars in outer space and the smallest sparrows on earth. And the universe—the stars and planets, the hills and rivers, the trees and stars, the people and other animals—is itself the body of this consciousness.

What does this have to do with listening? It suggests that God listens to the universe in an ongoing and continuous way, and therefore that God is perpetually affected by what happens. The falling of the sparrow and the stumbling of the child, but also the cruelty of the warrior and the suffering of his victim, are known by God because they happen inside God. In physiological psychology the process of listening to what happens inside one's own body is called "kinesthesia" or "proprioception" (from Latin *proprius*, meaning "one's own"). Sight, taste, smell, touch, and hearing are called "exteroceptive" senses by physiological psychologists because they tell us about the world outside our bodies. Proprioception is an interoceptive sense because it provides feedback solely on what is happening inside one's body. Divine Listening, then, is proprioceptive or kinesthetic.

Of course, this, too, can seem anthropocentric, or at least biomorphic. If we assume that molecules and atoms and subatomic particles are the "really real" things of the universe and that all living beings are made of them, then it can seem as if we are rendering unto God that which belongs only to living beings: namely, some capacity for taking into account other things from a subjective point of view. But in process theology the molecules and atoms and subatomic particles are themselves expressions of energy, and energy itself is not lifeless. Rather, it is creative and responsive, as evidenced in the fact that molecules and atoms respond to their environmental conditions. What we call energy at the microscopic level is what we call feeling at the psychic level. To say that there is a consciousness everywhere is not to render unto God what happens to living beings alone. It is to render unto God what also happens to atoms and molecules. Everywhere we look, say process theologians, we see expressions of feeling. God, then, is not the absence of feeling, but the fullness of feeling.

This does not mean that God is all-powerful or all-knowing in traditional senses. In process theology the mother of the universe knows what is possible in the future, but not what is actual until it is actual. Prior to the decisions of finite creatures, the future remains open, even for God. Moreover, in their freedom, finite creatures can actualize themselves in ways that even God cannot prevent. What makes God divine, at least for process thinkers, is not that God controls everything that happens and knows all things in advance. What makes God divine is that, whatever happens, God will be present in steadfast love—in empathy and in continuous yet noncontrolling action aimed at the world's well-being.

This action is the outcome of God's listening. God responds to what God hears by providing the world with hopeful possibilities for the present and future, relative to the situation at hand. These possibilities are what the biblical traditions name the "call"—or better, the "callings"—of God. They are discovered through a combination of reason and intuition, imagination and feeling. The callings change from moment to moment because what is needed changes from moment to moment. The divine call is sometimes to laugh, to cry, to sleep, to work, to play, but always to love. Of course, we humans are not always responsive to these callings. In the immediacy of each moment, we have a freedom to choose between options, and even God must wait and see what we choose, or perhaps, wait and *listen* to what we say and feel. This is one way that process theology is controversial to some Christians. Some Christians believe that, even before we were born, God knew and even chose the exact moment of our death. Process theologians believe we have more options. God doesn't know when or how we will die until we die, and God doesn't know precisely what we do and feel in each moment until we decide what to do or feel. Our decision may be conscious or unconscious, deliberative or instinctive. It may be largely shaped by social conditions, brain chemistry, past personal experiences, and, if we are open, the leadings of the Spirit itself. Still, it is an act of freedom, of cutting off certain possibilities for responding to the circumstances of our lives and thereby actualizing other possibilities. We can make decisions in which our own will is guided by divine yearnings, such that we say, with Jesus in Gethsemani, not my will but Thy Will. But the very act of choosing Thy Will over our own will is an act of choice. The will of God cannot be accomplished on earth as it is in heaven until and unless earthly beings choose to assist God in the accomplishment.

This language could suggest, of course, that God is a personified entity in the sky with a will of God's own. It is important to note, though, that in the process perspective as in many other theological points of view, God is not a thing among things. Process theology proposes that we avoid what might be called "the fallacy of the self-contained subject." This fallacy lies in assuming that the various entities of the universe—including even the divine reality—are akin to the subject of a sentence that exists all by itself apart from relations to the world, to which predicates can then be added. On this view, a human being exists all by himself or herself and then enters into relationship as if those relationships were mere predicates added to a subject. The same grammar would apply to God: God would be the subject, and God's relations with the world would be the predicates. If the predicates are taken away, so the thinking goes, the subject would still exist. In process theology, this is not the way things are. God is not the subject of a sentence to which the predicate *love* happens to be attached. Rather, God is the predicate itself. God *is* the Love and this love includes a listening. This means that the very essence of God includes deep receptivity, deep feeling, deep listening. Without the Listening, there would be no God. God *is* Deep Listening.

LISTENING TO GOD

The life of love includes listening to other people; to animals and the earth; and also to relevant possibilities for their well-being, given their immediate and historical situations. This is the second commandment: to love our neighbors as ourselves. But the life of love must finally be grounded in the first commandment: to love God with the whole of our hearts and souls and minds. What might it mean, then, to love God?

In keeping with the definition of love offered earlier, this love of God will involve sympathetic response to the Deep Listening, as well as intentional action aimed at enriching the very life of this Listening. What might it mean to act in ways that promote the well-being of God?

From a process perspective, we promote the well-being of God when we live with respect and care for the community of life, since this community of life is itself the very body of God. In living with respect and care, we protect and add beauty to the developing embryo within the divine womb. Such respect and care includes loving others and loving ourselves, who are also part of the divine body. When our actions are guided by impulses to respect and care for the community of life, including special attention to the victims of unnecessary abuse and suffering, we are, in biblical terminology, pleasing God. Of course, the language of pleasing God can be understood monarchically. We can picture God as an entity residing off the planet whose subjective condition is enriched by our actions. But the language can also be understood panentheistically. We can envision God as Deep Listening whose quality of consciousness becomes less burdened, and more joyful, by the happiness of the world itself. To please God is to add pleasure to the Deep Listening and thereby contribute to the glory of God. Just as a mother is pleased by the health of a child in her womb, so God is pleased by the health of life on earth and the health of the wider universe, including perhaps the health of other kinds of living beings—carbon-based or otherwise—who may inhabit other planes and dimensions of the universe. Just as a mother is herself glorified—not by having people pretend that she is the source of all that is happening in her womb, but by having people share or at least try to understand both the joys and the sufferings of being pregnant—so humans glorify God by sharing in the joys and sufferings of life in its various dimensions. While God is more than the universe, the universe itself is part of God's glory.

And what might it mean to respond sympathetically to God? From a process point of view, such response would lie in being open and responsive to the callings of God as they are discovered intuitively and imaginatively in the course of life. In the Christian tradition this openness is called discernment. It can be a particular act that one undertakes in the immediacy of a given situation, and it can also be, more importantly, a habit that one develops over time. When we are gifted with the habit of discernment, we make decisions moment by moment, not in dramatic and highly self-conscious ways, but in intuitive and spontaneous ways that are consonant with the leadings of the Spirit, the callings of the Listening. In addition, we become listeners ourselves, thus sharing in the deeper Listening that is everywhere at once. Most deeply, then, I believe this is what it means to listen to God: it is to accept our own calling to listen, to walk through life with a willingness to be touched—even if it causes us sometimes to fall down in despair or sadness, after which, with God's help, we get up and begin again, committed to a life of listening.

Given that the divine reality is an inclusive Listening, though, our own ongoing conversion into a life of listening must itself become more inclusive over time, in expanding circles of empathy. For practical purposes, this means that many Christians and others as well are beckoned to listen not simply to friends and families and coworkers and neighbors, but to what is happening on Earth as a whole. If we listen to what is happening to the Earth as a whole, what do we hear?

The first thing to note is that some of what we hear is quite beautiful: the rhythms of the seasons, the beauty of music, the purring of cats, the laughter of children, the poems of elders, the stories of communities, the sounds of creation itself, including its human participants. There is much to be heard and seen that is a source of delight, and good listeners do the earth a tremendous disservice if they—we—focus only on the more problematic dimensions of the state of the world. Buddhists tell us that one of the highest and most difficult forms of love is sympathetic joy, where we share in the happiness of others. It is easier, they say, to share in the sufferings of others, because we are in positions of power. But in sharing in the joys of others, we become liberated from one of the most destructive of attachments: debilitating envy. If we forget the good, if we ignore the happiness of others and focus only on the negative, we forget that the earth itself is a sacrament: a visible sign of an invisible and holy grace.

Still, there are indeed problematic dimensions of life on Earth, and the Earth is done a disservice if these are neglected. Perhaps the best single one-paragraph explanation is found in the following paragraph of the preamble to the Earth Charter developed by the United Nations. According to the Earth Charter, if we ask "what is happening" in the world today, we must note that

> The dominant patterns of production and consumption are causing environmental devastation, the depletion of resources, and a massive extinction of species. Communities are being undermined. The benefits of development are not shared equitably and the gap between rich and poor is widening. Injustice, poverty, ignorance, and violent conflict are widespread and the cause of great suffering. An unprecedented rise in human population has overburdened ecological and social systems. The foundations of global security are threatened. These trends are perilous—but not inevitable.[4]

It is in light of these trends that process theologians and many others today propose that religious people in the world face five serious challenges, all of which, from a process perspective, form five callings to which people must rightly respond. The callings are

(1) to live lovingly: that is, to highlight love as a defining characteristic of the healthy religious life, recognizing that love itself involves not only

one-on-one acts of kindness, but also a building of communities that are ecologically sustainable and socially just. This requires listening to others and finding out what they need and want.

(2) to live self-critically: that is, to acknowledge inherited teachings and practices that have lent themselves to arrogance, prejudice, violence, and ignorance, and to repent from those teachings and practices by adding new chapters to their religious histories. This requires listening to criticisms and listening to possibilities for new ways of living in the world.

(3) to live simply: that is, to offer a meaningful alternative to what is arguably the dominant religion of our time—consumerism—by showing that once basic needs are met, life can focus on *being* more rather than on having more. This need applies primarily to the one-fifth of the world's population who consume beyond the carrying capacity of the planet, depleting resources beyond the planet's capacities to renew them. If we are among the world's overconsumers, responding to this call to simplicity requires listening to the possibility of a "middle way" between the tragedies of poverty and the trappings of affluence, learning to live more simply for the sake of a flourishing life community. A commitment to frugality requires listening to the needs of others and also to the quiet call within human life to live simply once basic needs are met.

(4) to live ecologically: that is, to affirm that we are creatures among creatures on a small but gorgeous planet, who have ethical responsibilities not only to fellow humans but also to other creatures and the wider web of life. This requires listening to the Earth in its myriad expressions and especially to other animals with whom we share the gift of life. This calling is rightly met by spending time in and with nature and getting to know other animals, recognizing that they have gifts that humans often lack.

(5) to welcome religious diversity: that is, to recognize that all religions contain certain kinds of saving truth, even as none possess all the truth, such that the truths are many and all make the whole richer. This requires listening to people of other religions and honoring the various forms of good news that they, too, bring to the world.

To the degree that Christians and others respond to these challenges, there will be hope for the world, and religion will be part of the solution. And to the degree that they do not, there will be tragedy in the world, and religion will be part of the problem. The need, then, is to offer an image of the religious life in which it is natural to address these challenges. This means that the need is to develop an image of the Christian life in which listening is a sign of authentic Christian living.

Accordingly, we need mentors, and for many Christians in North America, Sallie McFague is a tremendously important voice. In her many works, she has highlighted love as the defining characteristic of Christian life. She has criticized aspects of traditional Christian thinking—its monarchical understandings of God, its patriarchal habits of thought, its anthropocentrism, its literalisms—that have obstructed a life of love. McFague has called affluent Christians to live more simply so that others might simply live, lifting up examples of Christians who abandon affluence in the interests of simpler and more loving ways of living in the world. She has encouraged us to recognize our ethical responsibilities to the rest of creation by speaking of the rights of nature, and she has rejected forms of Christian thinking that privilege Christianity over other religions as the one true religion. Strikingly, she has done these things by being open to the wisdom of the sciences, which have helped her affirm that the universe itself is the glory and body of God.

THE LOVING EYE

It is best to conclude by elaborating on one of my primary sources: the theology of Sallie McFague. In *Super, Natural Christians* McFague shows how a certain way of looking at the world undergirds many forms of exploitation, including the exploitation of people, other animals, and the earth. She calls it the "arrogant eye" and explains that it is not simply a way of thinking about the world, but also, more deeply, a way of perceiving it—of seeing it with our physical eyes. When we look at things with an arrogant eye, she says, we objectify and enframe them within our own internal frame of reference, thus making them objects of control and domination. The arrogant eye would be illustrated, for example, in the way we sometimes perceive animals in zoos, namely as curious spectacles for human viewing, but not as subjects of their own lives.[5] And it would also be illustrated in the way we sometimes perceive other human beings who are different from us: people of other religions, for example. So often we look at them through the lens of preexisting stereotypes, amid which they are disallowed their various kinds of individuality and uniqueness.

As an alternative to the arrogant eye, then, McFague recommends a "loving eye." She sees this way of looking at the world embodied, among other ways, in the careful and sensitive perceptions of naturalists and nature writers, the most gifted of whom see the world with empathy and patience, delight and openness. Whereas an arrogant eye looks at people and other living beings as objects to be manipulated and controlled, the loving eye looks at them like we might look at an old cedar tree or newborn baby: that is, in a way that appreciates them but does not need to control or own them. Part of the secret to having a loving eye, she explains, is that it is schooled in the wisdom of touch.[6] When we touch a tree carefully or hold a baby tenderly, we both know them through touch and realize that they transcend us. Analogously, when we look at the world with the eyes of touch, we know that it has its own beauty which cannot be reduced to our perceptions but with which we nevertheless feel a sense of intimacy and respect. What the world needs now, says McFague, is people who recognize the primacy of touch in human life and then learn to see in ways informed by touch.

McFague's insights concerning vision are especially important to philosophers and theologians in the West, who so often rely on vision for the metaphors of how the world works. In Western philosophy and theology we typically speak of worldviews, but not of world-odors or world-sounds or world-touches. We want to see truth, but we are not quite sure about smelling it. We want to get the big picture of how the world works, but somewhere in the process we forget that when we are touched by others in palpable and felt ways, we know something about reality that cannot be reduced to pictures. Touch reveals an aspect of reality that is lost to the arrogant eye: namely, that our very selves come into being, moment by moment, not by seeing others from a distance, but by being held by others, and by holding them, too.

My aim is to add to McFague's emphasis on the loving eye with a complementary emphasis on the listening heart. Just as we might learn to see the world with eyes informed by touch, so perhaps we can see the world with eyes informed by listening. Whereas touch reveals a unique relationship between intimacy and resistance, deep listening reveals a unique relationship between inner and outer. When we truly listen to another person speaking to us, for example, the tone of that person's voice is both inside us and outside of us at the same time. In the immediacy of the moment, the rhythms of the person's voice compose us, such that she is present inside us, and yet we also realize that she is more than us. This dialectic between inner and outer reveals something about the universe itself: namely that it is composed of entities—rocks and trees, hills and rivers, plants and animals—that are present in one another even as they are independent from one another. What emerges is what we might call an acoustic vision of reality. In such a vision, we see the world through the analogy of music: with notes being unique and different, and yet flowing into and out of each other in a continuous way. And we realize that we ourselves, moment by moment, are among the notes in the flow. The listening heart is the experiential complement to an acoustic vision of reality. Just as the loving eye can be informed by sensitive touch, so it can be informed by the listening heart.[7] The listening heart is an antidote to the mouth that speaks in primarily assertive discourse. It is a way of acting in the world that is patient, that can wait until the other speaks before acting in response. This kind of listening, as combined with a loving eye schooled in touch, is itself the best hope for the world.

Of course, hope has many levels. There is the hope that individual human beings and other animals have for their own lives: namely, to live with satisfaction and meaning relative to the situation at hand. There is the hope that communities have for their lives: namely, that they can flourish with a meaningful degree of ecological integrity, economic and social justice, democracy, nonviolence, and peace. There is the hope for the world as a whole: namely, that it can become a community of communities, some of which are nations and some of which are neighborhoods, but all of which live in maximum possible harmony with one another. And there may even be the hope for the universe as a whole: namely, that it can continue to evolve, despite the inevitability of entropy at a strictly material level, into a deeper experiment in love at the psychic level. This latter hope may include the possibility that humans are themselves stages along the way in forms of development that can be succeeded by transhuman forms of existence, whatever they might be.

All of these hopes are included within a wider hope that listens to each circumstance as it occurs, on its own terms and for its own sake, incorporating that circumstance into a larger adventure, which is the universe as a whole. This whole is not simply a mechanical whole composed of different parts. It is life that includes the universe much as a living cell includes its organelles, or the sky includes clouds, or, to repeat once again the metaphor used so often in this essay, a mother includes the embryo within her womb. I have emphasized that the inclusion can be understood as divine proprioception, a feeling of what is happening inside one's own body. I have called it divine Listening. My focus has been on how all living beings are present in God and can participate in God. In the last analysis, though, the hope of the universe cannot simply be that we humans cooperate with the Listening. It must also be that, even when we fail to cooperate, even when we have the arrogant eye, the Listening does not give up on us, but remains steadfast in its love. This steadfastness is itself part of what Christians can mean by grace. Traditionally, grace has been understood as a gift from God that is unmerited by its recipients. Perhaps this gift is not that God will make everything all right in the end, but that no matter what happens, God will be present to help whatever remains to begin again. Joan Chittister's words ring true: "The listener can always learn and turn and begin again." This is the heart of Christian faith. It is that the universe is encompassed by a Spirit who can turn and begin again and that we live and move and have our being inside this Spirit. In the beginning, but also in the middle and at the end, is this Spirit, this Listening.

TOWARD AN ELEMENTAL THEOLOGY
A Constructive Proposal

Ellen T. Armour

Without doubt, Sallie McFague's *oeuvre* (especially *Metaphorical Theology* through *The Body of God*) would appear on any list of the most important set of theological texts produced in recent decades.[1] Always a stickler for clear and forthright prose, she produces texts that are at once accessible to students, laypeople, and generalists and compelling to her fellow academic theologians. Beneath her constructive proposals lies a complex matrix full of literary and theological references as well as theories of religious language, metaphor, science, and, in her later work, metaphysics. McFague's work is driven by a deep concern for ecological and social justice. It offers a diagnosis and suggests partial cures for what ails us globally. Her diagnosis zeroes in on how Christians imagine God, ourselves, and the world. In *Metaphorical Theology* (published in 1982), McFague first articulates her potent critique of traditional patriarchal and monarchic God-language. She argues that the model of God as Father, Lord, and King that dominates Christian theology is not only anachronistic (given contemporary political systems) but dangerous. It justifies a system of domination that grounds and sustains social hierarchies (patriarchy, for one) and a hierarchical relationship between humanity and nature. Nature (imaged as female) is understood as a raw material to be exploited by its human master (imaged as male), made in the image of God. McFague claims that the patriarchal, monarchical model of God has helped to bring us to the nuclear and ecological crises that our age confronts. Christianity's ability to respond to these crises will surely be hampered, she goes on to suggest, if it persists in thinking of God in these terms. McFague turns to the theological tradition and to other cultural resources in order to sketch alternative metaphors for God (as lover, mother, and friend). In *Models of God* (awarded the 1988 American Academy of Religion Award for Excellence), McFague develops those sketches into full-fledged models. *The Body of God* finds her in full metaphysical mode as she argues in favor of conceiving of the natural world as God's body. Her latest two books, *Super, Natural Christians* and *Life Abundant,* describe the contours of a Christian ethos grounded in and arising out of her constructive theology.[2] In the former, she advocates a reorientation of First-World Christianity from an individualistic religion that looks primarily heavenward to one that begins with the interrelationality and diversity of all that is and recognizes the inherent goodness therein. McFague encourages Christians to look around them—to see deeply (and thereby love deeply) the wonders that surround us. Doing so will enable us to enter into a new relationship with nature—a subject-subjects relationship—modeled on interpersonal relationships and the relationship with God. Such practices and ways of thinking are the contribution that Christians in the "First World" (the top industrialized nations), especially, can make toward ecological (and social) justice. In *Life Abundant*, McFague turns toward theological anthropology as she seeks out the theological and economic roots of First-Worlders' sense of entitlement. She offers theological justifications for sacrificial changes to the materially abundant life that we pursue, largely without thinking, to create a truly abundant life for all.

Like McFague, I see a deep connection between how we think about God and how we live in the world. I share her conviction that living within the traditional monarchical model for God is in part responsible for the ecological and social injustices that constitute some of the world's most serious challenges. I admire the care, attention to detail, and nuance with which she has crafted alternative ways of thinking about God and am encouraged by the impact her work has made in Christian circles. In what follows, I will sketch my own constructive proposal. In many ways, what I have to say is deeply indebted to McFague's work as both a teacher (I was her student at Vanderbilt) and a scholar. Her influence will, no doubt, be readily apparent. If I learned anything from her, though, it is the value of critically engaging other scholars' work—including her own. What follows is both inspired by her work and, at points, parts ways with it. I trust that this double movement both compliments and, ultimately, complements her important work.

BEYOND MODERNITY

It has become commonplace in contemporary scholarship to describe our current *zeitgeist,* our era, as "postmodern." Indeed, McFague describes her task as speaking to an audience steeped in postmodernity, whether aware of it or not. Although the specific symptoms of modernity's passing vary, scholars with some consistency identify "post" with a certain suspicion of modernity's aims and projects—its confidence in human progress and rationality, and in particular, its way of dividing up the world.

Central to the modern map of reality is a particularly strong landmark that will not be easily eroded: namely, the place it has assigned to religion. Modernity responded to the challenges that modern science and history posed to traditional religious authorities by separating the secular from the sacred, faith from reason, theism from atheism. The effects on theology—and religion's place within philosophy—were profound in both method and content. Whereas the first topic in Thomas Aquinas's *Summa Theologica* and John Calvin's *Institutes* was knowledge of God, Friedrich Schleiermacher, the so-called father of modern theology, had first to establish the boundaries of the religious *per se*. Religion, he argued, was first and foremost neither a matter of theoretical knowledge nor practical wisdom, but a distinctive form of human consciousness: a feeling (or intuition) of absolute dependence.[3] Though quite contrary to the overall thrust of *The Christian Faith*, one can see in this methodological shift an opening through which emerged the impasses of modernity. In the United States especially, religion has come to be thought of as first and foremost a matter of private belief rather than public practice. It is surely not coincidental that the U.S. Constitution, itself a product of modernity, defines religious freedom as an individual right to be protected in part by separating "church" from "state."

I see the impact of this legacy in my classroom. Mostly from the Bible Belt, students in my classes at Rhodes College (a church-related college in Tennessee) are largely Christians of various stripes and levels of devotion. However, to a person, they conceive of religion as primarily a matter of faith, which they define as belief in something even though it cannot be proven. God's existence is the quintessential case in point. The project of proving God's existence is, to their minds, fruitless. One either chooses to believe or one doesn't, but reason has little if anything to do with it. Being religious (in its Christian form) is, to their minds, fundamentally a matter of believing that God exists and that Jesus died for their sins. That is, what is fundamental—and salvific—is holding certain *ideas* to be true, whether they accord with reason or not. When pushed, they admit that certain practical actions follow from faith commitments, but those practical actions are largely matters of personal morality, only secondarily social policy or communal commitments. To be "post"-modern, then, is not necessarily to have left modernity behind.

The bifurcation between faith and reason that is symptomatic of modernity would be quite foreign to figures like Anselm and Thomas Aquinas. Famous for their proofs for God's existence, they confidently assumed faith and reason's compatibility and saw belief and practice as inseparable and communal, not divisible and personal. Anselm grounds his ontological argument for God's existence in the practice of prayer. The *Proslogion* opens with an address to God in which Anselm says he does not "seek to understand so that I can believe, but rather I believe so that I can understand."[4] Aquinas found Anselm's ontological argument deeply flawed, but not the project of establishing rational grounds for affirming the existence of God. Aquinas sought and found those grounds in the natural order. His cosmological proofs argue that phenomena like causality and motion require a preexistent unoriginated origin—an uncaused cause, an unmoved mover—ultimately singular, infinite, and eternal.[5] To know that God exists is not to "know" God, however, Aquinas insisted. It is not to know God as God is in Godself (*in esse*), nor is it the knowledge of God that is essential to human existence.[6] Aquinas understood union with God to be the *telos* (end or goal) for which human beings were created.[7] Though fully available only after death, the gift of faith brings about a foretaste of union with God; in doing so, it completes reason rather than opposing it.[8] Thus, to "have faith" in Aquinas's theological vision is something quite different from simply holding as true the existence of God.

Other premodern Christian thinkers would trouble the modern line of demarcation separating theism and atheism. The British monk Pseudo-Dionysius (or Dionysius the Aeropagite), anonymous author of *Mystical Theology* and *The Divine Names* and important influence on Aquinas, distinguished between two ways of talking about God: the *via affirmative* and the *via negativa*. The affirmative approach uses "supererogatory" language (called by Ed Farley "omni-language") to assert the difference between God and the created order. In this mode, Christians say that God is omnipotent (all-powerful), omniscient (all-knowing), eternal (not subject to time). However, these words have little positive content since, as finite beings, we cannot know what it is to be "omni" anything. Moreover, the point of Dionysian theology is not simply to name God correctly in order to ensure that we hold proper ideas about divinity in our heads; it is, rather, to know and experience God. This requires the supplement of the negative approach, which denies *all* attributes of God—including the positive ones. Pseudo-Dionysius's theology is no "mere" intellectual exercise but quite literally a *via* (road or path) toward mystical union with the divine. It is a way of ascent that takes the supplicant to the experience of ineffability, to the point where words are exhausted.[9] This is what it is to know God, according to the Christian mystical tradition, which reached its apex in the medieval period. Mystics and visionaries—male and female—saw this path as bodily as well as intellectual. Specific bodily practices and disciplines prepared one for divine union; the experience of divine union brought with it, on occasion, certain bodily manifestations and obligations.

I am not advocating that we somehow turn the theological clock backward and reenter a premodern mind-set. I mention these strands of the tradition for two reasons: first, contextualizing the present via a glance at the past counters our cultural and historical myopia; we tend to think that Christians have always thought as we think, done as we do. It is important to see that they have not. Second, like McFague, I understand constructive theology as addressed to contemporary concerns but always in conversation with "the tradition"; that is, the various currents and crosscurrents of inherited Christian thought and practice. Moreover, as useful as epochal designations may be, they also often obscure the ebb and flow of ideas and practices across the lines that seem so clearly to distinguish the modern from the medieval, for example. Another feature of the contemporary Christian scene is the interest in "spirituality." To return to my students again, I find that they distinguish frequently between "spirituality" and "religion." The legacy of modernity is evident in what they seem to mean by this distinction, but their terminology also blurs the lines between modernity, what preceded it, and what may be succeeding it. "Spirituality" is their term for one's private religious life. It includes beliefs, but also one's devotional practices (mostly but not exclusively private). "Religion" is their term for corporate or institutionalized religious life. It includes doctrines and Scripture, church services, congregational and denominational structures. One can be spiritual without being religious; one can also be religious without being spiritual. However, genuine religion is spiritual.

In using this terminology, my students are reflecting a current trend in contemporary religious life: the renewed interest in "spirituality" evident both within and outside even the Protestant church, within and outside Christianity. Outside Christianity, the neo-pagan movement, for example, defines itself as spirituality rather than religion. Among the mainline Protestant churches in my own city, at least one has constructed a labyrinth for walking meditation, at least one has hired a minister of spiritual formation, at least two sponsor weekly Taizé services (musically based meditation services). Christians are turning as well to yoga and to Buddhist meditational practices as resources for cultivating a religious sensibility. Not coincidentally (and not solely for this reason), we have witnessed a resurgence of interest in medieval Christian mysticism. Note, for example, the recent popularity of medieval Christian religious music (the album *Chant* by the Benedictine monks of Santo Domingo de Silos and music by the medieval female visionary Hildegard of Bingen come immediately to mind). Witness as well the interest in secular academic circles in medieval mysticism.[10]

Insofar as this terminology follows the split between public and private (which it does, to a large degree), it reflects the contours of modernity. However, to the degree that this terminology foregrounds practices as well as beliefs, communal activities as well as individual ones, we see in it perhaps the beginnings of a break with modernity. Following this trend, then, may present opportunities for taking constructive theological reflection beyond the division between faith and reason and the stark alternative it offers between atheism and theism.

Before exploring resources for a cure, however, the scope of the disease must be more fully explored. This division between faith and reason, atheism and theism, afflicts not only mainstream theology, but feminist theology as well, I would argue. As early as the 1970s, Mary Daly put it succinctly: "If God is male, then the male is God."[11] Patriarchal authority and privilege and divine authority and privilege are mirror images of each other. This insight owes much to the nineteenth-century philosopher of religion, Ludwig Feuerbach, who first described monotheism as rooted in human psychology. According to Feuerbach, theology is nothing but anthropology; God is man writ large and purified of all his limitations. The attributes traditionally ascribed to God (omniscience, omnipresence, eternality, perfect goodness, and so forth) are attributes of the human species—not any of us individually, but all of us collectively. Rather than projecting these attributes onto an imaginary being, we should embrace the collective project of making them real in ourselves. To invoke "God's will" when faced with seemingly incorrigible social ills is to make a false excuse that results ultimately in paralysis. Instead, Feuerbach urged Christians to make the ideal real by working for the improvement of the human condition.[12]

Feminist theologians, of course, maintain a distinction between *images* (models and metaphors, in McFague's case) of God and God in Godself. Here, they draw on the long tradition within Christian monotheism (as well as Jewish and Islamic) that affirms the ultimate inaccessibility of the divine to human knowledge. The Feuerbachian critique applies to how human beings image God, but it has no purchase on ultimate divine reality, according to this view. Yet, to the degree that feminist theology embraces Feuerbach, does it not also endorse—or at least fail to displace—the modernist paradigm that divides faith from reason? The dividing line fills in the empty space between image and reality. Reason aligns with images (which are produced through and subjected to rational analysis) but the existence of a God beyond image, insofar as it is simply assumed or asserted, is relegated by default if not by intention to "faith." Within the premodern *episteme,* or base of knowledge, "faith" was associated with suprarationality, but the modern *episteme* offers only two options, it seems: irrationality or, at best, arationality, an association that remains in play by default if unchallenged.

I also worry that feminist theology implicitly if not explicitly endorses projection as an adequate account of the way images of God function in religious communities and the lives of faithful individuals. Certainly, as compelling as Daly's critique of masculine God-talk is, the obverse is not necessarily true. Scholarship in the history of religions casts doubt on any simple correspondence between worshiping female deities and higher social status for women. My work with the Project on Lived Theology also casts doubt on projection's adequacy as a description of what the interaction between the faithful individual and her image of deity can yield. The Project was designed to bring together academic theologians and Christian social activists working across racial lines. Most of the activists we met found their motivation for social justice work of this sort in their obligations as disciples to a sovereign male God. Barbara Skinner, formerly chief staffer for the Black Congressional Caucus and now working with at-risk youth in Washington, D.C., is a case in point. Her understanding of the divine command to love one's neighbor motivated her to work on overcoming her longstanding self-described hatred of white people.[13] Clearly, submission and discipleship can work by means other than projection and can produce laudable results. It seems to me, then, that feminist constructive theology needs two things: (1) a more complex theoretical account of the interaction between religious imagery and religious practice, and (2) ways of imaging the divine that bypass the split between faith and reason, theism and atheism. My focus in the remainder of this chapter will be on the latter, but in ways that indicate what I think would be a useful avenue for the former.

BEYOND PROJECTION

It is in suggesting a move beyond projection that I part company with McFague, at least for a while. She takes for granted—indeed sees no way around—projection as the fundamental mechanism for producing metaphors and models. Arguably, her theory of religious language as based in metaphor demands it. Metaphors are born when we apply the known to the unknown, the familiar to the unfamiliar. That we would use relationships we know (father, mother, friend, lover) to frame the divine is only natural, especially given the centrality of a personal, agential God to the Christian tradition. That said, McFague is also deeply aware of some of the dangers inherent in projection—and, as we'll see in a minute, of its limits. McFague seeks to balance (traditionally Catholic) sacramentalism with (traditionally Protestant) iconoclasm. She always insists on both the aptness and the inaptness, the "is" and "is not," of all models and metaphors. Keeping this fact before us provides a check on any tendency to assume that models and metaphors name (rather than frame) the divine. Furthermore, she recommends that Christianity keep a number of models in play. Using a variety of human metaphors for God undercuts androcentrism, but using *only* human metaphors perpetuates anthropomorphism, a point that McFague acknowledges in *The Body of God*. I would contend that, in addition to risking idolatry, anthropomorphism keeps us in thrall to modernity and its divide between faith and reason as well as theism and atheism. Although images of God survive and even thrive under its scrutiny, the clear light of reason renders Christian "faith in God" irrational and illusory. The claim that God is nothing more than the human writ large and religion merely a function of human psychology goes unchallenged.

In developing the model of the world as God's body, McFague pushes beyond the anthropomorphic. Chapter 5 of *The Body of God* focuses on fleshing out what this model would look like, where it fits within the Christian tradition, and establishing its usefulness (and the limits thereof) for our time. McFague distinguishes five models within the tradition for understanding God's relationship to the world: monarchical, deistic, dialogic, agential, and organic. She argues that a combination of the latter two (agential and organic) is best for our time. Such a composite model is more compatible with (which is not to say justified by) the portrait of the cosmos provided by postmodern science than the monarchical and deistic models. It also places front and center the importance of addressing the ecological and nuclear crises of our time. Individually, of course, the two models that she brings together exhibit strengths and weaknesses. She recognizes that the Hebrew and Christian traditions are "indelibly agential" in their understandings of God, hence the importance of retaining that model.[14] However, the agential model seems, on the surface at least, to conflict with postmodern science. All causes are local, according to science, a view that seems irreconcilable with the idea of a divine agent. McFague notes that some have argued for relinquishing all personal language for God except in worship for this reason. While she acknowledges the conflict, she is rightly troubled by the fact that such a response leaves in place very traditional personal language for God with all of its inherent problems. Furthermore, wouldn't rejecting all personal images for God itself be a further refusal of embodiment? The organic model, which sees God as intrinsically connected to nature, is potentially more compatible with postmodern science but tends toward pantheism. Within such models, "the world is, becomes, divine."[15] Combining the two not only allows each to correct the other's excesses, but transforms them, thereby producing in the end a more fully developed model for God that, while not without its limitations, is compelling in its own right.

McFague traces the agential model's problem to its anthropomorphism. That is, it tends to understand divine agency in terms of human agency conceived as mind over matter, in a sense. Over against this model of God as exercising supernatural control over nature, McFague proposes understanding God as the spirit that breathes life into nature. This route is opened up by the organic model and preserves that model's stress on God's connection to *all* that is (not just to humanity) without collapsing God and the cosmos. As in the theologies of Tielhard de Chardin and process thinkers, the agential-organic model of God is pan*en*theistic, not pantheistic, since "the universe is dependent on God in a way that God is not dependent on the universe."[16]

Several aspects of this model are of particular interest to me. First, thinking of God as the enspirited cosmos moves beyond both androcentrism and anthropocentrism. "Spirit" is neither male nor female; there is value, McFague argues, in the spirit's status as "it." When it comes time to fill in the contours of this model with greater detail, McFague turns not to specific features of human beings, but to wind and breath. Rather than the Holy Spirit of trinitarian thought, McFague harkens back to the creation stories in Genesis, which image God as the divine wind blowing across the face of the deep and as breathing life into animals and "adam."[17] Spirit-as-breath decenters human beings in a way that Holy Spirit cannot, McFague argues. All creatures breathe; indeed, human beings are dependent on the breathing of plants (and vice versa) for every breath. Moreover, spirit-as-breath reminds us of our finitude, a condition we also share with the other creatures. "We literally live from breath to breath and can survive only a few minutes without breathing. Our lives are enclosed by two breaths—our first when we emerge from our mother's womb and our last when we 'give up the ghost' (spirit)."[18] Spirit-as-breath is literally that in which we live, move, and have our being, McFague reminds us.

Moreover, this model reframes divine transcendence and immanence in ways that I find particularly suggestive. If the agential model stresses transcendence and risks sundering God from the world, the organic model's stress on immanence risks conflating God with the world. The agential-organic model repositions both. Conceiving of the cosmos as God's enspirited body figures divine transcendence as a fifteen-billion-year-old ever-expanding cosmos. God isn't just "up there," but everywhere, in everything, as everything is in God. Recall, of course, that God transcends this model, as well. McFague stresses throughout her work the "is not" of all models, including this one. Drawing on the famous passage in Exodus in which YHWH shows Moses only his back (Exod. 33:20-23), McFague insists that we "see" only God's back via this model, not God's face. Thus, God as the enspiriting/enspirited cosmos figures divine transcendence in a double sense: as the spirit of the cosmos, God makes the cosmos possible *and* exceeds it. McFague's model has the virtue, I think, of figuring both transcendences in bodily terms.

BEYOND GOD

I want to extend the line of argument that McFague develops here toward a more intentional and intensive development of nonanthropomorphic ways of conceiving the divine. I say "the divine" rather than "God" for strategic reasons. Given the long history and deep roots that entwine "God" and "man," I suspect that anthropomorphism will always exercise a certain pull on "God." I recognize that, in abandoning "God" in favor of "the divine," I court the question McFague asks: can a theology without a personal, agential God truly claim to be Christian? My answer to that will be "yes," as we will see.

I will draw on the work of the so-called "French feminist" philosopher, linguistic theorist, and psychoanalyst Luce Irigaray.[19] The complexities of her thought mean that I cannot do it justice in the limited space available to me, but I will do what I can to sketch out the insights that are most pertinent to the constructive project that engages me here. Irigaray uses her three areas of expertise and training to develop strategies for promoting "sexual difference"—that is, an "economy" (monetary, linguistic, sexual, and so forth) that makes space for genuine difference between the sexes.[20] (Our current economy, she argues, construes woman as nothing more than man's other. It defines her in terms of what she lacks that he has; it construes her as incomplete without him, and so forth.) Religion is integral both to Irigaray's critique of the current economy and to her imagining of what will replace it. Like Daly, McFague, and other feminist theologians, Irigaray sees a connection between imaging God in masculine terms and the current economy of sexual indifference. Similar to Feuerbach, though with a psychoanalytic twist, she argues that the male God is simply the male subject purified of limitations and flaws and projected onto a divine other. By reflecting man back to himself in idealized form, God reassures man that he really does have what the economy tells him he has, even if only in derivative measure (compared to God). That central "good" is the standard of value in our sexual economy, the phallus, which grounds "man's" ability to know, speak, and approximate truth. That economy is "hom(m)osexual," Irigaray writes; that is, it generates and perpetuates exchanges between men; women are the mirrors and the raw material in the economy that keep it going. In this respect, religion (specifically, Christianity) plays a central role in sustaining the economy of sexual indifference.

The economy of sexual indifference affects more than just relations between the sexes. As many feminist theologians (including McFague) have argued, Irigaray also claims it affects the relationship between nature (often gendered feminine) and culture (governed by masculine values) and the circulation of cultural as well as financial capital. Irigaray is perhaps best known for locating evidence of this economy in textual traditions that Western culture values highly. She uses a method she calls *mimetisme* (mimicry), in which the female reader/writer "resubmits herself—inasmuch as she is on the side of the 'perceptible,' of 'matter'—to 'ideas,' in particular to ideas about herself, that are elaborated in/by a masculine logic, but so as to make 'visible,' by an effect of playful repetition, what was supposed to remain invisible: the cover-up of a possible operation of the feminine in language."[21] The method owes a great deal to psychoanalysis in that it seeks access to a kind of textual unconscious via the traces left on the surface. Her ultimate aim is therapeutic, in a sense: she seeks to undo the cultural damage that these symptoms reflect. Significantly, given my engagement with McFague here, these traces often take the form of the metaphors and other figures used by a writer. In the work of the canonical philosophers of the Western tradition, for example, Irigaray uncovers the raw materials (earth, water, air, fire—the pre-Socratic elements) out of which Nietzsche (water) and Heidegger (air), for example, unwittingly construct their work.[22] These materials are transcendent in at least two senses. The work of these philosophers would collapse without the material infrastructure that sustains them. That these elements perform this essential labor goes unnoticed by the philosophers and thus, in a certain sense, exceeds their control. Their presence in the philosophical tradition enables subversive readings of that tradition in order to gather resources for constructing a symbolic economy that makes place for sexual difference.

Irigaray suggests two routes by which religion could play a role in constructing such an economy. One involves an appropriation of the mechanism of projection on women's behalf. In her essay "Divine Women," Irigaray argues that women need a god of their own to sustain their subjectivity like God-the-Father sustains men's subjectivity.[23] Readers will not be surprised to learn that I do not find this proposal persuasive. Irigaray would certainly be vulnerable to the critique of projection I make above.[24] Moreover, I have argued elsewhere that this aspect of her work does nothing to address issues of diversity between women.[25] In *An Ethics of Sexual Difference,* however, Irigaray offers another, more intriguing proposal. Noting that divinity is the open horizon that is essential to all human becoming, she envisions the inauguration of "another epoch in history" in which religion plays a vital role. This new epoch would come about "by means of the opening of a *sensible transcendental* that ad-vents through us, for which *we would be* the mediators and bridges. Not only in mourning for the dead God of Nietzsche, not waiting passively for the god to come, but by conjuring it up among and across us, within and between us, as resurrection or transfiguration of blood, of flesh, through a language and an ethics that is ours."[26]

Theologians Serene Jones and Grace Jantzen both view Irigaray's evocation of a sensible transcendental as caught up in the cycle of projection.[27] Indeed, when considered in the abstract, I think they are right. However, when concretized in the form of specific metaphors for the divine—and deployed in conjunction with McFague's theory of metaphor—the sensible transcendental provides a way out of the cycle of projection. I have argued elsewhere that the pre-Socratic elements are good candidates for sensible transcendentals and thus for concrete figurations of the divine. They exhibit the paradoxical configuration of transcendence and immanence that the term "sensible transcendental" itself embodies. Within the Western philosophical tradition, transcendence has usually been associated with breaking the bonds of the sensible, the material. Yet, as we saw above, the elements embody a material transcendence. The traditional concept of transcendence implicitly and often explicitly denigrates or devalues materiality. To the degree that materiality (like nature) is associated with femininity, such denigration is arguably a symptom of the economy of sexual indifference. Thus, the elements function like the "sensible transcendental" Irigaray envisions—as interventions in the economy of sexual indifference. Potentially, they "transfigure . . . flesh . . . through a language," if not yet an ethics (more about that later), "that is ours".[28]

AN ELEMENTAL THEOLOGY

In the space remaining, I want to sketch the outlines of this theological proposal, drawing attention to and drawing on connections with McFague's work. The reframing of immanence and transcendence that the sensible transcendentals engender resonates with and potentially extends McFague's own reframing. That one of the sensible transcendentals is air, a central detail in McFague's sketch of the model of God as enspirited cosmos provides another point of contact. But it is also the differences between these sensible transcendentals and McFague's model that draw me to them as routes for getting beyond the impasses of modernity. Since they neither arise from nor invoke the mechanism of projection, they bypass the problems of anthropocentrism. Thus, a theological appropriation of these particular sensible transcendentals renders moot certain aspects of the conflict between faith and reason and its limited choices between theism and atheism. One does not have to decide whether or not to believe in the existence of earth, fire, air, or water. Furthermore, they are not easily assigned a place on one side or the other of the divide between theism and atheism. Admittedly, we are indeed at a considerable distance from the notion of a personal, agential deity.[29] But we have not crossed over into a pure and simple atheism, especially if we read the elements through McFague's theory of religious language.

Like the human relationships that McFague develops into models of God, sensible transcendentals frame rather than name the divine. As McFague notes, the frame matters a great deal to what you see. Since the elements are not anthropomorphic in origin, they rather dramatically torque traditional Christian theism. Their particular combination of "is" and "is not," aptness and inaptness, in relationship to theism needs to be highlighted. Sensible transcendentals retain certain aspects of traditional Christian theism's insistence on divine transcendence; we are utterly dependent on them for our existence, and yet they exceed our grasp. Without air, for example, we literally could not exist, yet it does its work almost invisibly. The deepest parts of the oceans, the molten center of the earth, are literally inaccessible to us. The elements "are not" a God, properly speaking, yet they "are" that in which we "live, move, and have our being."

Elemental theology, then, refocuses attention from an invisible, disembodied-but-agential transcendence to a (more or less) visible, embodied, impersonal transcendence.

Moreover, we are not as far as it might at first appear from the Christian tradition. Framing the divine through sensible transcendentals draws our attention to ritual rather than doctrine. The central Christian rituals, baptism and eucharist, connect immediately with water and earth. The waters of baptism signify the move from sin to redemption, death to rebirth. The grain and grapes that become bread and wine (and ultimately body and blood) are products of earth and water. The Feast of Pentecost celebrates the descent of the Holy Spirit—in the form of "divided tongues, as of fire" (Acts 2:3)—on Christ's apostles, endowing their ministry with new authority as each listener heard the gospel message in his or her own native tongue. The Feast of the Ascension calls attention to air as the medium through which Christ ascends, thus linking the heavens and the Earth, the human and the divine.

What work would elemental theology do? What implications for Christian life arise from such a theology? Taking sensible transcendentals as figures of the divine offers resources to address the ecological crisis that motivates McFague's work. We are quite literally sustained by air, water, and earth—physically and, if we adopt this way of thinking, spiritually. We have, then, religious and moral obligations to the natural world. Elemental theology repositions the relationship between divinity, humanity, and the natural world in ways that further complement McFague's vision. The elements bind all three together in a fragile network of interdependency rather than domination. This way of thinking reconfigures the relationship between religiosity and mortality. Again, if my students are reliable examples, many Christians think of their religion as a matter of a vertical relationship between individuals and God whose ultimate payoff is life after death. When the next world becomes one's ultimate concern, it is all too easy to ignore the needs of this world. Elemental theology offers a different, even shocking, relationship to mortality. Rather than focusing on escaping it, figuring the divine as the air we breathe, for example, confronts us with our own finitude, a condition we share with all of nature (including the air itself), thus raising the stakes in ecological justice.[30]

So far, I have focused on only three of the four pre-Socratic elements. Fire opens up a different path for elemental theology, one that refigures the relationship between unity and diversity. In the event of Pentecost, community is produced not in spite of (linguistic) difference, but through it. When viewed against this background, the implications of figuring the divine as fire are potentially quite helpful. Christianity is, after all, a global religion and thus diverse in cultural shape and theological perspective. As the recent and ongoing debates within the Anglican communion over homosexuality make clear, dealing with diversity is not always easy or peaceful. Fire is at one and the same time among the most helpful and the most dangerous of the pre-Socratic elements, as the ancient Greek myth of Prometheus, the giver of fire, attests. When carefully tended, it provides warmth and comfort, but it can easily get out of hand and become violent and violating. Its paradoxical combination of the domestic and the feral is particularly salient for our time. If modernity aimed to domesticate religion (partly in response to the religious wars in seventeenth-century Europe), the events of September 11, 2001, were a violent reminder (though hardly the first) of religion's slumbering ferocity. We lie to ourselves if we think that Islam is the only monotheistic tradition open to such violence; familiarity with the most basic features of Christianity proves otherwise. Imaging the divine as fire speaks to the dangers and risks of religious zeal; real destruction can result. We should be careful, then, to claim that the divine fire flames in us.

Diversity is, of course, not only internal to Christianity. Another feature of the so-called "global village" is religious pluralism. While hardly a new feature of human culture, it poses distinctive challenges and offers new opportunities for contemporary Christian theology. Religious pluralism is a lived daily reality for many of us. In Memphis, Tennessee, where I live, one can find not just a church on every street corner (along with at least three synagogues), but mosques and Hindu and Buddhist temples, as well as a Church of Scientology (thanks to Isaac Hayes and Lisa Marie Presley's Memphis ties). Many Americans practice an amalgamation of religious traditions. They may attend an Episcopal service on Sunday morning, participate in a Native American drum circle on Wednesday evening, and go to yoga class on Saturday. Christian theology has been rather slow to provide critical and constructive reflection on this aspect of religiosity. Elemental theology can help jump-start that process.

The elements do not map neatly onto a unitary deity. Indeed, I would argue that this is part of their value to us. Insofar as Christianity's ability to engage deeply with nontheistic or polytheistic religious traditions is hampered by its enthrallment to personal, agential, monotheistic understandings of divinity, then thinking outside the bounds of that understanding could go some distance in furthering interreligious dialogue. Its reorientation of theology toward practices should be particularly helpful since the boundary crossings between religious traditions are occurring there.

CONCLUSION

No doubt, some will resist my proposal of an elemental theology as an unwelcome "regression" to some form of "primitive nature religion," a particularly wrong-headed move in the wake of a recent series of natural disasters. I write only months after the tsunami that devastated much of South Asia, and in the more immediate wake of a horrific hurricane season (which included Katrina, a storm that all but destroyed much of the U.S. Gulf Coast), and an earthquake in Kashmir that killed at least 50,000 people. Whatever value might reside in my proposal for an elemental theology, surely its "is" meets its limit in its "is not" here.

Perhaps, but not yet. I note first of all that such a criticism draws on yet another modernist narrative, that of the progression in human culture from "primitive" nature religion to Christianity, a teleology familiar to us in various forms of post-Kantian theology, philosophy, and theories of religion. I trust I need not repeat here the well-established criticisms of that trajectory. Moreover, I would argue that to promote an elemental theology in the wake of modernity— even were such a move motivated by nostalgic interests—is not to recapitulate the past. We cannot return to a premodern perspective, however appealing (or not) that might be. Moreover, elemental theology's effects will be conditioned necessarily by its deployment in modernity's wake. Let me illustrate by considering one of these recent catastrophic events, Hurricane Katrina, through the lens of this kind of theology.

Hurricane Katrina threw its full fury at the Gulf Coast, leaving thousands dead and tens of thousands homeless. The horror that unfolded in the immediate aftermath of the storm caught the nation up short. Those of us watching at home on TV were horrified at the level of human (and animal) suffering that appeared on our screens, particularly in New Orleans. We were astounded as much by the ineptitude of the federal government's response to a catastrophic event that it knew was on the way as by the devastation wrought by "Mother Nature."

It should come as no surprise that, fast on the heels of the storm's fury came public figures who pronounced the storm an act of divine judgment. In *Come Hell or High Water: Hurricane Katrina and the Color of Disaster,* cultural critic and scholar Michael Eric Dyson documents several of these pronouncements from on high.[31] Not coincidentally, the theodicies they deploy are rooted in the traditional theologies that McFague critiques. In addition to offering his own trenchant critiques of the inadequacy and injustice of these pronouncements, Dyson endorses the call to take the question of theodicy seriously. Questions of God's role in catastrophic events give particular depth to inquiries into the way we understand—or ought to understand—the relationship between the divine, the human, and nature.

Elemental theology as I have sketched it out can be helpful here because of the way it reframes those very fundamental relationships. To the degree that it pushes us to think of the divine as "in" nature and nature "in" the divine, elemental theology reframes our approach to nature in ways that resonate with McFague's insights. Rather than raw material that human beings are entitled by divine mandate to master and exhaust, elemental theology acknowledges that "nature" transcends humanity's ability to subject it to our will. Our divine mandate should be reframed as cooperation rather than conquest, it suggests. Elemental theology also counters the tendency of modern theology to domesticate the divine. To think divinity *as if* it were wild winds and water is undoubtedly jolting and jarring, but good metaphors often are, as McFague has taught us. Recall that the book of Job, itself a stringent critique of retributive theodicies such as those employed in Katrina's wake, concludes with God addressing Job out of a whirlwind. Via a series of poetic figures that recall the making and remaking of creation, God reminds Job not to presume that he knows how the divine mind works—a bracing tonic for us after modernity, perhaps.

Elemental theology also complements McFague's call for a theology that places humanity within nature rather than outside it—a particularly useful insight here. In the days, weeks, and months that have followed, journalists have unpacked layer upon layer of the realities that laid the groundwork for catastrophic devastation and suffering. Dyson's analysis calls on much of that work to depict Hurricane Katrina as a "perfect storm" formed by the intersection of a powerful hurricane with decades of environmental exploitation, systemic poverty and racism, and government ineptitude at all levels. Whatever the role of the wind and water in the violent storm itself, the catastrophe of Hurricane Katrina is not *merely* natural. Human hubris, greed, and negligence laid the groundwork for and exacerbated the extent of the damage.

In reframing the relationship between humanity, nature, and the divine, elemental theology heeds McFague's call for a theology that disables escape from responsibility in hope for divine rescue. Rather, we are called to acknowledge our responsibilities, our power and its limits—essential insights that we must continue to plumb as we live further into this postmodern, ecological, nuclear age.

GOD AND POWER, PROPHETS, AND NATIVE LANDS

Joerg Rieger

GOD'S POWER AND OUR POWER

"We must do all we can to help those who have no power, to empower those who are powerless. We need to use power for the powerless," the preacher passionately proclaimed to the congregation. Reminders of this kind—that the Christian faith cannot just be a private matter and that we must be there for the disadvantaged—were not unfamiliar to our inner-city congregation. Yet somehow there was a tension in this sermon and, in fact, in the whole worship service that Sunday morning, something that I suspect might be indicative of a much deeper problem in many of our churches and theological efforts in the United States today.

At a time when the imbalances and gaps of our society become ever more pronounced, many well-meaning Christians feel called to respond. A large number of churches have been getting ready for quite some time to step into the gaps created by cuts in the nation's welfare system. In fact, the role of the churches takes on more and more importance because the Bush administration continues to increase funding to faith-based programs while cutting funding to most other existing governmental programs. In their well-meaning efforts to help, some of the leaders of the church might even recall a few vague memories about liberation theology from their seminary days, now faded away into some kind of advocacy language. But something is not quite right with this picture.

THE POWER OF THE PROPHET

The biblical text on which the above sermon was based might help us understand the problem. The story of Naboth's Vineyard (1 Kings 21:1-29) tells of King Ahab's schemes to extend his backyard and to acquire the vineyard of Naboth, an ordinary citizen. As the story unfolds, the king's power prevails, Ahab gets the vineyard, and Naboth ends up dead. In the final scene, the prophet Elijah is sent by God to pronounce judgment against Ahab and his household. The sermon raised the question of where the church would be in the story.

We quickly found ourselves in the role of Elijah. The reasons for that decision seemed so obvious that the preacher did not seem to feel a need to address them explicitly. Who else but the church could be proclaiming with the prophets, "Thus says the Lord"? And have we not, in recent decades, begun to focus more on the prophetic ministry of the church?

However, despite the logic of the argument and its resonance with some established theological and ethical schools, something is not quite right with this reference to prophecy. The order of worship that Sunday morning could have given us a clue. In the liturgy of Holy Communion, the confession of sin was dropped. Then, during the time when people in the congregation select two or three hymns, someone suggested the classic "America the Beautiful," to which the pastor, against custom, had the whole congregation rise. In this context, things were not helped by the fact that the Social Creed of the United Methodist Church was recited with its emphasis on commitment to social action.[1]

All these elements in one way or another affirm the church in the role of the prophet Elijah. The church harbors few doubts that it is, by and large, a decent institution and that most of its pronouncements are, by default, on the same level as prophetic speech introduced by "Thus says the Lord." Dropping the confession of sin, as in this particular worship service, reassures us that we are good people and that God is always on *our* side, no matter what. Of course, even if we had followed the traditional liturgy and confessed our sins, one wonders whether our generic confessions of sin go very far in helping us understand the particular shape of our sinfulness. Generic confessions normalize the situation by creating the impression that not much can be done anyway; everyone knows that we will confess the same things again next time. In addition, singing triumphalist hymns like "America the Beautiful" and many others affirms the church's self-confidence of being in tune with God's will and proclamation. In this context, proclaiming our social commitments and prophetic tasks (all the way to the "elimination of economic and social distress") may lead us in the wrong direction. What if the church is not in the role of the prophet Elijah to begin with? Worse yet, what if we are in the role of King Ahab?

THE POWER OF THE SOVEREIGN

The story of Naboth's vineyard might help us to come to a different perspective on ourselves and on power. In this story, the top-down power of the sovereign prevails, even though he has to resort to a trick. Ahab's wife, Jezebel, helps the frustrated king to get rid of Naboth and to acquire his vineyard through a deceptive scheme. She arranges for a false accusation against Naboth, blaming him for blaspheming God and the king. Naboth is accused before the assembly of elders "in the presence of the people" (21:13) and then stoned to death. The scheme works on the basis of a theology that leaves no doubt that God is on the side of the king. As a result, God is claimed for the sovereign, and generally for those in power, and God blesses their endeavors and possessions. It is not hard to imagine King Ahab singing "My vineyard, 'tis of thee." The plot of the story shifts only when the prophet Elijah enters the scene and pronounces the judgment of God on the injustice done by Ahab.[2]

When contemporary Christians in the United States read this story, we quickly identify with the prophet Elijah and share his outrage. Yet, unlike Elijah, we cannot claim to enter the scene of the crime from the outside. We live in a country that is built on a history of expropriated land, and we find ourselves in a world where land and much else continues to be expropriated in the name of globalization. When we sing the hymn "My country, 'tis of thee," we sing of expropriated land. While the hymn only mentions God and us, assuming that God gave us the land, what about those Native Americans who used to live in this land and who continue to live here?

While the story seems to be settled when the prophet Elijah pronounces the judgment on King Ahab, we need to take a closer look at what is going on. If we want to find out the full truth about the story we need to include the perspective of Naboth. From this perspective the question of power becomes clearer. The clash of Naboth and Ahab is a clash of two different kinds of power. Naboth's stubborn refusal to sell his land creates serious headaches for Ahab—to the point of a severe depression manifested by Ahab's refusal to eat (21:4). After all, Naboth has the backing of the traditions of the land—the land is his ancestral inheritance (21:3). Naboth also has the backing of the ancient legal tradition of Israel that limits the powers of the king in relation to the people.[3] Naboth's power is strong enough to resist a profitable trade (Ahab promises him an even better vineyard or money [21:2]) and a king who is obviously leaning on him to sell.[4] Nevertheless, in the end the power of the sovereign is able to enforce the transaction and Naboth is killed. This marks the historical transition to a more absolute form of royal power in Israel that, while rejected not only by Naboth and Elijah but also by the writer of the text, is nevertheless acknowledged by the "elders and nobles who lived with Naboth in his city" (21:8).[5]

Naboth's story—which presents most likely a pattern in old Israel rather than an isolated incident—can teach us some important insights about power.[6] The top-down power of the sovereign tends to move toward more and more absolute forms, but it does so in different ways. Top-down power, particularly in the stages before it has reached more absolute forms, does not always present itself in clearly visible forms, nor does it always achieve its goals by open battles. If Ahab's actions were clear and for all to see, there might have been trouble. If

Ahab had simply sent his army to kill Naboth and to take over the vineyard, the people might have rebelled. No doubt, in our own U.S. history some battles for land have been fought in precisely that way, but always at a certain risk of resistance and criticism. Even today, in the midst of open warfare in Iraq, the U.S. government cannot afford to have too many pictures shown, let alone to announce how many Iraqi people have died. At the same time, we have become more sophisticated than Ahab in our hidden moves of top-down power. Our absolute top-down power no longer needs to be demonstrated by confiscating the land of others since we have learned that we do not need to own the vineyard in order to profit from the grapes (or oil, as the matter may be). We now have other modes of power, some of which work through economic registers rather than through direct political ones.

In the case of Naboth's vineyard, top-down power proceeds under the guise of legitimacy. Naboth's sentencing to death appears to be just according to the law, which states that those who curse God and the king must die. The earlier history of our own appropriation of the land in the United States also appeared just according to the law and some law-like doctrines. Much of the land of the United States has been appropriated through official treaties and other actions that had the appearance of legitimacy. Legitimacy was also provided by the doctrine of Manifest Destiny, which said that Europeans were charged by God to take over the North American continent.[7] In the more recent case of the war against Iraq, legitimacy was claimed to a large degree because the enemy was said to have illegitimate weapons of mass destruction. That nothing has changed in this war even though the charge turned out to be false (the search for weapons of mass destruction was discontinued in April 2005) shows that legitimacy has never been the real foundation of top-down power. The same is true for the doctrine of Manifest Destiny: the fact that it is no longer officially proclaimed does not mean that its outcomes are challenged. Legitimacy is thus not the basis of the exercise of top-down power, but merely its guise.

All this has theological implications. The power that crushed Naboth and all the others who are usually classified as the "losers" of history is easily equated with God's power. God tends to be located on the side of the winners. Might makes right, as the saying goes. Today we might add a general feeling that success is what makes things right. There is a long tradition that assumes that God's power works from the top down. Despite many complaints about the loss of traditional imagery in Christianity, these traditional modes of thinking are alive and well. Frequently, these images are so engrained that they are not even recognized as images any more. The hierarchical dualism connected to this approach, according to Sallie McFague, "is so widespread in Western thought that it is usually not perceived to be a pattern but is felt to be simply the way things are."[8] It is taken for granted that God moves from the top down. If God fails to proceed from the top down on occasions, that is reason enough to doubt and to turn away in disappointment and disgust. No wonder that, consciously or unconsciously, we tend to resonate with successful actions from the top down. In its most extreme forms, the bombing campaigns of the three most recent U.S. wars, one in Afghanistan and two in Iraq, represent this logic. While the ancient Romans ascribed to God's action the top-down phenomena of thunder, lightning, and other celestial affairs, today we ascribe to God's actions other top-down phenomena. In situations of military conflict, dropping bombs straight from the sky is not only the most dramatic top-down action available to us but hints at divine imagery. Imitating God's perceived actions in thunder and lightning—or perhaps even in the great flood that fell from the sky—gives contemporary bombing campaigns an aura that is hard to resist. Unlike a dirty ground war that tests the limits of our control, as over two years of messy and rather unsuccessful combat in Iraq demonstrate, an air war keeps things safe, clean, and in control. Proceeding from the top down without getting our hands dirty seems to send a clear message as to who is right.

Power, whether the power of God or the power of the sovereign, appears to be safeguarded best when affirmed from the top down. This logic is hard to resist. Even the voices of dissent to the recent wars initiated by the United States are usually tied to other concerns that do not necessarily question this top-down logic of power—for instance, to humanitarian concerns for the victims or to pacifist agendas. Few doubt that the United States has a right to use top-down power—even though there might be disagreement as to when to use it. Closer to home, and back to the issue of the expropriation of land within our own borders, top-down power has clearly been at work in our relation to Native Americans. More than simply legitimizing top-down power, the legalization of this power surfaced in 1903, when the Supreme Court affirmed in the *Lonewolf* case that the United States had a right to disregard a treaty with the Indian nations while the Indians were bound by it because the United States wielded "plenary power." In other words, treaties were not binding on the United States because it was the stronger nation.[9]

At present, talk about the United States as empire, fiercely rejected just a few years ago, is openly embraced. This empire differs from empires in the past—for instance, by not directly controlling external colonies. Power is projected differently, often through economic and police-style military actions. Nevertheless, like the story of Naboth, the story of Native America allows us to take a closer look at our own reality. There is an internal form of colonialism that must not be overlooked.[10] The Native American struggle is different from the African American, Asian American, and Latino American ones insofar as there is a struggle, as Ward Churchill has put it, "for the liberation of our homelands rather than for the liberation of land on which to build our homes."[11]

THE POWER OF HELPERS

When the churches thus seek to "help those who have no power" and "to empower the powerless," it makes a difference what kind of power is discussed. We should not too quickly assume that our vision of power differs much from the dominant models of power. If everything around us—from political, economic, and cultural forces (including the mainline Christian churches)—operates in terms of top-down power, how can we escape? Furthermore, if we benefit in our own ways from top-down power, how could we possibly assume the position of the prophet Elijah, pronouncing judgment from the outside?

Churches are quick to embrace the language of helping others, of benevolence, and of charity. We Christians see ourselves as compassionate people and most of us mean well. There are many examples of help provided by Christians, from inner-city soup kitchens and homeless shelters to the free medical and legal clinics that are often housed in and supported by churches. Yet this sort of help, while much needed and in great demand, is characterized by the fact that it mostly does not challenge and often works alongside the powers that be. The goal is to lift people out of their misery and to give them their own share in the top-down power of the status quo. After all, some top-down power seems to be better than none at all. These models are built on the assumption that those who seek to help are located further up along the spectrum of power. The power that they share, therefore, is a mode of top-down power. Nevertheless, the power of the helper continues to be seen in a top-down way, as benevolent leverage or control over others for their own good. This is what "using power for the powerless" tends to mean in our context. Here, top-down power is preserved—which might be the reason for the Bush administration's strong support of faith-based programs.

A more interesting alternative to the power of the sovereign is sometimes defined as "power for" or "power to," in contradistinction to the top-down forms of "power over."[12] "Power to" refers to the empowerment of people who have been deprived of the power of the status quo, particularly along the lines of gender, race, and class. "Power to" also entails a refusal to control others and the willingness to share power with others. We will come back to the power of the people in the next part, but we need to note here that even this form of power can be co-opted by the status quo, especially if it is driven by people further up on the spectrum of (top-down) power who seek to "empower" those further down. Liberation projects that are not ultimately driven by those who seek liberation but by self-declared liberators might not get very far beyond the prevailing forms of top-down power.

The virtual omnipresence of top-down power, which we tend to take for granted like the air we breathe, shapes even our most benevolent projects and messes up our efforts at being in solidarity. As Edward Said has pointed out, "the rhetoric of power all too easily produces an illusion of benevolence when developed in an imperial setting."[13] Said goes on to point out that this rhetoric, which characterizes the contemporary situation in the United States, has been used frequently by other modern empires, including the British and the French. Domination is often disguised as benevolent leadership.

Domination as top-down power is of course more easily recognized: actions like the dropping of bombs are for all to see, and even deceptive schemes that claim legitimacy become clear when exposed by the prophets. But, as Michel Foucault has taught us, there has been a shift in how power is exercised in modernity, beginning in the seventeenth and eighteenth centuries. One of the "great inventions of bourgeoisie," to use Foucault's own words, mentions "a type of power which is constantly exercised by means of surveillance rather than in a discontinuous manner by means of a system of levies or obligations distributed over time. It presupposes a tightly knit grid of material coercions rather than the physical existence of a sovereign."[14] The logic of power shifts from the logic of top-down control to the logic of discipline, which proceeds by using techniques of everyday discipline (including education, supervision, social norms, etc.) that interiorize power. Michael Hardt and Antonio Negri add that the logic of Foucault's work points to a logic of control "in which mechanisms of command become ever more 'democratic,' ever more immanent to the social field, distributed throughout the brains and bodies of the citizens."[15] They connect this observation to the notion of "biopolitical power"—a situation where "the whole social body is comprised by power's machine and developed in its virtuality."[16] In this context, the effort to help others and to empower people tends to become an extension of top-down power, which produces more people in sync with the system. Even our most intimate personal relationships are affected by the logic of discipline. As feminists have reminded us for decades: the personal is political.[17]

Another manifestation of this dispersed form of power can be found in the global economy. The global markets—while undergirded by particular forms of top-down political and military power—proceed according to another logic that does not move straight from the top down. Here, success appears to be based on the free movement of capital across borders, and fixed hierarchies and boundaries are considered harmful (except for the boundaries that prevent the free movement of workers).[18] Power is projected according to the free-floating laws of supply and demand that seem to know no top and no bottom. Both capitalists and consumers are supposedly free to determine their own lives—a freedom that is deeply determined, of course, by the world of advertising. No wonder that, as Hardt and Negri observe, the world market "establishes a real politics of difference" which promotes antifoundationalism and antiessentialism, that is, a view that reality is constructed independently of hard facts and that ultimately no such facts exist. The market functions in terms of "circulation, mobility, diversity, and mixture."[19] Nevertheless, even this more free-floating organization of power continues in the traditions of top-down power. Despite hopes that "a rising tide will lift all boats," the global markets continue to favor the rich at the expense of the poor. The seemingly free-floating power of the market flows much stronger at the top than at the bottom.

As in the story of Ahab and Naboth, we find the full truth only when we look from the perspective of those who suffer the ultimate consequences. The suffering produced by the (softer) power exerted by the global economy is enormous, and there are many examples, including the phenomenon of a new slavery.[20] In this chapter, however, the theme of the extortion of land suggests that we listen to Native American stories. Their situation in the United States has worsened significantly since the 1980s. In 1983, the Reagan administration cut Indian programs from $3.5 billion to $2 billion.[21] Attempting to reduce government involvement across the board (though not in matters of military and defense), Reagan pursued the economic development of Native Americans instead of political interaction. The expectation was that economic development would result in the adjustment of Indian society to the standards of white U.S. society, bringing in line polity, religion, community, education, and even family structure. Obviously, the softer forms of economic power could be trusted to work in sync with top-down power. Even approaches that are widely seen as economic empowerment lead to further domination. The encouragement of Indian-run casino gambling, for instance, often results in destructive adaptations to dominant culture and divisions among Indian nations.

Nevertheless, while power has become ever more dispersed and encroaches in the most hidden ways on our relationships, we must not forget that the various forms of top-down power are not mutually exclusive—an issue at the heart of much recent debate.[22] Despite the emphasis on economic development that would give some (top-down) power to the Native Americans, the U.S. government has also continued earlier patterns of expropriating resources, as when it allowed oil companies to take billions of barrels of oil and gas from federal and Indian lands. At the beginning of the twenty-first century, as much as $10 billion are owed to American Indians for resources taken from their lands.[23]

ANOTHER KIND OF POWER

Prophets who do not understand how they are immersed in the kind of powers that move from the top down will not make much progress in challenging the system. Benevolent intentions and a concern for the empowerment of the disempowered are not enough and may even be harmful. We need to align ourselves with a different sort of power—one that is substantially different from the derivatives of the power of the status quo. As Jonathan Schell has pointed out: "The power that flows upward from the consent, support, and nonviolent activity of the people is not the same as the power that flows downward from the state by virtue of its command of the instruments of force, and yet the two kinds of power contend in the same world for the upper hand, and the seemingly weaker one can, it turns out, defeat the seemingly stronger, as the downfall of the British Raj and the Soviet Union showed."[24] From the Native American perspective, Vine Deloria notes that we have changed the world irreversibly through nonviolent actions and have thus created a new way of transforming the world.[25] Hannah Arendt's distinction between power and violence applies here, noting that "the extreme form of power is All against One, the extreme form of violence is One against All." Power—as opposed to violence—is not the ability to act but the ability to "act in concert."[26] But is it true that the origin of this power is "the heart and mind of each ordinary person," as Schell claims?[27]

In search for this other kind of power, we can once again learn from people who have to bear the brunt of top-down power. Since they have very little share in the powers that be, they are often considered to be powerless. But they share in a different power that is frequently overlooked. Native America can be our guide again. While there are significant differences between the many Native American nations in both Americas that must not be overlooked, there are common historical strands that are, in the words of Guillermo Bonfil Batalla, "reinforced by the common experience of almost five centuries of domination."[28]

Common experiences of domination and repression not only produce strong bonds extending across substantial differences; they also produce a different kind of power. Power growing out of experiences of repression is diametrically opposed to top-down power. While both types of power presuppose a relationship of at least two parties, according to the model of top-down power, one party always seeks to control the others. On the other hand, the "power that flows upward" (Schell), for instance, the power of the repressed, is not built on the desire to control others and it does not depend on the approval by the status quo.[29] Positively speaking, the power of the repressed possesses its own kind of energy—an alternative energy that is often lacking with those who want to help and who thus frequently burn out. The power of the repressed is not a sheer reaction to the power of the status quo. It manifests itself in registers that are simply not available to top-down wielders of power who have created their own empires, which have become their prisons.[30] Perhaps this is what the apostle Paul meant when he noted that "power is made perfect in weakness" (2 Cor. 12:9).

A common objection to any alternative to the top-down flow of power is that the result will be a simple reversal of power. In other words, does the flow of power from the bottom up simply mirror the flow of power from the top down? This objection touches on a real problem, but it fails to realize that power that truly flows from the bottom up is qualitatively different.[31] From the Native American perspective, Deloria has identified the problem with such objections, noting that "Western peoples" "assume that we know the structure of reality and must only make certain minor adjustments in the machinery that operates it in order to bring our institutions into line."[32] In this case, the shift from one mode of power to another one is not a "minor adjustment." The new kind of power reshapes and extends our horizons in every respect. There is an epistemological gain, for instance, when those who have been repressed begin to speak in their own distinct ways.[33] It is not that the repressed know everything, but they know a few decisive things about reality that no one else knows, having to do with the repressed truths that are at the core of what drives the status quo. They also know that the repressions produced by the system are not isolated incidences but the foundation on which the system is built. Furthermore, there is an onto-logical gain because the kind of power that flows from the underside has a more acute awareness of its limits—knowing full well that it cannot control the whole world—and thus does not need to pose as the only and absolute representative of ultimate reality. This awareness of limits is often missing when power moves from the top down; such power is usually coupled with a sense of being the primary representative of ultimate reality. If other forms of top-down power are acknowledged at all, they are seen as derivatives and spin-offs. In Christian theology, this failure to recognize limits is called idolatry, defined by the apostle Paul as worshiping and serving "the creature rather than the Creator" (Rom. 1:25). Power exercised from below, by people who know that they are neither almighty nor God, is qualitatively different.

One of the most important characteristics of power from below is that it cannot present itself as absolute since it is always a product of pressure and repression. It does not mimic omnipotence and provides alternative visions of power that might ultimately be more helpful when searching for and envision-ing the power of God. Power from below is aware of how it is produced in the tensions and struggles of power (and thus provisional) and how it needs to be sustained by community and solidarity. This different sort of power is mirrored in Friedrich Engels's insight that revolutions are not made intentionally and arbitrarily but emerge out of the tensions of the historical situation. Intentional top-down actions where people take things into their own hands, such as conspiracies and political assassinations—the tools of the political right—do not share in this alternative power, and neither do the kinds of revolutions of the left that glorify violence.[34]

It is no coincidence that many of these themes resonate with Native American traditions; there is an ancient wisdom informing these alternative perspectives on power. Among the most widely known Native American traditions in this respect are the emphasis on community and relationality and the emphasis on the limits of life.[35] Still, even those emphases can be misused by top-down power. Deloria's rejoinder needs to be kept in mind, that the proclamation of "sacred circularity" and the message that "everything is related" are not necessarily "particularly revolutionary" in and of themselves.[36] What makes these emphases revolutionary in the sense of power flowing from below, however, is the ways in which they are tied into the struggles of the people and what challenges they pose for the powers that flow from the top. While there is a sense of community and relationality in the circles of the powerful as well—the exclusive clubs of the rich and the networks of the international business world come to mind—there is a different sense of community and relationality among those who struggle for survival. Not only is there a different sense of urgency, there is also a different sense of the place and value of the individual in relation to the whole.

In the Native American tradition, community and relationality are tied to the struggles of the people and the land. Community here is not a luxury or a way to expand one's personal power base. Community is a matter of life and death, both for the people and for the land.[37] Even the land cannot survive without being included in our relationships—a truth of which our self-produced ecological crises keep reminding us. For Native Americans, community has nothing to do with the optional communities that many Americans choose voluntarily, including religious communities; rather, community includes every aspect of life, such as politics, economics, ecology, and spirituality. Because of this all-inclusive notion of community, Native Americans have not given up the idea of recovering their nationhood.[38] Native American nationhood stands for truly alternative communities that would challenge the top-down registers of powers of the superpower states and push toward what Ward Churchill describes as "voluntary, consensual interdependence between formerly dominated and dominating nations and a redefinition of the word 'nation' itself to conform to its original meaning: bodies of people bound together by their bioregional and other natural cultural affinities."[39] In a similar spirit, George Tinker proposes "small, local, autonomous communities as the basic political unit recognized and respected by everyone, with tolerance for a wide variety of politically organized configurations."[40]

To be sure, this understanding of community and relationality has broad implications. Just as one cannot own and control another person—an important lesson of power from below—neither can one own the land.[41] Including the land in alternative visions of power ties this discussion back to the struggle between Ahab and Naboth and adds an important aspect to the understanding of our current situation. The land reminds us of the implications of power that take us beyond the anthropological lenses of many of our current liberation struggles.[42] The community that shares the land shares all resources, as well as the means of production. Those issues might well pose the strongest challenges to our contemporary top-down empires, and they remind us in no uncertain terms of the tremendous difference between community as choice and community as the basic structure of life. Community, understood in those terms, poses the ultimate challenge to hierarchical class structures and top-down governance.[43]

None of these reflections seek to romanticize Native Americans. Whatever their inevitable shortcomings may be, Native American perspectives pose a challenge to the top-down powers that have been at work in varying degrees during various periods of history and which are on an all-out attack in our own times.

We must not forget that at the heart of the matter is, ultimately, a theological issue. Just as top-down power draws on images of God that are deeply engrained in the Western world, power that moves from the bottom up is tied to different images of God. George Tinker points out that if we acknowledge being created by God, one of the deep insights of Native American traditions, the "Creator's hegemony over all" leaves no basis for exploitation and oppression.[44] Going one step further than Tinker, how we imagine God's "hegemony," or authority, also changes when we consider models of power that flow from the bottom up. The prophets who challenged the top-down powers of the kings in the Hebrew Scriptures, and the disciples who followed Jesus Christ, had a sense that God's power was sufficiently different from any form of top-down power. God's own power, seen most clearly in the startling resistance of the Crucified and of the "crucified people" like Naboth and all those who suffer injustice to this day, continues to confront top-down power in surprising ways.

LIBERATING THE PROPHET

In our time, when top-down power is taking over the globe more and more, the potential prophets need liberation as well. Mainline Christians need to be liberated from our imprisonment by the powers that be. First, of course, we need to realize our imprisonment. Going back to the old story of Ahab, Naboth, and Elijah, we finally notice how even the prophet Elijah might have been imprisoned by top-down power. While he is the only one to protest—the elders and even the people are on the side of the king—he is unable to address the bigger problem. Elijah's protest remains limited to one particular and obvious crime—much like in our own situation where many protest the unethical excesses of big business but not the bigger problem of top-down power that pursues the interests of the business world at the expense of the people. Elijah lives at a time—not unlike our own—when the popular alliance of citizens that could challenge the power of the king had been severely damaged, resulting in a victory of the top-down power of the king who was able to split the population by aligning himself with the wealthiest groups.[45]

Thus, reading between the lines of the relation of Ahab, Naboth, and Elijah, the true extent of the problem finally becomes clear. Likewise, reading between the lines of our own relationships with the U.S. empire and our Native American neighbors helps clarify what is at stake. There is a bigger problem that points beyond the obvious crimes and betrayals committed against Native Americans. We can see the bigger problem when we realize that individualism, one of the most cherished principles of top-down power, is really a myth. The individualism that tells us that we are self-made people simply covers up the fact that our success is produced on the backs of others—in Ahab's case, on the back of Naboth and probably many others like him; in our case, on the backs of Native Americans and many others. In the Americas, we have never lived as "individuals," independent from Native Americans. This is true even for the most individualistic of pioneers. If this reality is overlooked, all appeals to be in solidarity with others and to build community will be counterproductive since they reinforce the belief in the myth of individualism.

Just as we cannot truly be in community without first acknowledging our distorted relationships, we cannot appreciate Indian traditions without understanding the distortions of top-down power. No wonder that the growing appreciation of Native traditions has too often led to consumerist appropriations.[46] Such superficial appreciation amounts to other forms of exploitation, creating for instance a spirit of codependency among Native Americans that manifests itself in the search for approval. Superficial appreciation is counterproductive also for those who appropriate Native American tradition as individual choice (comparable to "church shopping") since they remain caught in the status quo. Such false appreciation repeats parts of the story of the missionaries of old, who in their own ways failed to listen to the Natives and thus ended up supporting their exploitation, despite good intentions and despite the fact that the missionaries themselves did not personally gain from it.[47]

The task of the prophet has thus become more challenging and complex. Prophecy can no longer do without self-critique. We need to realize that we do not live in a power vacuum. No one can claim the role of a neutral spectator, watching the game from the sidelines as it were, or intervening "from above." The task of the prophet thus begins with very specific confessions and repentance, and leads to a genuine conversion from one model of power to another.[48] And while all these steps are personal, they cannot be taken in isolation from the struggles of the community. Following the flow of power from the bottom up is not a matter of special interest. We are not talking about the liberation of some at the expense of others. This conversion aims at the liberation of everyone.[49]

These reflections lead us back to the image of God who, according to the Christian tradition, initiates the process of conversion. God does not tolerate the usurpation of power by the kings and sovereigns, and God rejects not only blatant evil such as the murder of Naboth but also any form of absolute power that does not respect the people. Such fresh encounters with God in the midst of the struggle call for an end to forms of religion that merely support and legitimate the status quo. Vine Deloria's observation still applies, that "religion has become a comfortable ethic and a comforting aesthetic for Westerners, not a force of undetermined intensity and unsuspected origin that may break in on them."[50] Prophetic critique and empowerment become more real when, as mainline churches and theologians, we begin by applying Elijah's prophetic critiques to ourselves, and when we join in the unsuspected and startling dynamics of God's own power, which does not exclude but rather works through the witness of the Naboths, the Native Americans, and the Crucified. Perhaps this will lead to an invitation to join Elijah in proclaiming, "Thus says the Lord."

PART TWO

ECOLOGY

FROM METAPHORS AND MODELS TO MAPS

Thinking Theology with an Archipelagic Imagination

Nancy M. Victorin-Vangerud

Archipelago:

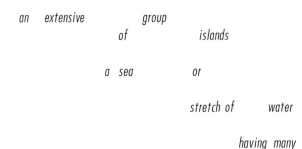

—NEW OXFORD DICTIONARY OF ENGLISH[1]

Because religions, including Christianity, are not incidentally imagistic but centrally and necessarily so, theology must also be an affair of the imagination.
—SALLIE MCFAGUE[2]

This chapter muses on maritime mystery mediated through personal narrative, cross-cultural exploration, and theological reflection drawing on the image of an archipelago. I hope the currents of this chapter will evoke a new way of seeing—and *sea-ing*—so that in relation to the Mystery, we might "override conventional thinking and see ourselves as part of a whole to which we have been taught, unwittingly, that we do not belong."[3]

AFFAIR OF THE IMAGINATION

Over the last twenty years, Sallie McFague has encouraged us to see theological thinking in a new way—as an imagistic, constructive, and experimental venture whereby we as individuals and communities express Christian faith by drawing on language relevant for our time and place.[4] Today, we live in an evolutionary, ecological world, where human beings bear great responsibility for the possibilities of life now and in the future of "our" blue-green planet, Earth. In McFague's view, thinking theologically moves us beyond interpreting biblical and traditional metaphors to exploring the metaphors of contemporary life that locate us within this holistic, interdependent picture of reality. Thinking theologically about the God-world relation, including human beings, means we can navigate between the "is" and the "is not" character of our metaphors and models for a credible way of speaking and enacting Christian faith.[5] Through her own imaginative explorations of metaphors for God, McFague dares us to imagine novel possibilities and play with them for their illuminating and persuasive impact. Yet, this is serious work, playing at the "foundational level of the imagination." She claims, "Metaphorical theology is a kind of heuristic construction that in focusing on the imaginative construal of the God-world relationship, attempts to remythologize Christian faith through metaphors and models appropriate for an ecological, nuclear age."[6]

But McFague has also taught us to see theological thinking in another way—with "loving eyes." In contrast to acquiring objective knowledge as uninvolved observers, we can seek theological understanding using all our senses from *within* our ecological context. The point is not using the mind's eye to grasp and classify objects into discrete categories according to universal definitions, so that we can control or manipulate these objects for our own (arrogant) purposes. According to McFague, understanding others with embodied, loving eyes involves an "in-touch attitude," especially sensitive to differences and aware of empathetic connections between beings, subject to subject. With an "in-touch" model of being and knowing, the world becomes, in McFague's view, a "neighborhood . . . a place where one listens and looks in order to learn who one is, who the others are, and how all fit together in one place . . . The neighborhood encloses us within a particular space where many live together, inviting us to pay close attention in order to learn more about our neighbors."[7]

A NEW NEIGHBORHOOD

> Going to the beach was the excitement of the year. We would be driven to Midland Junction by horse and buggy, then by train to Perth and by tram to the end of the line . . . The plank road was fairly smooth, but the block was very bumpy. To spare the horse, we walked up all the inclines, and there was great excitement when we came to the hill with the bend, for then we knew we would see the sea.
>
> —ROSE FARRINGTON, *RECOLLECTIONS FROM A SHORELINE*[8]

It was seeing my new neighborhood in Perth, Western Australia (WA), with loving eyes that engaged me in exploring a constructive expansion from theological
metaphors and models to maps. As new residents, my family and I went everywhere with our road atlas. Yet, no matter where we traveled north and south
along the coast, one prominent feature of the WA neighborhood beckoned—the
sea. As Annie Dillard said of her welcome to the Puget Sound neighborhood,
"[E]verything in the landscape points to the sea."[9] Certainly, Australia is known
for its vast, red-hearted desertlands, but when one begins to pay attention, to
look and listen, one learns that one cannot understand much about Australia
and Australians—indigenous and nonindigenous—without understanding the
sea and that cerulean and white littoral space of "is" and "is not"—the coast.
In WA, I learned to "see the sea," not just the cold horizon of my childhood
memories (growing up near the gray waters of the Atlantic), but the warm, shim-
mering neighborhood paved in shifting sand *under* the wave-surface, with its
towering tenements of staghorn coral and oyster stacks, undulating fields of sea
grass, and bustling residents of parrotfish, neons, painted sweet-lips, dolphins,
and green turtles. Under the waves, being "in touch" is elusive, humbling, and
ultimately risky with stinging jellies, rippling rays, and even great white point-
ers scouring the neighborhood. Who was I, this floating, fin-ing, sometimes
flailing, newcomer without a proper visa?

Becoming immersed (baptized?) in what Rachel Carson termed "the world
of waters" brought about a "sea-change" in my perception.[10] I realized I needed
a new "imaginative cartography" to reorient myself—locally, globally, especially theologically—in this water-world.[11] But I was a constructive theologian
schooled in the metaphorical terrain of a land-lubber God; with salty tears in my
eyes, I wondered, What might it mean to construct theology, not from the edge
of the sea, but from "land's edge," as Western Australian novelist Tim Winton
suggests?[12] What might it mean not only to see the sea differently, but to be
in touch with the sea, in the sea, like—or even as—the sea? Theologian Sheila
Greeve Davaney claims that "as our vistas change so will our sense of what is
important and what is peripheral, what is at the center and what resides at the
perimeter."[13] Yet, in the sea there is no center, no perimeter to mark, even daily
tidal transformations—especially as the threat of global warming looms.

Amazing! Beneath the waves, "land" continues from the sandy reefs and
rocky cliffs of "my" shallows, to the canyons, plains, mountain ranges, and
trenches of the deep, according to new maps of the ocean floor. And there is
life all the way down, even surrounding the eerie hot water chimneys streaming
darkly from the benthic bottom! Yet, the sea also filters through the land and
rivers to influence the estuaries and underground aquifers of the coast. Looking at my travel map, I had seen only those dry surfaces sticking up above the

water in the air. But when I became in touch with the ebbing and flowing of a water-world, I began drawing "imaginative pictures" of an archipelago.[14] Maybe the sea doesn't so much separate us from others as it connects us with others. We can think of the nautical neighborhoods of sand, rock, and coral; the great gyral patterns of upwelling and downwelling seawater in thermohaline circulation; the global hydrological cycle of evaporation and condensation; as well as the "transgressive" migration of whales, eels, and seabirds across latitudes and longitudes. Maritime enchantment prompted me to wonder, What if we began "thinking like an archipelago" for constructing theology?[15] What if we read our maps for an archipelagic adventure? As Jay McDaniel claims, "We need new maps of God, ways of thinking about God . . . They help orient us, however fallible and finite, to the Mystery."[16]

SEA-ING THE ISLANDS

His days are lived according to the tide. From the spit he casts for queenfish and trevally . . . He labours all one morning to make the mesa's summit and traverse its windblown gutters to look out oceanward and see the archipelago backed up like a jack-knifed train in the gulf below . . . Fox begins to grow expansive.
— TIM WINTON, *DIRT MUSIC*[17]

Eight years ago, when my family and I first traveled out to Perth from Rochester, Minnesota, we felt acutely what Australian historian Geoffrey Blainey classically termed "the tyranny of distance."[18] We had moved to the great "island continent," certainly under different conditions than the British colonialists and convicts faced in the era of "transportation."[19] But like them, traveling thousands of miles from home across the sea, we thought we were the farthest distance we could be from the center of our world. We had sailed out to the margins, "down under" as many North Americans and Europeans say, to the western frontier edge of the Great South Land, where even toilet water flows in reverse.

But then a good friend, Eleazar Fernandez, from the island of Leyte in the Philippines—itself an archipelago of 7,100 islands—told me to look up, and he was not only talking about attitude! He suggested a simple "thought experiment" to me.[20] I was to pick up a map and put my finger on Perth, then move my finger straight up, following the lines of the time zone. On the way, I traveled to Jakarta, Hong Kong, Ho Chi Min City, Beijing, Nanjing, and many other cities large and small. The scales fell from my eyes—I was not alone (no woman is an island, remember?). I just needed to get out and meet my new neighbors. Through this thought experiment of sailing up the confluence of the Indian and Pacific Oceans, Eleazar showed me that I was living in the most populous neighborhood on the planet! With over 71 percent of Earth's surface covered with saltwater, the coast of WA is connected to the coasts of many other places and people. I began to learn what island people know by heart, "The sea unites the entire world."[21]

Fortunately, I had washed up on the coast of very hospitable people. One new friend, storyteller Liana Christensen, shared her WA water-wisdom for making the paradigm shift from "distant frontier" to "new neighborhood." She believes the epistemological problem, the thinking or knowing problem, lies in simple definitions. When those of us with an Enlightenment sensibility think of an archipelago, we think of discrete islands. We see the dry land as isolated bits and ourselves as one of the individual parts (in what McFague calls an "atomistic or "mechanistic" paradigm).[22] We can think of Kant's image of the human being standing on an island, separate, self-contained, and tenaciously moored to the ground of Divine Reason, away from the lapping, changing, and chaotic waves surrounding him. But as Christensen discovered, archipelago has another, older meaning:

> When I started writing natural history stories from the southwest of Western Australia, I thought an archipelago was a group of islands—and so it is. Yet along the way I discovered the original meaning of archipelago was 'a sea studded with islands.' This holistic definition conjures for me the experiences that cause the greatest passion, the ideas that matter most. My original concern for islands on land and sea expanded to embrace the corridors and currents that connect these apparently isolated places.[23]

Through Liana's stories, I learned we can see islands from a holistic perspective, one that "seas" them immersed and connected within larger bodies.[24] Rather than paddling in the shallows, on the surface, we need to dive deeper into the "corridors and currents" to understand ourselves and all things in relation to others. With an archipelagic imagination, what at first may appear in isolation, determined in its aseity, may become understood as embodied, complex, and interdependent. Thus, when we think like an archipelago, we seek not to dissolve or merge identities, but to "grow expansive"—to understand both the particular and the holistic character of planetary life (in what McFague calls the "organic model").[25] Liana's stories of island life in WA sent me "world-traveling" again, to learn from the oceanic wisdom of others.[26]

SALTWATER SPEAKING

> *If you do not respect the sea which holds our life, it will take you. Where the sea has the power to heal or to claim you and you must learn to live with it, its power is felt elementally as part of people's blood and body.*
> —MARY YARMIRR, *CROKER ISLAND*[27]

In northern Australia live the people of saltwater country. As Nonie Sharp knows, "The indigenous peoples of these areas are themselves rich and diverse. In their world, threads of association join people with the sea as well as the land, imprinting them as sea peoples."[28] Thus, in saltwater country, belonging involves learning the "Dreaming" of the land and the sea, which communicates the sacred identity, memories, and future of sea people. Seascapes bear the rights and responsibilities of particular people for particular places, and they speak to those who listen attentively. Colors, shapes, and sounds of saltwater bear special significance for those who "learn the language of the sea," because different waters speak in different ways—in hope and in sorrow.[29] Saltwater people have an in-touch knowledge of the "seamarks"—how the world looks from the sea, according to cloud formations; islands; rocks; shifts in the wind; light patterns on the waves; tidal flows; star pathways; birds in flight or resting; drifting seaweed; flashes of bio-luminescence; crab and shellfish movements; flying fish leaping; waters roaring and murmuring; and even the smells of the reef at various times of day and night.[30]

In saltwater country, the sea is not a void or chaos in contrast to the land; the sea embodies a sacred cosmology of kinship. As Sharp explains:

> The patterns of movement given in sacred designs passed down from ancestors are those of cosmic cycles, and these continue to find artistic expression today as sacred political geographies. These geographies encompass sites, people, their languages and the sea. Dreaming figures who speak 'to and through' local people.[31]

Saltwater geographies map seascapes as a vast interconnection of people and spirits, ancestors and sea creatures, who are responsible for different country in different ways, yet they all flow together in the Dreaming. Lanani Marika shares her holistic sense of belonging in Yolŋu country:

> I will say this with my own feelings. How I am feeling toward this saltwater . . . We sing from the shore to where the clouds rise on the horizon. And from where the clouds rise we sing of the seaweed and of the clouds rising. Clouds

always rising and raining on the ocean. And then after the rain the calm sea will sleep there. The song cycle of the sea starts there; of this water, of this saltwater, for this country . . . Everything that exists in the sea has a place in the sacred Songs.[32]

In an era of rising sea levels, ocean pollution, depleted fish stocks, dying mangroves, and coral bleaching, will we listen to the songs of saltwater? We live in a world where individualism and neoclassical economics rule the day, rather than environmental sustainability and kinship. Thus, who will understand the deep archipelagic connections of an ecological, evolutionary world? Who will learn the language of the sea?

HOME IN THE SEA

> [O]nly those who make the ocean their home and love it, can really claim it theirs. Conquerors come, conquerors go, the ocean remains, mother only to her children. This mother has a big heart though, she adopts anyone who loves her.
> —EPELI HAUʻOFA, "OUR SEA OF ISLANDS," *A NEW OCEANIA: REDISCOVERING OUR SEA OF ISLANDS*[33]

In March of 1993, on the way from Kona to Hilo on the Big Island of Hawaiʻi, historical geographer Epeli Hauʻofa had what he calls his "road to Damascus" experience.[34] He had presented a paper at the University of the South Pacific in Suva, in which he struggled with the image of islands in the Pacific as "too small, too poorly endowed with resources, and too isolated from the centers of economic growth for their inhabitants ever to be able to rise above their present condition of dependence on the largesse of wealthy nations" (4). He worried that throughout his academic career, he had been promoting this "belittlement" view, which consigns island people to despair, passivity, and wardship. But on the road to Hilo, he saw again the majesty of Mauna Loa and the craters of Kilauea, and he realized: "The Big Island was growing, rising from the depths of a mighty sea. The world of Oceania is not small; it is huge and growing bigger every day" (6).

Hauʻofa admitted he had been intellectually formed by the colonialist cartography of the Pacific as "islands in a far sea," which placed the dry, land surfaces far across a foreboding ocean from the civilized centers of power (7). In the eyes of European explorers and contemporary economists, the islands of the Pacific Ocean seem small and remote, fragmented and disparate. Mapmakers in the service of colonial empires drew measurements of longitude and latitude across the sea to determine boundaries and territorial claims, which confined people to such small locations. In contrast, Hau'ofa's ancestors thought of themselves as "ocean peoples," who lived in "a sea of islands" and circulated throughout the region (7). Reflecting on the myths, oral traditions, and cosmologies of the peoples of Oceania, Hau'ofa remembered:

> Their universe comprised not only the land surfaces, but the surrounding ocean as far as they could traverse and exploit it, the underworld with its fire-controlling and earth-shaking denizens, and the heavens above with their hierarchies of powerful gods and named stars and constellations that people could count on to guide their ways across the seas. Their world was anything but tiny. (7)

The culture of ocean peoples could be characterized as "world enlargement," with people traveling from island to island for the purposes of trade, marriage, art, education, adventure, and politics (6). Instead of feeling themselves in an alien environment, ocean peoples lived from their deep sense of place:

> People raised in this environment were at home with the sea. They played in it as soon as they could walk steadily, they worked in it, they fought on it. They developed great skills for navigating their waters, and the spirit to traverse even the few large gaps that separated their island groups . . . The sea was open to anyone who could navigate . . . [a] way through. (8–9)

As Hau'ofa watched the living, volcanic landscape rising from the sea, a new identity rose within the depths of himself. He contemplated: "The ocean unites us, and is our common heritage . . . The sea is constantly flowing. No boundary can contain it, or stop its movement within a confine. The same body of water washes all our shores . . . The ocean is our supreme metaphor."[35] Despite the attempts of nineteenth-century imperialism to erect boundaries and confine people to remote spaces, the people of Oceania continued to travel across the sea, even to the farthest cities of power. They continued to flow and return, enlarging their worlds, sustaining connections between homelands near and far. Hau'ofa re-imagined Oceania as a "sea of interdependence," based on "the social centrality of the ancient practice of reciprocity" (12–13). Today, living in a sea of islands provides the people of Oceania the cultural basis of identity and dignity needed for collective action on their own behalf.

But in reimagining the sea as his home, Hau'ofa saw further that the people of the Pacific need to link up with the people of the Indian Ocean, the Atlantic Ocean, and beyond, for at stake is life's sustainability on Earth:

Oceania is not a world of its own. Although it is ours in the sense that it is our home, it also belongs to the rest of humanity. The sea flows in and out of Oceania, and into the other bodies of water that connect all the land masses of our planet. The sea unites the entire world.[36]

On the road to Hilo, Epeli Hau'ofa experienced his own sea-change in identity. In reading his map with postcolonial eyes, the "islands in a far sea" became "a sea of islands . . . in which things are seen in the totality of their relationships" (7). He now sees the planet as a vast archipelago, with one ocean connecting all of life. For Hau'ofa, "center" and "periphery" have become relative concepts, as he recovers images from his culture to empower and sustain practical strategies for Oceania's future in the hope of mutual reciprocity with others. Will we respond from our own homes in the archipelago?

FOCUSING ON THE LIQUID

Christensen's stories, Marika's songs, and Hau'ofa's journey helped me see/sea my neighborhood in God's blue-green "household" or *oikoumene*. I began learning that maps can be drawn and read in many ways. As historical geographer J. B. Harley comments:

> Much of the power of the map, as a representation of social geography, is that it operates behind a mask of a seemingly neutral science. It hides and denies its social dimensions at the same time as it legitimates. Yet whichever way we look at it the rules of society will surface.[37]

I had been reading my maps in terms of land, ground, and property, from within a culture that day by day seems to think and act in ways that continually places itself at the center of empire, with nothing real or known beyond its own boundaries (from its perspective). As neoconservative political movements claim, the United States needs to pursue "a unipolar era" because "a multipolar world . . . would be far more dangerous" for the country's "benevolent global hegemony."[38] I wondered if Hau'ofa's ocean-mother would adopt me too.

Yet, on one of my coastal journeys, I found myself near where I grew up in northern New Jersey. Naturalist Mary Parker Buckles went to live along the Long Island Sound, and after attending closely to her neighborhood, she too came to see/sea the islands in a new way:

> I can't find the right pronoun for the land around me. It can't be an "it" which implies constancy and continuity. "I love it" or "I see it" involves an

objective case that stays put, or at least stays visible. Is the ground a "them,"
which acknowledges the minute-by-minute mutability of the islands in my
view? This will lead to trouble. The islands, plural, are already a "them," a
shorthand archipelago. How will I distinguish between this "them" and the
upstart one?

The problem is not really one of number. It lies in my early perception
of tides. Being a landlubber, I watched land shrink and swell when I went to
the shore. I didn't see water rise and fall.

The Sound has slowly changed me.

Now I focus on the liquid.[39]

Here was a hint, whispered from the "pneumatic foam" of coastlines I
thought I had known and would come to love anew. Focus on the liquid.
Buckles's clue streamed with the clues of Hau'ofa, Marika, and Christensen.
Make a new home. Learn the sea's language. Follow the currents.

Living on the coast of WA was changing me, and it would change my
theological map too. God, the grounded source of our being, was beginning to
ebb and flow through an "oceanically widened experience of self." [40] With the
yearnings of fellow sea-farers I prayed, "You are the ocean that laps my being, in
you I dwell." [41] This archipelagic yearning to love the "depths of God" (1 Cor.
2:10) was no subliminal urge to oblivion, avoidance of responsibility, or infantile regression. The wind of another Spirit moved across the face of the waters.
Catherine Keller wrote to me (though she did not know it): "Has the death of
God viewed from *down under*, (un)veiled instead another depth of 'God'?"[42]

MYSTERY DOWN UNDER

Nanarup	Garden Island
Woodman's Point	Two People's Bay
Cottesloe	Marmion Marine Park
Coogee	Ningaloo
South Beach	Monkey Mia
Yallingup	Hamlin Pool
Turquiose Bay	Canal Rocks
Rottnest Island	Leighton Beach

Living along the coast of WA, I affirmed the wise words of nature writer Terry
Tempest Williams: "Spirituality is not a belief. It is a place."[43] And there are
many places along the coast, named with the tongues of Nyoongar, Yamachi,
Dutch, French, English, and others offering seascapes of memory. In WA, a

"sense of place" has been vital for reimagining and contextualizing Australian culture, as George Seddon realized in his classic story of coming to WA from Victoria: "It slowly became clear to me that I wasn't an Australian at all, but a Victorian . . . So my first job was to understand this land. I was lucky in the people I met, and I began to learn . . . For me, it was learning to see."[44]

Learning to see the sea came in many waves for me. Once I was taken by a strong current off the reef at Yallingup, only to glimpse the vast inverted cathedral of the cavern below me. My sons and I swam with dolphins at Peppermint Grove Beach and then with green turtles at Turquoise Bay, at Ningaloo. On "Sorry Day," we listened carefully to the mournful story of a Nyoongar woman remembering how she used to call the whales from Bathers Beach, now overrun with fast-food joints, yachts, and tourist buses. I remember the day swimming at Coogee when I first sensed the wind had shifted, from the warm morning breeze flowing down from the hills to the refreshing "Fremantle Doctor," blowing in from the sea, stirring up whitecaps. Then there was the Leighton Beach Rally when thousands chanted "Beach for all!" against the plans of corporate developers interested in remapping coastal places for high-rises for the few.

Place is essential for cultural meaning and practice; as John Inge writes, "Our existence as embodied beings means that place is as necessary to us as the air we breathe but, more than that, it seems to me that our human experience is shaped by place."[45] Why not for theology, too? Unfortunately, theology (like much of Western thought) has subordinated place to space and time, which Inge believes has led to a "dehumanizing loss."[46] Fortunately, literature on the "fate of place" and its recovery has been growing, with contextual theologians beginning to speak from place within a more nuanced and complex understanding of culture.[47] For example, Sigurd Bergmann claims that contextual theology can only form a "manifold interpretation pattern of . . . God in function today" when "traditions in the cultural environment of human beings and the natural environments are part of one single common biospherical history." Thus the environmental surroundings of individuals and communities contribute to the construction of theological meaning through "the production of inner visual pictures for orientation."[48]

Contextual theologians in Australia have been doing their own analysis, attending to their surroundings and inner visual pictures.[49] Yearning for a new poetics, Geof Lilburne notes the "triumph of homogeneous space" in the Western tradition and calls for a "reconstitution of place" through particular attentiveness to the land.[50] For many contextual theologians, poets, novelists, and spiritual seekers, the wide brown land and red-hearted desert provide the sense of place needed for renewing the Australian cultural imagination. As mapped by Jungian theorist David Tacey, the iconic spiritual journey entails traveling physically, psychologically, and politically from the crowded, urbane edge-skin to the sacred, soul-center of Australia: Uhluru, or Ayers Rock.[51]

But in attending to my new neighborhood, I found that when I asked people about important places, most talked about the coast. As I came to understand, it was the simple sea pleasures and practices that people talked about—walking their dogs on the beach, swimming in the early morning, sitting on the verandah catching the breeze, meeting friends for a cup of coffee, fishing from the jetties, surfing, and snorkeling—these comprised the colorful grains of "sand in [their] souls."[52] I listened as cultural-studies theorists mused, "We all dream of the sand and the sea in Australia."[53] As Meaghan Morris claims, the beach is "one of the deepest-laid 'realities of life' in Australia."[54] And as novelist David Malouf observes, "Once again the idea of ocean has been essential to how we define who we are and who we are most closely related to."[55]

Yet, Tacey's map charts the coastal edge as a shallow, secular space. Are there other ways of mapping Australian senses of spiritual place? I began pursuing the question posed by ethnographer Margaret Somerville: "Can our stories of pleasure and bodies, and the landscape of our sea, give rise to a different spirituality?"[56] Thus, what if the "edge of the sacred" is reimagined as a "sacred edge"?[57] A cue came from Davaney: "Theologians need to contend with vastly more materials than that of, say, the plural Christian tradition; we must also engage the material realities and traditions of nation, ideology, gender, race, and class as well as other religions and cultures with their concrete particularities."[58] What if as a constructive theologian I began contending with the "vastly more materials" of *place*—sand and surf, blue horizons, sorrowful loss, and salt-blessed skin?

As a "spiritual ethnographer," I talked with people about their "ordinary" experiences of the coast and their spiritual senses of place. I heard many sacred-edge narratives, some of which I share here.[59] They continue to engage me in thinking like an archipelago:

> *It's a place where I've made connections at key times in my life, especially in crisis. My healing place is by the sea. It's renewing.*

> *To me, the ocean represents something about God's personality. It's there, it's beauty, it's love, but it needs to be respected.*

> *There's this sense of being part of it all. It comes out of respect for the sea and the relationship that I have had over so many years.*

It's not that the land is the light and the water is the darkness. There is light and dark in each. And we can have our storms within. The storms are important . . . they lead to transformation.

I can't remember a time when there wasn't the beach. The expanse of the ocean to the west is as important to me as the expanse of the land. There's meaning in both directions. I'm not on the edge of something, so much as in the middle of something.

In these small grains of conversation, I sensed a different way to map the God-world relation. The spiritual edge doesn't end in the shallows, but flows as a place of possibility for deep connection, within oneself, with others, and with Sacred Presence. On the edge, all things belong, even the storms, as water-wisdom incorporates both light and darkness. Spiritual deepening involves humility, as we receive ourselves anew embraced within a Mystery larger than ourselves, yet welling up from the abyss within ourselves. We can't anchor for too long—the sea-changes keep flowing, and there's meaning in both directions. Novelist Tim Winton's words map a coastal spiritual journey:

> Australians are surrounded by ocean and ambushed from behind by desert—a war of mystery on two fronts . . . Of the two mysteries, the sea is more forthcoming; its miracles and wonders are occasionally more palpable, however inexplicable they be. There is more bounty, more possibility for us in a vista that moves, rolls, surges, twists, rears up, and changes from minute to minute . . . The sea is the supreme metaphor for change.[60]

From down under, the yearning of an archipelagic imagination for fluidity, connection, and transformation can help us see/sea ourselves in the God-world relation anew. Living along the coast of WA was changing me, eroding and reconnecting me in a water-world. We may have been taught to be divided by species, class, race, culture, sexuality, gender, and passport, but perhaps these coastlines can become sacred edges for diving deeper into the multipolar, maritime Mystery we all share.

MAPS OF MYSTERY

I have always been moved by the ocean—its sounds, the topography of the sometimes sandy and sometimes rocky land surrounding it . . . The sight, smell, sound, fluidity and changing nature of the ocean—especially preserved, undeveloped stretches—have always

been a symbol of God who has many gifts, many strengths, and the power to adapt to life's
circumstances.
　　　　—KAREN BAKER-FLETCHER, *SISTERS OF DUST, SISTERS OF SPIRIT*[61]

For her constructive theology, womanist Karen Baker-Fletcher draws on the
"oceanic memory" of her coastal sense of place to reimagine the "wildness" of
God, the natal source of creation's being and becoming.[62] The ocean symbolizes the God human beings can never domesticate, yet must learn to respect,
so that we might honor all of life. From an archipelagic horizon, can we begin
to imagine ourselves as islands within the ocean of God? With seascapes of suffering and destruction still before us following the Indian Ocean tsunami, this
may be difficult to do. Yet, in terms of religious metaphors and maps, mountains slide, rivers flood, and fires obliterate. Our impersonal metaphors for the
Divine remain vulnerable to limitation. But we know this to be true of personal
metaphors as well—fathers, mothers, lovers, and friends can be destructive and
life threatening. McFague acknowledges this, yet argues that personal metaphors
"arise from the most basic level of physical existence," and persons are "the most
sophisticated, complex, and unified part of an organic whole that embraces all
that is."[63] She distinguishes her metaphorical pathway from Gordon Kaufman,
who argues from a similar evolutionary, ecological perspective that personal
images are unable to serve as the symbolic center of a cosmos "grounded" in
"serendipitous creativity."[64]

　　Curiously, in sea literature, the ocean is imagined and related to in both
personal and impersonal ways. For Hau'ofa, the ocean is Mother, and saltwater speaks with Marika daily. But here I am exploring a sacred archipelago, an
impersonal image, but one that I believe helps us map interdependence, mutual
vulnerability, cultural diversity, and ecological ontology in a way that honors
both the local and the global. As environmental anthropologist Veronica Strang
suggests, encoded in water are the meanings of "a connective medium" and
"essence of life," for water provides a vision of collective existence through its
"circulation" as a "shared substance."[65] With the map of an archipelago, God's
vast body (of water) circulates and connects all things, even within our bodies,
as our cells are constituted by saltwater. Though oceanic maps have been drawn
and interpreted in ways amplifying the distance, smallness, and exotic difference of others, we can also create "imaginative geographies . . . not to drama-
tize the distance between what is close and what is far away, or to contain and
incorporate 'the Other,' but to produce constellations of relations that are never
bounded, never inhibited."[66] In a sacred archipelago of relations that are never
bounded, never inhibited, God the Spirit invites us out farther, and like another
wonderland character who dives head over heels, Alice of Winton's children's

story learns, "You could swim in the deep just as easily as in the shallows . . . To the deep, the deep, the deep!"[67] Perhaps from the shore we can begin to see the sea already flowing, but overlooked, within Christian imaginative geographies of Mystery. Here Karl Rahner brings his snorkel and fins to the coast:

> In the ultimate depths of [our] being [we know] nothing more surely than that [our] knowledge, that is, what is called knowledge in everyday parlance, is only a small island in a vast sea that has not been traveled. It is a floating island, and it might be more familiar to us than the sea, but ultimately it is borne by the sea . . . hence the [deepest] question for [we humans] is this. Which [do we] love more, the small island of [our] so-called knowledge or the sea of infinite mystery?[68]

Why do we continue to anchor ourselves in grounded images of God when archipelagic thinking offers another compelling map of Mystery?

ANOTHER THOUGHT EXPERIMENT

And what is more is islands: sea . . . Here is the fringey edge where elements meet and realms mingle, where time and eternity spatter each other with foam . . . We have less time than we know.

—ANNIE DILLARD, *HOLY THE FIRM*[69]

Ever since leaving the blue coast of Perth, Western Australia, a year and a half ago for the pine trees of central Minnesota, not a day goes by when I don't muse over in my mind another simple thought experiment. I walk down to the creek from the lodge, a few provisions in hand, put in the canoe, and paddle downstream through the forest to Little Stanchfield Lake. After crossing the lake, I then portage the canoe over County Road 6 and put in again where the creek picks up and winds through the wetlands that drain into the Rum River. Then I head southeast, down the Rum to the Mississippi, hang a right and paddle south, where I finally meet the Gulf of Mexico.

But now comes the hard part. I could go east along the coastline of the southern states, round the tip of Florida, shoot through the islands of the Caribbean, cross the Atlantic, curve around the Cape of Good Hope, and paddle directly across the Indian Ocean to Fremantle. I would put in at Leighton Beach, walk up to The Surf Club, and order a proper cup of coffee. Or, at the Gulf of Mexico, I could choose to go west, down along Texas and Mexico, through the Panama Canal (or all the way around the tip of South America) and then cross the Pacific Ocean, past Aoteroa/New Zealand, through the Tasman Sea, along the southern coast of Australia, around Augusta and Dunsborough to Fremantle, walk up the beach, and savor that cup of coffee. Like I say, this is a thought experiment, a very simplistic venture of imagination and yearning that reminds me daily: we live in an archipelagic world.

THE FLESH OF GOD
A Metaphor in the Wild

Catherine Keller

The human race is one of God's sense-organs,
Immoderately alerted to feel good and evil
And pain and pleasure. It is a nerve-ending,
Like eye, ear, taste-buds (hardly able to endure
The nauseous draught) it is a sensory organ of God's.
—ROBINSON JEFFERS

THEOPOETICS IN THE STREAM

Without some metaphor of the world as God's body, "God" becomes for me a gallery of distant icons, a rehearsal of relentless projections, or a minefield of apocalyptic contestations. In other words, "God" becomes a disembodied abstraction. To put it bluntly: if God is immaterial, God doesn't matter. I first encountered the figure of "God's cosmic body" in Charles Hartshorne's work, as an analogical argument against "the disembodied spirit with power to determine all becoming."[1] As to God's body—the body of Jesus as the incarnation of God, re-membered in the Body of Christ, surely demands (at least) one. But the hints as to the cosmic body of God, beginning with Plato, Tertullian, and Irenaeus, remain scattered and sparse, until the writings of process theologians and, above all, Sallie McFague. It is McFague's *The Body of God* that has given the metaphor an ecological birth and a systematic framework as a model for Christian theology.[2] This chapter affords an opportunity to reflect on the metaphor with primary reference to her work. My work has been more oblique in its reference to the metaphor, and so it is high time that I contribute to the theopoetic flesh of "God's body." This will develop here in relation to complexity theory, a fleshed-out pneumatology, an open-system panentheism, and Job's whirlwind in/sight into the creation.

Let me start again, less abstractly: I am sitting in a brook as I write. I know of McFague's predilection for mountain hikes in northerly zones. I don't know how many books have been written in brooks. But in this environmental congruence,

I am settled (almost too happily to write) on a hospitable boulder, softened by aeons of stream running down from the northern face of the Catskills.

It is almost too easy to meditate on the universe as God's body, here. Yet it does not occur to me that this rock *is* God, this water *is* God. These neighborly pines rooted stubbornly amid the layers of rock bed; this waterskimmer floating with such elegant insouciance on the water—ah, no, it is a couple, a coupling, a water-waltz, limbs forming delicate pontoons that rest, speed, and fish upon the surface. They do not announce to me, "We are God." When my (human) friend Mary glances over at me from a neighboring boulder, I do not think, "She is God." It is always a different sort of thought—and a *thought* it is, a way of seeing in thought, an in-sight, never a *knowledge.* If *God* is the right word for it, God is somehow somewhere *in* this all, every ripple and rill, every bite, flight, scramble, or stillness of it.

This thought appears in other sorts of wild spaces, like on a subway ride in Brooklyn, with God peeking through our eyes at each other. In our aggressive differences, our alien asymmetries, we cannot get out of the skin of this social body we share.[3] Yet here by the stream, these particular nonhumans in their shrinking woodland habitat bear their elemental clues about a universe that precedes and exceeds our input. However recklessly we have done in their dwelling places for the sake of our own constructions, however nonexistent is a pure or objective "nature"—these poignant relations persist. Without them theology can hardly breathe.

WHAT'S IN THE "IN"?

This God-in-them: what am I putting "in" the scene, "in" this niche of universe, "in" each element of the world, then? An image of a person, an artist, vaguely parental, knowing—one beginning already to nag me about all the suffering people elsewhere, unable to enjoy contemplative time by a clean stream? Am I injecting something only imaginable in a human body into all these other bodies—even as I project something too human into God? But then all it takes is—omi*god*—those pink daubs of wildflower, there, sparkling over the mossy face of rock, and the humanoid God dissipates. The intuition trickles in again, then: if "God" has a meaning beyond our collective wishes, our historical debt, and our professional commitments, then God is in and through and around all of this. This is a little complex bit of God's infinitely complex body. This rock is God's tough flesh, this stream God's fluid, this insect God's sprightliness, this friend God's thoughtfulness.

And my own pleasure amid this scene: is it part of the humanity Robinson Jeffers poetically imagines as "one of God's sense-organs"? Perhaps I am like a nerve ending or brain cell, conveying a pulse of the world's feeling to the world's ultimate Feeler. Might we imagine this subject as enfleshed in the universe, as a body of bodies within bodies within bodies: an infinite regress of "withins"? Would "the flesh of God" suggest something less like Chinese boxes and more like a shared matrix of materialization? But would it then fail to include the inorganic bodies, down to the molecules, the atoms, the charmed quarks? All these events of the divine flesh—these bodies interacting with grace and verve—retain plenty of room for breakdown, surprise, and shift.

The biologist Stuart Kauffman asks, wonderfully: "Whence cometh all this bubbling activity, complexity, and *chutzpah*?"[4] Science, he argues, has no answer yet to the question of the emergence of life, of creative complexity, in the universe.[5] In the meantime, all these bodies dwell in and as complex life-systems poised on the "edge of chaos."[6] McFague's model never attempts to use God to fill in the gaps of science; her models, insistently, claim no power to explain or even to describe. These are imaginative constructs helping us to see the world differently—and to act in it with trust, love, and a widening ethics.

But here is the rub: if this universe can be imagined as God's *body*, aren't I saying after all that this universe *is* God? How else can this metaphor actually transfer its meaning, as it must, by a process of analogy, from my body to God's? My body is, after all, not something separate from "me." "I"—subject, self, or spirit—am not something "in" my body. What does it mean to say that God is "in" the body-world? Neither contemporary thinking—biological, philosophical, theological—nor biblical anthropology suggests a soul that is "in" the body, like a jack-in-the-box to be released upon death or a person who dwells in one house and then moves to another. In the interest of an ecological nondualism, do we end up reinscribing the dualism of spirit and body at a higher level?

Sallie McFague is all too familiar with this problem, which she has in an important sense solved. "With the metaphor of the world as God's body, God as the agent or spirit in and through all that is (as our spirits are the energizers of our bodies), we can imagine a unified view of God and the world, which does not, however, identify them."[7] Yet the dilemma accompanies and is restimulated by the terms of the model and so cannot be solved once and for all. For to stress that "God is not only the universe," but "also (and primarily) the breath that gives it life, the spirit that transforms it" still presupposes the binary language of spirit and matter that will always again need deconstructing. And to claim that "every creature, thing, and process in the universe has value because it is an aspect of God, it is part of God's body"—is a *valuable* step for ecology.[8] But process theologians would object that each creature has *intrinsic* value and *therefore* is valuable to God. The challenge is to think the difference of "God" and "world" with a radicality that actually deepens their interdependence. Or put differently, we will want to complicate the boundaries by which these two terms are opposed, while releasing mystery into the first term and creativity into every level of the second.

If the model's potential has still barely been realized in Christianity, however, it is not because of its inadequate development so far, but because of the sheer force of the resistance it faces. Process theology, like McFague, has been skittish about the risk of pantheism that the model invokes—the danger of in effect making God a metaphor for the universe, and therefore undercutting the basis for *relationship* with God. McFague's own pneumatology already initiates the biblical hermeneutic of creation needed to relax the fear of pantheism. I share that hermeneutic. But it is in a greater *wildness* of the Spirit—indeed its creative vibration at the edge of what the sciences of complexity call "chaos"— that I have found the "energizer" of a theology of creation.

Here's my hunch: that metaphor of the edge of chaos may designate the very space of the "in" of all-*in*-God. That space, that "in," that distinguishes but does not separate God from world, would not designate a clean boundary, as though God is a vessel containing world, or as though God is distributed in neat metaphysical pellets, one per being. The "in" suggests an edgy, interconnective, and unpredictable difference.

FLESHING OUT THE SPIRIT

I am to my body as God is to the universe. Therefore if I "am" my body, then God "is" the universe: *is* this stone, this stream. Or rather their totality: would God perhaps only be "in" the bug as the whole is "in" the part, or as "I" am in each part of a body that is not just "mine" but *me*. It is when the analogy drifts toward this mind-body identism that the alarms go off for Christian theology, ever fearful of pantheism, of simply identifying God with the creation, of reducing God to nothing more than a name for the totality of creatures.

So either God is one with the universe as I am with my body, or I must resort to a mind-body dualism of self *in* the body in order to guard against a reductive pantheism. Yet the hermeneutical motivation of the model, at least in McFague's version, is ecological. And what could be more detrimental to the cultivation of an ecological consciousness than a reinscription of a Cartesian subjectivity, the self or spirit as a metaphysical substance that is qualitatively different from the mechanical, merely material substance of the body?

McFague wrote *The Body of God* fully attentive to this problem. She proposed a sound solution, one that avoids both undesirable outcomes. The key is pneumatology: "We are suggesting, then, that we think of God metaphorically as the spirit that is the breath, the life, of the universe, a universe that comes from

God and could be seen as the body of God."[9] God as Spirit is not identical with the material world or any part of it—but also never separable from it. Such a God "is not primarily the orderer and controller of the universe but its source and empowerment, the breath that enlivens and energizes it."[10] This line of thinking resonates with my own intuitions. If God is Spirit, which of course is confirmed by the sole Gospel "definition" of God (in John 4), the Spirit is the very life and energy of the universe-body and of its innumerable bodies. Everything, of course, depends on how we read the relationship of God the Spirit to the world.

Once we shift to the language of this blowing Spirit, we are less able to resort to the old habit of theistic dualism, less able to fantasize a disembodied God up and outside of the universe, micromanaging it from above. But of course that fantasy always exports its own body—the white-skinned, old, bearded one—so we seek to correct it here in its own rhetorical milieu, to counter it with the equally biblical and far less anthropomorphic imagery of the wind/bird/breath Spirit. This Spirit is promising in its nondualistic potential for God-talk. Yet McFague has noted, the spirit language is itself capable of the most radical dualisms in theological anthropology, especially when it comes to traditional deployments of the Pauline spirit vs. flesh. So while I think the key to the metaphor of the body of God indeed lies in pneumatology, the doctrine of the Spirit must itself be opened up, released from its own doctrinal confinements.[11]

The biblical version of the spirit/body binary then actually begins to break down our lingering dualism. Scripturally speaking, there is no rigid spirit/body binary, not in any metaphysical sense—though its likelihood is instigated by the Pauline duality. But theologically we can only deconstruct the *spirit/body* dualism by first deconstructing the *Spirit/spirit* dualism that links the terms of the analogy. Then we are working by a reverse analogy, one that might please a Barthian (with the *analogia fides*), as it moves at this crucial point not from world to God but from God to world: for the very metaphor of a human spirit, as the self (later *Geist*-mind) of the person, can only be thought in dependence upon the metaphor of the Spirit of God. If God's Spirit is to the world as our spirits are to our bodies, then how is God's Spirit related to our spirits? What kind of analogy is being drawn?

The problematic of "spirit" is complex biblically—in other words, theopoetically—but that complexity, we will see, is the heart of the matter. There is a strong distinction but no sharp line between the Spirit that is God, named finally the Holy Spirit, and the spirits of creatures, including humans. That distinction, however, must not be interpreted dualistically, nor monistically flattened. And the third way between the dualism of classical theism and the monism of so-called pantheism is the method of panentheism, which McFague deploys skillfully.[12]

We live each of us as spirited flesh, enfleshments of a single spirit of All—creatively differentiated into the many spirited bodies as our "own," as our selves. Only so can our spirits—the spirits of our flesh, the life and breath and animation of our bodies—enter into relation with each other and, theologically, with their creator. But this is precisely not the classical dualism of spirit vs. flesh—this is the creation as the very enfleshment of spirit, the *spiritus creator* stirring up the energies of the deep to flow into the bodies of the creation. Without trumping scientific speculation, without imposing an external Designer, we can imagine the work of a Wisdom from the start, or from the start we know anything about—a Wisdom by which, for instance, the universe at its Big Bang expands at the impossibly exact speed, enabling matter to clump into stars and us, rather than to dissipate into the cosmic soup or collapse back in a big crunch. This is an awesomely open-ended, spontaneous process—not a divine dictation but a creative in-spiration.

In the inspiriting of the universe, no dualistic dividing line is possible between Spirit and the spirits (including our spirits) of the world. The divine breath that enlivens each creature, that is the creature's own spirit, *is* the breath of God, is as such God's spirit. Try putting a boundary around a breath—I think that is called strangulation! Yet a breath has its uniqueness. The individual human spirit in the biblical imaginary can be wise or vexed, faithful or lying—and the Spirit of God "rests upon" persons in moments of in-spiration and prophecy, reviving, lifting, or stirring their own spirits. And despite the "restful" image, it invariably causes trouble. For the movement of the Spirit, the movement indeed of God in the world, invariably comes up against the established orders. It is not accidental to the Spirit that it provokes disorderly conduct, but of its very dynamism of risky embodiment. Spirit can only materialize at the edge of chaos.

The difference of our spirits to the Spirit of God is then not one of *ontological separation*—as though once the divine breath has filled our bodies it remains then separate, no longer divine, sealed off like air in a balloon. The crass version of divine transcendence that increasingly characterized classical theism, and locked into place in the Reformation, produced the fantasy of a God "outside" the world (occasionally making helpful or angry forays into it) and the presumption of the divine omnipresence. This version of divinity as separation purports to honor the transcendence of God, but in fact it is far more preoccupied with our own human honors—that is, with establishing a "heaven" beyond this world of dying bodies, where we will be "saved" when we die. Too much Christianity has disguised greed for the rewards of private immortality as praise of the Creator—as though the higher we lift God, the higher we too shall soar. The idea of the bodiliness of God lets this fantasy down; the balloon deflates.

The grounding of God, however, implies no reductionism.[13] The pathos of hope, for those whose lives are rude or short, cannot be disregarded. Nor does the re-embodiment of faith exclude some rich sense of the resurrection of our bodies in the body of Christ, indeed of an eternal life in which we may, in the spirit, *participate.* In the meantime, however, we may with McFague be especially interested in awakening Christians from their ecocidal slumbers. Any eternal life of our spirits will depend in any case on our ability to live, in the spirit of life, within our living bodies and their lifetimes, which is to say, in such a way as to make our lives count *within* the creation. The more we look to a disembodied immortality, the *less God-like* we become—and so, ironically, the less capable of what the Bible means by *eternal life.* It is a Johannine concept that can only be read as the qualitative change designated by life "in spirit," partaking of "living waters," and paradigmatically exemplifed by the word, the logos, "*become flesh.*"

The biblical imaginary, to the extent one can draw theological generalizations from it, constructs the universe as all-together inspirited, from the first hovering of the spirit over the prematerial waters through every phase of creaturely life. The divine breath of life, the *ruach,* not a thing but rather an activity, a breathing—is endlessly released into the free agents of creation, enlivening the unfathomable multiplicity, the poignant complexity, of the *genesis collective.* There is nothing disembodied about this spirit; as God's it is embodied as the world, and in each of us it is—with all its moody, moral, personal, and indeed "spiritual" qualities—the spirit of material life itself. As Job proclaimed, "As long as my breath is in me, and the Spirit of God is in my nostrils, my lips will not speak falsehood" (Job 27:3). In other words, this divine immanence is not a metaphysical fact, a presence of God transparently available, like air, but rather a quality of relationship. I am not breathing in God if I am speaking out with dishonesty; with hypocrisy; with a dispiriting certainty, like Job's comforters, as to the truth (a perpetual temptation for theologians).

A full-bodied ecotheology will embrace a wider, more ancient Spirit. McFague articulates its pneumatology in terms of a *nouveau* Augustinianism: "As the embodied spirit of all that is, God would be closer to us than we are to ourselves, for God would be the very breath of our breath."[14]

OPEN-SYSTEM PANENTHEISM

For God is the God of life, and those who love this God love all God's creation, tend to it, heal it, feel it, enhance it, feed it: for "the body of God must be fed."[15] *That* primal piety wakes me up. Not only does it allow one to understand the near universality of blood sacrifices in the older religions of the world, but it brings theology into resonance with the ecological realism of Whitehead's "life feeds on life."[16] But McFague's point is that the care for the material needs of all is key to the gospel.

Process theology has taught for half a century, depending on the White-headian-Hartshornian-Cobbsian model of divine-world interdependence, that at every moment "the consequent nature of God" absorbs in itself the spontaneous self-actualizations of the world, toxic or nourishing. This model suffers the world to come unto God. God internalizes as part of this "nature"—a sensitive, receptive nature itself open to surprise, disappointment, curiosity—the input of the wild and open universe. If God has first, at any moment, lured forth a world, there is no place "outside" of God from which the world could have been called. Yet the world comprises its own alterity, its otherness, not by some spatial abstraction of exteriority, but by its *freedom.* The world would have no interest to God—could offer no companionship, neither love nor worship—were this freedom not irreducibly streaming through the becoming world. In the creative processes that God invites—and then receives, moment by moment—this autochthonous spontaneity expresses itself. Its effects may be good, bad, or bland. But it makes possible a relationship of true reciprocity, and it interrupts the theological production of the closed circle of omnipotence, predetermining providence, and final bodiless salvation. The alternative becomes ever more thinkable: that of the positive feedback loops of an open system of "self-organizing complexity."[17]

And so the "in" of God "in" the world cannot be tidily contained, as though God's transcendence balances out this immanence (a way one might read McFague's apologetic moves, like those of Moltmann, asserting immanent transcendence and, unlike him, transcendent immanence); as though really this panentheism were not so different from the classical closed system. For the difference is in a certain sense radical—precisely the difference between a closed and an open system. In a closed system, the entropy of the world will gradually overpower the complexity—hence the dependence on a God "outside." In any open system, the divine "outside" is one of moving relationship, not fixed ontology, or else the system would not be open. Nonetheless, like McFague's, this reading of God's body does maintain certain classical Christian values: for instance, those of a personal relationship to a God who remains transcendent of—that is, irreducible to—all creaturely knowledge or categories, and whose immanence is revealed in a unique way in the incarnation of Christ but has always already pervaded the creation as the Spirit, the very immanence of God.

However, in a different, perhaps more postmodern mood, we may intensify the wilder, flesh-loving, world-desiring Spirit. It also blows through the figure of God's Body. I am indeed wanting to stir up the wilder energies enfolded in the model, without meaning to subvert its own care for the doctrinal history. The difference of this mood of the Spirit registers as the boundary zone *between* God and world: precisely the domain of pneumatology. This spirit is "in" the world in a way that does not reinscribe the classical boundaries dividing God from the All, a pan/en/theism indistinguishable at the slash-boundaries of its "in" from classical theism. The "in," however, remains, or else the relationship drops out.[18] Spinozan metaphysics is not the other pole of our problem. The reduction of spirit to any modern closed system of the world by which it collapses quickly and entropically toward a flat materialism—*that* is the problem of the other pole, the opposite of classical theism. Pantheism is not materialism but idealism, and materialism may have its own biblically inspired forms. The problem is of a monistic materialism in which the complex can be reduced to the simple. "Pantheism" is not a serious problem theologically simply because almost no one pursues it. So while it is useful pedagogically to demonstrate how, structurally, panentheism represents a third way between and beyond both classical theism and pantheism, this strategy remains a rather abstract doctrinal argument.

Yet the "in" of panentheism, of "the world *in* God," does indeed meaningfully mark itself off from pantheism in another, less obsolete sense. For "the world *as* God" can symbolize the most globally potent of all current ideologies—the capitalist materialism that performs, in current cahoots with the bastardized form of classical theism known as fundamentalism, the secular idolization of the world. The flattened, dreary mechanisms and materialisms of a closed system universe—the "classical" physics of Newton—of course are deeply indebted to their opposite, to the classical theism that construed the creation as little more than a sign of the Creator's power to save us all *from* the world, from our bodies, in the *afterworld*. This Augustinian sense of the world as mere site of pilgrims passing through—to be loved only in passing, as a means to the love of the creator—already flattened the first creation to a mere prelude for the new, the supernatural, creation.[19] How much further the flattening of the world has gone in its desacramentalization, in the Protestant destruction of the iconography and the cosmology of medieval Christianity. The "spirit of capitalism" under the regime of Protestant modernity yielded new levels of both Christian and materialist literalism, presumably at odds but ultimately in solidarity, as we witness now in the love affair of late capitalist and fundamentalist Christian politics. In their shared antiecological commitments, they have merged notions of our "dominion" as warrant to use up the bodies of the world.[20]

There is a wilder wind that blows through the biblical text, a Spirit that was too readily domesticated and disembodied as the Holy Spirit and cut off from our own breathy life—as though air, breath, or wind can be cut off without asphyxiation![21] So the body of God lives from that Spirit; or that metaphor, at any rate, lives from the inspiriting force of a breath that is always at once material and spiritual, my own and God's own—an "inspiracy" of cosmological proportions! For just to release the caught breath of the Spirit once again—always, again, breathe—before we suffocate the atmosphere of this living planet means to cross the metaphysical boundaries of God/world, God/human, spirit/flesh, individual/collective. It means to cross the boundaries without destroying them; that is, it means to deconstruct the classical separations while actually enhancing *difference*. For if the difference between God and world is a matter of relationship rather than opposition, then there is after all not such a problem in imagining how the world could be at once the body of God—a God whose spirit is not the opposite of materiality but its source and resource—and at the same time *in relation to* God. So then the "in" of *the spirit in flesh* resembles at one and the same time the *relational "in"* of intimacy, of the lover in the beloved, or the babe in arms; and the *organic "in"* of the sap in the tree, the blood in the veins, the fetus in the womb.

For the otherness, the outsideness, of this different one—this lover, this baby—is all the more intense for its intimacy. The other who becomes part of my reality, even of my body, remains other, remains in relationship—indeed far more meaningfully in relationship than are the billions of others who will remain outside of my consciousness. And as the example of the maternal relation to an infant suggests, the fetus that is "part" of the mother (at some point that no political campaign can designate) becomes its "own" person, and thus an other, perhaps a friend of the mother; or from the other direction, the other who is the tomato in living integrity comes "into" me and is organically part of me, even in its difference; or I become part of a community or an ecosystem, without ceasing to be my self. The boundary of in/out can only be fixed arbitrarily. So "God" then names a perspective not "outside" of the creation but embracing it—not something on the other side of a boundary theologians set, but rather the inconceivable edge of the universe itself. It is a bounding embrace that turns back in at every point, the outside that encompasses all differences—and that touches each. But then God touches each not from a vertical outside but from the point of contact between the creatures themselves, the point of interdependency, where boundaries might get hardened, or where, alternatively, a creative interchange might take place. This God then dwells within the creatures as they dwell in God: or in medieval mystic Nicholas of Cusa's language, "But everything that actually exists is in God, for God is the actuality of all things . . . Since the universe is contracted in each actually existing thing, it is obvious that God, who is the universe, is in each thing and each actually existing thing is immediately in God, as is the universe. Therefore, to say that 'each thing is in each thing' is not other than to say that 'through all things God is in all things' and that 'through all things all are in God.'" This is not a simple pantheism, but rather a consequent panentheism, which recognizes that whatever is "in" God is part of God, and therefore as universe "is" not other *(non aliud)* than God.[22]

My point is simply analogical: *if God is in the universe as I am in my body, this does not mean that God is not in relationship to the universe.* The universe can remain—as a whole and in every part—an other to God; analogically, the others with whom I most intimately relate do not remain outside of my personal boundaries. As to my body, I do experience myself as relating *to* it, however unfashionable that may sound. I tried for a couple decades to rehearse the simplicity of "I am my body." *My Body, Myself,* after all![23] It always felt forced. But a complex version might not. The comma in "my body, myself" need not after all indicate synonymity but internal relation. I emerge—I become—within, from, *and* as my body. I relate more or less healthfully to it, I identify more with certain parts (brain, nerve feelings, eyes, heart) than with others (toes, fingernails, nose), and yet this pattern of experience is constantly shifting, entering into its own internal tensions, contradictions, occasional moments of coordinated grace. And for me to insist on this distinction of "I" from my body is precisely not to separate from the body or even from a part of it. It is to acknowledge a certain roving difference. By this way of reasoning, then, we may relativize the separation of spirit from flesh so that the difference is neither a separation nor an identity, but a relation—a differential relation of embodiment. *The spirit embodies itself through difference,* and it inspires the dis-spirited body as best it can, within the indeterminate varieties of bodies in time and in freedom.

In other words, we do not have to stick to a classically theist notion of God as an external, all-controlling Creator of the world *ex nihilo* in order to assure that God and the world are *other* enough to be in relationship. *Au contraire:* it is the rhetoric of God as omnipotent Creator/Governor that belies the personal relationship with God. The language of that personal relationship—of covenant, faithfulness, and love—has borne the cross of a later language, that of the immutable omnipotence of an extrinsic transcendence. Might theology be starting to reimagine this personal relationship—not to a Superperson but to *a mystery that encompasses the personal and the impersonal,* an honest transcendence, to which we can only relate *as persons*? Such a personal relationship is not therefore an anthropomorphic person-to-person relationship, in which we fantasize an infinitely expanded divine male Person (or two of them), and call it/them Lord. It is time for Christianity to outgrow its dishonest deployments of the rhetoric of divine transcendence. This pseudo-transcendence, in the name of its "personal relationship to the Lord," conveniently declares Him [sic] radically other than bodily creatures while surreptitiously uploading a masculine anatomy onto "Him." For we can imagine no personal relationship with the bottomless mystery of life if we seal it off with all-too-human-immanent images of power as paternity or royalty. This is mere incoherence—that which is transcendent in God is truly that which we must leave to negative theology, to the unspeakable alterity. And if we are going to go ahead and speak—as all apophatic theologians have done—then our kataphatic affirmations will need to come from the best metaphors of relationship, not the worst (the dominative, the oppressive, the patriarchal). And those metaphors, drawn from human and nonhuman life, will intensify relationship in difference and difference in relation.

An alternative rhetoric, a process ontology of radical relationality, kicks in to support this affirmative God-talk: it is contiguous with McFague's model of construction and lends it needed conceptual strength. It offers a cosmological account, like hers in dialogue with postmodern science, of a universe where each being is constituted by its relations, emergent within a matrix of physical potentialities. This is an open-system panentheism. Each being takes place as a singularity, a becoming, lured toward greater complexity by the divine eros—and received into the consequent nature of that divinity as the stuff (or food!) of the deity's own nonstatic genesis. This is not to say that God is fickle, or becomes someone else, or was inadequate and "had to" grow more perfect. This is to say, with Hartshorne's "logic of perfection," that as we draw our analogies from human experience, consider what growth means: the more perfect a being is, the more he or she grows, even showing curiosity and development on the death bed. The most mediocre models of the human are surely those who do not change—and who in apparent goodwill wish others, with high school yearbook wisdom, the same: "don't ever change." There is nothing static or immutable about the biblical deity. If some Hebrew could be translated to suggest God's changelessness (Ps. 102:27), the context in each case shows the meaning: God is not ontologically static, the unmoved mover, the immutable, not even "eternal" in the sense of residing outside of time—but rather the faithfully everlasting one.

As to this growth, look after all at this barely conceivable cosmos, more mysterious than is most current God-language, in which indeed the universe is growing, expanding—*nah,* wildly accelerating—in its rate of expansion! Isn't it the growing Body—all hundreds of billions of its galaxies each made of billions of stars—of a becoming God?

A WHIRLWIND LENS

We can no longer get our brains around the scales—macrocosmic or microcosmic—of the universe. We do not even know if there is just one and not a multiverse. Astrophysics or biology strain their own models in so many directions that we might want to counsel a scientific apophasis: the discipline, which we in theology have not performed with any great consistency, of acknowledging our utter incapacity in the face of mystery. Science, like theology (and therefore certainly ecological theologies, perched as is McFague's close to the edge between science and religion), would benefit from Cusa's *docta ignorantia*—the knowing ignorance: not to give up on our knowledge but to keep always in mind how humanly constructed are the models whereby we know anything at all. We are all loathe, however, to risk the authority of our models. To science, "God" still sounds largely like an excuse for ignorance, and faith still competes with science for an essential and unifying certainty.

We may step beyond such moribund pretenses into a confident uncertainty—a humble spirit that, just because it can no longer evacuate the mystery of existence, imagines boldly and with discipline. In this step we can make use, as does McFague and as all ecotheology must, of the models of natural science without succumbing to the temptation to "naturalize" or essentialize models constructed of human elements. We do not mirror the natural elements but rather admit their all-present efficacy; for the nonhuman infinitely precedes and exceeds the human, and the extralinguistic funds every tone and mark of language.

For faith this humility might mean to step into the pneumatological zone designated in complexity theory as the condition "far from equilibrium," where in Genesis 1:2 the spirit hovers, vibrates, oscillates upon the face of the chaos waters. Whether spiral galaxies, traffic jams, animal population patterns, the cerebral cortex, whirlpools, or leaky taps: "the most complex and interesting things in the Universe are happening at the edge of chaos, just before order is destroyed."[24] That is, between mere gaseous disorder and a rigid order, fluctuations and feedback generate the dissipative, far-from-equilibrium conditions and the fractal-like patterns that characterize so much of the material world. Chaos here means the "extreme sensitivity to initial conditions" symbolized by the butterfly effect: a butterfly flapping its wing outside my apartment window can set off—through the complex and indeed infinite chain of winds, currents, and other interconnected earth processes—an avalanche in the Himalayas. More to the point, my overdependence on fossil fuels to keep me writing in coolness can be a trigger in the disasters that global warming is beginning to produce. Or by contrast, your ecological action to support sustainable energy policies can produce a butterfly effect in your community, and so in the nation and the world.

The body of God, if it is a body of endless bodies within bodies, would be then most meaningfully imagined as the most open of systems—the host of a universe of systems far more open than we had until recently imagined. With the spiral arms of galaxies formed by the chaos-phenomenon of feedback, the map of the universe looks less like my childhood image of a set of balls rotating in a void, or a Chinese box of closed systems; the cosmos looks far more like a fractal, with its psychedelic beauty generated by multiple scales of iteration. This virtually infinite fractal model does not need "God" as an explanatory hypothesis. But it is fractured with its interdimensional spaces, riddled with openings, nonlinearities, and indeterminacies. For instance, our planet is "bathed in the flow of energy from a star, which makes the whole surface of the planet an open, dissipative system." Because the system is open, the second law of thermodynamics, dictating that entropy always increases, no longer automatically obtains. "All life on the surface of the Earth makes use of this energy to maintain itself far from equilibrium, on the edge of chaos."[25]

I have elsewhere developed a biblical theology of creation from chaos—the *tehom,* or the deep of Genesis 1:2—with reference to complexity theory. The spirit oscillating on "the face of the waters" rather precisely anticipates the life at "the edge of chaos."[26] But this is not a motion of unilateral determination; this is not a *creatio ex nihilo* or an omnipotent dictatorship. Attentive to the potentiality of the matter that is already divine flesh, the *spiritus creator* calls forth new levels of complexity—and therefore of spontaneity, even freedom. The divine invitation is not a coercion, nor is the divine reception a final closure. The panentheistic motion between the universe and God is a movement of spirit into emergent systems even as they emerge—and a reception of those creatures when they have emerged. It is what Wesley calls a mutual breathing, a breathing of God into the world and the world into God.[27]

This chapter has been a single meditation on the slim little slip of a word, the "in" of God-in-world, or the "en" of panentheism. I have suggested that we read that "in" as forming the kind of permeable, unsuffocating, intimate boundary or skin that distinguishes and connects God and world. But it is not then any more a spatial than a temporal boundary: it is a transition, edge, *eschatos* between phases. In other words, we may imagine the "in/en" of panentheism as forming the ultimate "edge of chaos"—a phase transition between moments of becoming: *God is in All* as the permeating possibility for the next moment, a possibility not yet actualized, open to divine surprise. *All is in God,* who receives the already actual in the embrace of everlastingness—and whose experience, whose "self," is thereby altered. Precisely in the intrinsic value of every creature's experience for-itself—for the most part oblivious of anything called "God"—the multiplicity of the "all" shifts, grows, evolves as God's own field of experience. What's in it for God? *Everything.* God's intensity of feeling depends upon the many animal and vegetable organs of experience evolved through the aeons of creation.

Without human sense organs of God, suggests the poet, God would be more like a serene rock—the Aristotelian ideal. But we only have passions of the heart through a physical heart, and gut-feelings by way of sensitive intestines, and thoughts by way of a brain, and sensuous touch by way of nerves. God may be imagined growing this ever more complex body, with its surprises of spontaneous agency, as a means of ever richer experience, ever more complex interrelations. One part of the highly cosmic body, which is, after all, a multibody, relates to every other part, and the spirit to the (open) whole. I do not "possess" my body as an external thing, nor am I in it as a mental, detachable substance thing. But, rather, spirit names a way—mine or God's—of being in the body. The Holy Spirit is the traditional language for God's way of being in the cosmos: God breathes into me my life, my spirit, that which has been traditionally individualized as soul. God names my way of being in the flesh, my way of being (in) the body.

God's incarnation throughout the universe may be uniquely intensified in the humanness we have symbolized in the life and suffering of Jesus; it may be distinctively transmitted in the Body of Christ. If, however, according to McFague's principle, we "maximize [the incarnation] in relation to the cosmos" then we may with less parochial competitiveness, with less infantile greed in the name of dominion, permit the stirrings of a love that will sustain our planetary life.[28] The "house rules" McFague suggests are what we need. But I think before the ethical responsibility of a mature sense of "stewardship," or of what enlightened evangelicals are calling "creation care" is likely to kick in, we will need as Christians to feel and practice the elemental love of the universe as our very love of God. No environmental moralism or apocalyptic threat will motivate the transformation. Love might. That elemental force of this love will perhaps be stimulated by a wilder spirit.[29] Rules are needed, but they will only be motivated by attraction; perhaps, indeed, the "strange attractor" of chaos theory, displaying the deep order within what appears to be chaos, can be one source of this elemental eros.

QUESTION TO JOB

Whirlwinds and whirlpools, patterns of vortices amid flow, suggest the strange order that can sustain itself over a long period without breaking up into randomness. From a tehomic theological perspective, there is no more important image of this strange attraction than that manifest in—not coincidentally—a whirlwind. Out of the honesty that kept Job's intolerable suffering throbbing with questions was first articulated the full possibility and, at the same time, the refusal of a classical theodicy: a justification of God's omnipotence in the face of human suffering. Intriguingly, it was the windy Spirit of God that prevented Job from acquiescing in the orthodoxy arguments of his friends. "As long as my breath is in me, and the *ruach* of God is in my nostrils, my lips will not speak falsehood" (27:3). And what no Christian orthodoxy since has come to terms with has been the terms of the answer he provokes—from that very *ruach*. The epiphany in the whirlwind, the turbulent wind of God, answers in a medium that is at the same time the message: for what is the content of the vision? Nothing but one long gorgeous poem of creation—a midrashic amplification of Genesis 1. But it is an iteration with a difference.

The whirlwind poetry stresses the wildness, the utterly undomesticated and untameable life of the creation—whether the morning stars singing or the baby sea bursting, squalling, "out from the womb"; the predations of the lion or the raven; the birthing of mountain goats and deer; the freedom of the wild ass and the forgetfulness of the ostrich, who nonetheless when it spreads its plumes aloft "laughs at the horse and its rider." On the epic monologue rushes, with its rhetorical questions, routinely misinterpreted by theologians tone-deaf to the poetry of creation as mere taunts of poor Job. "Can you lift up your voice to the clouds, so that a flood of waters may cover you?" (No, but apparently this is an activity God enjoys on a hot day!) "Who has the wisdom to number the clouds?" (Indeed, who? Are they countable? Do they have boundaries? Can God's wisdom count the uncountable?) YHWH poses questions more like Zen koans than courtroom interrogatories. Rather than the taunt of a bully God, displaying his omnipotent creator-power, I can only hear the teases of a divine artist, peeved at the disregard of her work, beginning with the difficult birth itself of the chaotic waters and proceeding to the ecstatic delight in the Leviathan, the witty and warning climax of the vision: "it leaves a shining wake behind it; one would think the deep to be white-haired." But warning—"will traders bargain over it? Will they divide it up among the merchants? Can you fill its skin with harpoons . . . any hope of capturing it will be disappointed. . . ." Well, this is a pre-Moby Dick perspective: the warning points right at us, who dare indeed to make merchandise of the wild itself, who commodify the incarnation of the deep.

I want to conclude with a question back to the poet of Job. McFague might well have asked it first. When, in the end, after the whirlwind has calmed, its climactic invocation of Leviathan having exhausted its artistic pride, Job repents his own interrogation of God. The tone is not of humiliation but of the wonder of one reborn against all expectations: "I had heard of you by the hearing of the ear, but now my eye sees you." Like most of us, God for Job had been a matter of theological hearsay. Now: what is it that he has *seen*? What "you" became visible to his "eye"? The Hebrews weren't much for seeing God—the eye is prone to idolatry. Job has received this speech from the whirlwind, the single longest soliloquy of God in the Bible. But what is, after all, its visual, visible content? There is no hint of God as such, as a figure—no glimpse even of throne, sword, or footstool. Not even McFague's favorite: the backside. Indeed, there is no description, let alone definition of God. God as such, the invisible, the unspeakable, remains bottomless mystery. What Job "sees" in the vision as narrated in such detail is only and precisely the multiplicity of untamed creatures. So, O Joban poet: does to "see" God then mean to see the creation? But to see with new eyes?

It would seem that in this turbulent poetry, even the fear of pagan idolatry could not inhibit this new in-sight: to see the creation is to see God's visible body. The All has spilled forth creatively, chaotically, procreatively from "the womb" (38:8). Surely the poet of Job does not mean to identify God (pantheistically) with any or all of the creatures. Yet the whirlwind blows away the foundations of any dualistic theism. Only a hint, a peek, of God's womb as the deep, the precreation *tehom*, and of God's body as the visible universe, comes through.[30] The in-sight comes in the extraordinary excitement with which the voice of the whirlwind describes the wild creatures. It expresses an utter captivation of the spirit in the details of their life and motion. It is through the symbols of the spirit of the whirlwind, the breath of life, and the *hochmah* (wisdom of God), that this uninhibited immanence come into play: "Is it by your wisdom that the hawk soars, and spreads its wings toward the south?" (39:26) The farcical, boastful element does not belie the honor of this maximum revelation offered to an honest and enraged sufferer. More importantly, the whirlwind spirit present in the wisdom in all things not only calls them forth but seems to soar and suck and run with them, with utter delight. Is YHWH insensitive to Job's suffering? Apparently not. The eye-opening dis/closure opens Job anew to his place amid the complexity and ambiguity of it all. It reopens existence itself. He gets a life. It is not the little narrative of reward stuck on the end, in an older, simpler Hebrew, that is the contribution of the poet. Rather, it is the elemental intensity of the vision, exploding with turbulence, vitality, and nutritive flesh, that offers the healing effect for the poet of the book of Job

Without the "immoderately alerted" capacity for pain and pleasure, good and evil, the universe would be a machine, and God's self-relation mere autoeroticism. The freedoms that keep life risky and worthwhile call us to an ethic that bursts with life, not with self-righteousness. This God seems hungry for life—"the body of God must be fed." It is not a matter of exacting sacrifices but of sharing the vision. The coupling insect skimming the brook feeds itself, the food chain, God's flesh, my eyes, these words. I offer this little exegesis in tribute and in gratitude for the "new lens for seeing" McFague has offered the future of Christianity.

7
THE HUMAN NICHE
IN EARTH'S ECOLOGICAL ORDER

Gordon D. Kaufman

I take it for granted, in this chapter, that human existence on planet Earth today must be understood in light of the theory of evolution. This is a sweeping conception that brings into interconnection and interdependence all forms of life that have appeared on our planet, interconnections grounded largely on developments in time over some billions of years. Life has evolved down many different lines, on one of which mammals appeared and eventually primates, including *homo sapiens*—us humans. I see no good reason—on theological or philosophical grounds, certainly not on biological grounds—to call into question this overall conceptual framework; I shall not, therefore, take up issues about evolution raised by so-called creationists.[1] But I do want to examine here some respects in which the evolutionary framework bears on our understanding of human existence, in particular on the understanding of our human niche in the natural order. I hope my remarks will throw light not only on what we humans *are*, but also on how we ought to live, and on some of the major goals humanity should set for itself today.

These are no longer matters that can be dealt with simply in terms of the needs and values of individuals or communities, or even of whole societies or cultures. We live within a rapidly deteriorating global environment, brought about at least to some extent by our own activity: it is a time of dangerous global warming, a time in which basic natural resources for ongoing life such as clean water and air are becoming exhausted; a time of an exploding human world population; a time in which one or another sort of nuclear catastrophe is possible—each of these matters being greatly complicated in many ways by global economic and political problems that no one seems to know how to address. It is essential that we learn to think about our human existence and its predicaments in ways that will provide us humans—humankind as a whole—with proper orientation in today's world, orientation enabling us to clearly identify and effectively address the major issues that we as a species now confront. If we can find a way to think more clearly about the place that human existence has in the overall economy of life on planet Earth—what niche humankind can properly occupy within Earth's ecological order—we may be able to begin bringing these complicated issues into clearer focus.

I

Current evolutionary theory obviously must be one of the major contributors to our thinking about these questions, but this theory does not (as I shall argue) supply us with a full answer to the question about our niche in the natural order. What I call a *biohistorical* understanding of human being—an understanding that emphasizes, and holds together in one, both the biological grounding of our human existence and the historico-cultural dimensions of human life—can, however, provide a way to think about these matters.

An adequate conception of the human niche will be qualitatively different, in some important respects, from that of any other form of life: we humans want to know—*need* to know—as much as we can about our place in the overall network of life. In the last hundred years or so, we have become aware that unless we live and act within the constraints that life's ecological order places upon us—unless we arrange our activities, our living and acting, in ways appropriate to the environmental context that supports and sustains us—we will not survive much longer. No other form of life—trees, dogs, other primates—needs this kind of information or would be able to make any use of it. We humans alone have available to ourselves technologies and knowledge that give us the power to destroy ourselves and many other of the complex forms of life on planet Earth; in fact, we are already engaged in such highly destructive activity. We humans alone are able to envision the enormity of these matters—to understand what all of this means (not only for ourselves but for other species as well); we alone are able to deliberately set ourselves to amend our ways in respects that may bring us into better harmony with the overall ecology of planet Earth. For us, thus, in contrast with every other species, gaining insight into our niche within the web of life has become a matter of life and death—not only for ourselves, but for much other life as well.

The facts just reviewed, well known to most educated modern/postmodern people, are the basis for my claim that the conception of our niche in Earth's ecology will necessarily be qualitatively different from that of any other species. It must help us understand not only how human existence came into the world and lives in the world: it must also facilitate our understanding of what is required if we are to continue to survive and flourish in this world. In close connection with our conception of the human niche, that is to say, we need to develop a distinctive species self-understanding—an understanding that, in broad outlines, makes clear how we must comport ourselves in life, how we must live and act—and our species self-understanding must include moral and ethical imperatives. Discernment of this sort is prerequisite to our moving more effectively into, and living within, our proper place on Earth. A conception of the human niche that does not interconnect with species self-understanding of this kind would not in fact be adequate for the kind of beings we humans actually are today.

The picture or conception of the human place in Earth's ecological order that I will present here will (*a*) help orient us with respect to major issues now demanding our most urgent attention, and (*b*) help motivate and energize us to address these issues. In the past this sort of double function—indispensable for self-conscious beings like us, who are capable of acting purposively and taking responsibility for our actions—has been performed largely by the religio-moral symbol-systems produced in human cultures everywhere. The various religions have presented quite diverse construals of the ultimate mystery within which human existence transpires, and they have generally succeeded in setting out pictures sufficiently intelligible and meaningful to enable women and men to come to some understanding of themselves in relation to the context in which they live—and to live out their lives more or less fruitfully and meaningfully within that context. It was their religion (as Durkheim saw) that gave a people its sense of solidarity as a group, uniting them in common cause and common sense of meaning. For many today, however, our traditional religious world-pictures no longer provide these indispensable orienting functions.

When we seek, now, to consider the proper niche for humans within the ecological order on planet Earth, we are in fact exploring one more way of construing human existence in the world—that ancient and profound mystery to which the religions have addressed themselves. Like the traditional religions, this vision will, we may hope, illuminate the situation of us humans today, with our wide range of knowledges and technologies, and our enormous ecological, political, economic, social, psychological, moral, and religious problems.

II

Let us begin with the general proposition that humankind has emerged, in the course of evolutionary developments on planet Earth over many millennia, out of less complex or (as some would say) "lower" forms of life, and that we cannot exist apart from this living web that continues to nourish and sustain us. This proposition is, however, too general (as it stands) for the project I am setting forth here, for it tells us nothing about the way in which—within this evolutionary setting—the uniquely *historical* features (that is, the sociocultural features) of human existence are to be understood. The natural order is, no doubt, the wider context within which human history has emerged. But it has been especially through our historical sociocultural development over many millennia—not our biological evolution alone—that we humans have acquired many of our most distinctive characteristics. Our increasingly comprehensive knowledge about the natural world in which we live, and about our human constitution and possibilities, has provided us with very considerable powers over our immediate environment and over the physical and biological (as well as sociocultural and psychological) conditions of our existence—powers that go far beyond those of any other animal. We human beings, and the further course of human history, are no longer completely at the disposal of the natural order and natural powers that brought us into being in the way we were, say, ten millennia ago. In the course of history we humans have gained, in and through our various knowledges, a measure of transcendence over the nature of which we are part; with our developing practices and skills—growing in modernity into enormously powerful technologies—we have utterly transformed the face of the earth and are beginning to push on into outer space.

How should we understand—in connection with our evolutionary story—these features of our humanity that have emerged largely in human history? Anthropologist Clifford Geertz has summed up what is at stake: the organism that has finally emerged as human is "both a cultural and a biological product," and our present biological organisms, if left simply to themselves, would be so seriously deficient that they could not function.[2] "We are . . . incomplete or unfinished animals who complete or finish ourselves through culture—and not through culture in general but through highly particular forms of it: Dobuan and Javanese, Hopi and Italian, upper-class, academic and commercial."[3] Thus, the various sorts of human culture that have appeared around the world must each be understood as an indispensable dimension, in its particular location, of the niche within which humankind is sustained. The growth of human cultures, moreover—and correspondingly, the growth and development of human symbolic behaviors—have affected significantly the actual biological development of the predecessors of today's *homo sapiens*. They have had particularly strong effects on the evolution of the human brain, as brain scientist Terrence Deacon has shown. Deacon argues that it was the emergence of symbolic behaviors—such as language, a central feature in the historical unfolding of human cultural life—that brought about the very evolution of our unusually large brains.[4] Thus, all the way down to the deepest roots of our distinctly *human* existence, we are not simply biological beings, animals; we are biohistorical beings.[5] And in significant respects, our growing historicalness—our *historicity*—is the most distinctive mark of our humanness.

How should we understand—within its context in nature—this historicity: that we are beings shaped decisively by a history that has given us power to shape future history in significant ways? On the one hand, in our transcendence (through our creation of complex cultures) of the natural order within which we emerged, we humans, as we know ourselves today, are radically different from any other living beings. On the other hand, in our "utter dependence" (to adopt a phrase of the nineteenth-century theologian Schleiermacher) on the web of life from which and within which we emerged, we humans are at one with every other species. How should we understand this peculiarity of ours—that we beings with historicity have such great creative (and destructive) power in the natural order? And how does this bear on our understanding of our niche within that order? Our human niche, it seems, without which we humans could never have come into being or been sustained in being, has itself come to have increasingly important historico-cultural features: that is, the human niche also is a developing biohistorical reality. To think intelligently about our niche within the evolutionary development on planet Earth, then, we must think throughout in biohistorical, not simply physical and/or biological, terms. The complex interconnection and interdependence of the "historical" with the "bio"—in ourselves as human, and also in our niche within nature—must be given its due, if our understanding is to be of help in addressing the complicated problems we humans today face.

We will not, for example, be able to deal effectively with our enormous environmental problems unless we simultaneously find ways to come to terms with the complex of political, social, economic, cultural, and religious matters—that is, with the *historical* issues—with which these problems are interconnected. These historical issues, it should be noted, are not only affairs internal to each nation or society; they are international and multicultural as well—*global*, as we increasingly have come to say. We must, therefore, find ways to think politically, economically, culturally, and religiously in global terms—terms that are simultaneously pluralistic terms, or they will not in fact be truly global. Human history has, from very early times, been thoroughly pluralized, and there is no reason to expect this condition to disappear in the foreseeable future. Our conception of the human (and of the human niche on earth) must be capacious enough to appreciate and accommodate this enormous cultural and religious diversity—including, for example, adequate space for those who thoroughly disagree with the basic evolutionary and historical premises on which this interpretation of the human niche is itself based. Only to the extent that our evolutionary understanding of human being is framed so as to help orient us with respect to this complex set of historical issues (in addition to the pertinent physical and biological questions)—that is, only to the extent that it is a thoroughly biohistorical understanding—will it help us identify our actual present position (or better put, perhaps: position*s*) in Earth's ecological order.

If there is any appropriate niche for modern/postmodern *homo sapiens* on planet Earth, it is clear that—given our extraordinary human creativity and powers, as well as the exceedingly diverse ways in which we have exercised that creativity and those powers—it will be quite distinctive.[6] We humans are the only animals able to ask about the appropriateness of our present niche(s), and the only ones capable of deliberately reshaping both the niche(s) and ourselves, so that we—and our distinctive, and potentially quite destructive, abilities—fit better into the natural world that is our home. Moreover, as has already been implied, our conception of the human niche(s) must concern itself not only with the human place in Earth's past and present; it must also take into account the various possible *futures* that we may have to face—a very weighty complication indeed!

III

What kind of moves is it possible for humans to make when confronted with questions like this that go well beyond our established knowledges? Our religious traditions have long understood that it is only in and through moves of faith that we address these deep but unavoidable mysteries that are connected with our distinctive human powers as self-conscious agents—beings who must act, must take responsibility for ourselves even though the future may be inscrutable, beings with historicity. That is, we can commit ourselves to this or that construal of the mystery that confronts us, and we can live and act in faithfulness to this commitment, but we must recognize that all such commitments go beyond the knowledges at our disposal. Human life is able to go on in face of profound bafflements of this sort only because of our will to believe (as William James called it), because of our deep-seated attitudes of faith and trust and loyalty that enable us to continue moving forward into uncertain futures even though adequate pertinent knowledge is unavailable.

Let us look briefly, then, at certain aspects of the religious framework that contributed to the birth of Western culture, and which subsequently has continued to nourish our culture (at least to some extent). Unlike most other religious traditions, the basic form of the Hebraic cosmic vision—a principal root of our Western religiousness—is that of a temporal/historical process. The biblical picture portrays human life as in a "created" world, a world that began at a particular point in time, a world that developed in important ways through time because of God's continuing activity within it. This human story includes both a fall away from God and the emergence of diverse human languages, cultures, and religious practices and beliefs, and it culminates in the expectation of God's overcoming the sin and evil that humanity has brought into the world, thus bringing it to the perfection originally intended. Although many of the details of the evolutionary conception on which we are focusing here differ sharply from the biblical story, the overall *form* of these two accounts is much the same: in both, human life is understood within the context of a larger cosmic temporal/historical/developmental picture.

The biblical account, however, in contrast with the evolutionary story as often presented, is able to give this developmental process profound human meaning. It displays (*a*) the human dimension of the story—human history—as possessing an overall unity from beginning to end, brought about by (*b*) God's continuing presence and activity throughout, an activity believed to be creatively and redemptively moving humankind toward the full realization of God's original loving purposes for humanity. It was the ongoing presence and humanizing activity of *God* in this story that brought the past, present, and future of the world, and of humankind within the world, together into a coherent whole of profound human meaning. Basic orientation for women and men was found, thus, in relation to God—God's purposes, God's ongoing activity, God's will for humankind. Motivation for humans to orient themselves in accordance with this vision was encouraged by the hope it offered of ultimate human realization and redemption, as God's purposes were consummated. The connection between how things are (in the world) and which things really matter for humans—what is truly of importance to humans—was brought about and secured by the central role in the story, and the specific character, of God, whose activity bound the human and cosmic past, present, and future together into a single coherent and humanly meaningful account.

Is there any way that the past, present, and future of human existence generally—and our lives in particular—can be situated within a similar unity of development in connection with the biohistorical evolutionary story? I believe there is. I would like to introduce two concepts here that bring out certain humanizing dimensions implicit in the biohistorical evolutionary process with which we are concerned. When our evolutionary picture is articulated in terms of these concepts, it can provide an orientation for human life and actions appropriate to our position(s) in Earth's ecological order—an orientation that, moreover, encourages motivation and commitment to live and act in accord with this order.

First, I want to point out what I call the "serendipitous creativity" manifest throughout the universe—that is, the ongoing coming-into-being through time of the new and the novel. In my opinion, it is precisely this serendipitous creativity that should be regarded today as God. Second, since the biblical idea of a powerful teleological movement (God's purposive activity), underlying and ordering all cosmic and historical processes, has become quite problematical in today's thinking about evolution and history, I shall replace it with a more modest conception—a conception of what I call *trajectories* or *directional movements* that spontaneously emerge in the course of evolutionary and historical developments. This more open (even random) notion—of serendipitous creativity manifesting itself in evolutionary and historical trajectories of various sorts—fits in with, but amplifies in important ways, our thinking about cosmic and historical processes. It is a notion that can be used to interpret the enormous expansion and complexification of the physical universe (from the Big Bang onward), as well as the evolution of life here on Earth and the gradual emergence of human historical existence. This whole vast cosmic process manifests serendipitous creativity, the coming into being through time of new modes of reality. This is a creativity that has frequently produced much more than would have been expected, given previously prevailing circumstances—indeed, more than might have seemed possible, even moving eventually, along one of its lines, into the creation of us human beings with our distinctive history and historicity.

There are, of course, other plausible ways to view today's universe. Taking up such a position as this, therefore—drawing all of this together in terms of the notion of cosmic serendipitous creativity—calls for a step of faith.[7] What does such a step of faith involve? What does it mean to think of the overarching context of human life—the universe—as a product of a serendipitously creative process or movement? We can begin to answer these questions if we take note of some important features of cosmic and (especially) biological evolution.

IV

Movement in and through time, as traced today through the long history of the universe and particularly through the evolution of life on Earth, seems frequently to eventuate in truly unprecedented happenings: the appearance of new—of novel—forms, not simply the repetition of already existing patterns. Moreover, these developments, to the extent they involve the emergence of new evolutionary lines—for example, new species on planet Earth—each have specific potentialities for developing further in some directions but not in others. Such tendencies, as biologist Ernst Mayr says, "are the necessary consequence of the unity of the genotype which greatly constrains evolutionary potential."[8] Ever more complex species have emerged along some evolutionary lines, and we can discern "trajectories" of a sort eventuating in these new forms. These trajectories are visible, of course, only to the retrospective or backward-looking view that we necessarily take up when we survey the past, and there is no reason (at least from a biological standpoint) to suppose that the process of evolution on Earth has actually been directed, somehow, toward this or that specific goal, or toward any goal whatsoever. The processes of natural selection, it appears, are themselves able to bring about the directional momentums that emerge along the various lines down which life has evolved.[9]

On one line (our own, as we have noted) what may be regarded as a new order of reality—history—has emerged. The order of history—which increasingly came to include flexible and complex languages, a great variety of forms of social organization, the development of skills of many different sorts, the creation of innumerable kinds of artifacts including tools that extend human powers in many new directions, and so on—is the only context (so far as we know) within which beings with freedom, creativity, self-consciousness, and responsible agency have appeared. It is not that the evolution of life has been a sort of straight-line movement, up from the primeval slime to humanity with its historicity and its complex histories: evolutionary developments have obviously gone in many directions. Moreover, it is not evident that the human form is as biologically viable as are many others. So from a strictly biological point of view (with its emphasis on survival, perpetuation of the species), there is little reason to think that human life is the most successful or important product of the evolutionary process. However, we are not confining ourselves here to strictly biological considerations: our principal concern in this essay is with our distinctly *human* need—as bio*historical* beings—to find an ecologically appropriate way to orient ourselves in this evolutionary world.

As we have noted, fully human beings (beings with great symbolic facility, beings with historicity) did not appear simply as the last stage of an exclusively biological process: it was only after many millennia of *historical* developments (in concert with continuing biological evolution) that human existence, as we know it today, came on the scene. Moreover, only with the emergence of the particular historical standpoint of late modernity has this biological-historical movement eventuating in contemporary humankind come into view. As we humans today look back at the gradually cumulating evolutionary and historical development that produced us, outlines of a cosmic trajectory, issuing in the creation of beings with historicity, become discernible.[10] There are, no doubt, many other cosmic trajectories as well, moving in quite different directions. For us men and women, however—with our specifically human needs and interests, and our many diverse configurations of human values and meanings—the emergence of this particular trajectory is obviously of great importance. This manifestation of the creativity in the cosmos has given us men and women our very existence, and it quite properly evokes from us both awe and gratitude. I am not claiming that we humans are the best or the highest or the most important of all species of life. I am claiming, however, that because of our great knowledge and power—especially our power to destroy so much of life—the question of our proper place in the ecological order on Earth is an extraordinarily important one, one unlike that of any other species.

To emphasize in this way the connection of our distinctly human existence with the creativity manifest throughout the universe clearly involves an act of faith of much greater specificity and human significance than our earlier general affirmation of pervasive creativity in the cosmos (our first step of faith). It is an act of faith resembling in some significant respects what in the past has been called faith in God. Unlike more traditional faith, however, in this case it remains unclear where the particular trajectory that brought human existence into being on our planet will move in the future—perhaps toward the opening of ever-new possibilities for human beings, as we increasingly take responsibility for our lives and our future; perhaps going beyond humanity and historicity altogether, however difficult it may be to image what that might be; perhaps coming to an end in the total destruction of the human project on planet Earth.

We are employing here a twofold idea: (*a*) the notion of cosmic serendipi-tous creativity (which, I suggest, is what we should today think of as "God"), and (*b*) the manifestations of this creativity in and through interconnected evolutionary trajectories of quite diverse sorts. This idea (consonant with mod-ern evolutionary thinking, as we have seen, though not necessary to it) can help us define our place within the evolutionary cosmos that is our home. Our human existence—its purposiveness, its social/moral/cultural/religious values and meanings, its glorious creativity and its horrible failures and gross evils, its historicity—has, as we have seen, a significantly distinctive position within the vast (seemingly) impersonal cosmic order. With the emergence of histori-cal modes of being (in humans), explicitly purposive patterns have appeared in the cosmos, as human intentions, consciousness, and actions began to become effective. We can say, then, that a cosmic trajectory, which had its origins in what seems to have been mere physical movement or vibration, has (in this particular instance) gradually developed increasing directionality, ultimately creating a context—a niche—within which deliberate *purposive* action could emerge and flourish.[11] Construing the universe in this way helps us see that our proper place in the world, our home in the universe, is the evolutionary-ecological trajectory on which we have emerged. With our two steps of faith, thus, we are beginning to gain some orientation in the universe (as we think of the universe today).

Let us note four points in this connection. First, this approach provides us with a frame within which we can characterize quite accurately, and can unify into an overall vision, what seems actually to have happened (so far as we know) in the course of cosmic evolution and history. It should be noted that the ancient cosmological dualisms—heaven and earth, God and the world, supernature and nature—which have shaped Christian thinking from early on and have become so problematic in our own time, are completely gone in this picture. Moreover, this is accomplished without dismantling the traditional sharp distinction between God (creativity) and the entire created order—perhaps the most important contribution of monotheistic religious traditions to human self-understanding.

Second, this approach gives a significant, but not dominant, place and meaning to the *biohistorical* character of human life and history within this cosmic process; in so doing, it identifies the niche that humankind occupies within this process as itself, necessarily, a biohistorical one. The traditional anthropological dualisms—body and soul (or spirit), mind and matter, those beings bearing the "image of God" and those that do not—similarly fall away in this picture. Moreover, this means, happily, that the basis on which the distinction of male from female has been elevated into a rigid gender dualism is also undercut here. It is important to note that the biohistorical ecological niche that is our home can be properly defined and described (as we have seen) only by carefully specifying not only the physical and biological features required for human life to go on, but the importance of certain historical features as well. It is, for example, only in sociocultural contexts in which some measure of justice, freedom, order, and mutual respect sufficiently prevail, and in which distribution of the goods of life (food, shelter, health, education, economic opportunity, and so on) is sufficiently equitable, that children in each new generation can be expected to have a reasonable chance of maturing into responsible and productive adult women and men—men and women, that is to say, who can take the sort of responsibility for their society and for planet Earth that is now required of human beings worldwide.

Third, awareness of these sorts of distinctive biohistorical features of ourselves and our ecological niche makes it possible to develop notions of value and meaning that will enable us to understand better, and assess more fully, both the adequacy of the biological context of our lives and the import of the historical sociocultural developments through which the various segments of humanity are moving, in this way enabling us to take up more responsible roles with respect to these contexts and developments. Thus, *normative thinking* directly appropriate to our varied human situations on planet Earth is facilitated by this biohistorical understanding, and the all-too-human-centered moralities and religions, politics and economics, of our various traditions can be more effectively called into question and significantly transformed.[12]

Fourth, because this approach highlights the linkage of serendipitous cosmic creativity (God) with both our humanness and the humane values so important to us, as well as with our ecological niche, it can support hope (but not certainty) for the future of our human world. It is a hope about the overall direction of future human history—hope for truly creative movements toward ecologically and morally responsible, pluralistic, human existence. A hope such as this, grounded on the creativity manifest throughout the cosmos (a creativity that, on our trajectory, evidences itself in part through our own human powers)—though carrying much less assurance than the traditional religious expectation of the coming of God's kingdom—can help motivate us men and women to devote our lives to bringing about this more humane and ecologically rightly-ordered world to which we all aspire. Thus, our human past, present, and future are drawn together in this overall vision of the ongoing creative biohistorical process in which we are situated—a vision that will help us identify and address the problems in today's world most urgently demanding our attention. From this vantage point we can see that what I have been calling "serendipitous creativity" actually performs, in many respects, the basic roles in human affairs traditionally attributed to God.

V

The frame of orientation or vision of reality that I am setting out here is not, of course, in any way forced upon us: it can be appropriated (as I have suggested) only by means of our own personal and collective decisions, our own steps of faith. This is a frame with sufficient richness and specification to provide significant orientation for our time, but it can accomplish this only if we decide to commit ourselves to it, ordering our lives and building our futures in the terms it prescribes. Acceptance of this vision can help women and men in our world—not only those who think of themselves as religious in some more or less traditional sense, but also modern/postmodern women and men of other quite different persuasions—to gain some sense of identity, some sense of who we humans are and what we ought to be doing with our lives. And the hope that our biohistorical trajectory may move forward creatively toward a more humane and ecologically well-ordered world can help motivate us men and women to give ourselves in strong commitment to its continuing growth and development.

I have deliberately refrained from forcefully arguing in this chapter that the ideas of serendipitous creativity and evolutionary and historical trajectories should be identified with the more traditional notions of God and God's activity. It has seemed to me important that the appropriateness and usefulness of these ideas be considered in their own right, as suggestive interpretations of the evolutionary-ecological universe in which we today take ourselves to be living, whatever may be their specifically theological significance. I hope, however, that it is clear by now that this world-picture can become religiously quite profound, if the ultimate point of reference to which it calls our attention—serendipitous creativity—is regarded as *God,* and faith in God is understood to be faith in the creativity manifest throughout our world. It is not difficult to set out the main outlines of this picture in terms of a theocentric—indeed, a specifically Christian—vision of the cosmos and human life.[13]

The world, I have been suggesting here, can best be understood today as a vast developing process of interconnected trajectories, in and through which ongoing creativity is often manifest. Life appeared on (at least) one of these trajectories, and in due course mammals and later on primates came into being; in a further evolution of one of the primate lines the historical order emerged, and it may be continuing on in further creative development. This trajectory, including its biohistorical extension on which we humans find ourselves, represents at least one significant direction in which cosmic creativity—*God*—has been moving in our region of the universe, a direction which, if and as it becomes increasingly attuned to the overall ecological order on planet Earth, may eventuate in the creation of a biohistorical niche that can sustain humankind through a long future. We humans are today being drawn beyond our present condition and order of life by creative impulses in this trajectory, suggesting some new movements now required of us. Moreover, if we fail to respond appropriately to these historical and ecological forces impinging on us today, we may not even survive. Are we willing to commit ourselves to live and act in accord with the imperatives laid upon us by the biohistorical situation in which we find ourselves, in the hope that our action may be supported and enhanced by further serendipitously creative developments? In my view it is to precisely this kind of hope and faith and commitment to which the biohistorical trajectory that has brought us into being—and thus God—now calls us.

CRUM CREEK SPIRITUALITY
Earth as a Living Sacrament

Mark I. Wallace

I enter a swamp as a sacred place,—a sanctum sanctorum.
—HENRY DAVID THOREAU[1]

If the world is God's body, then nothing happens to the world that does not also happen to God.
—SALLIE MCFAGUE[2]

Gentle Goddess,
who never asks for anything at all,
and gives us everything we have,
thank you for this sweet water,
and your fragrance.
—LEW WELCH[3]

Christianity has long been a religion that endows the natural world with sacred meaning. Every day, material existence—food and drink, life and death, humans and animals, earth and sky—is recalled in countless rituals and stories as the primary medium through which God relates to humankind and the wider earth community. Christianity's central ritual is a group meal that remembers the saving death of Jesus by celebrating the good gifts of creation—eating bread and drinking wine. Its central symbol is a cross of wood—two pieces of lumber lashed together as the means and site of Jesus' crucifixion. Its central belief focuses on the body—namely, that God became flesh in Jesus and thereby became one of us, a mortal, breathing life-form who experiences the joy and suffering of life on earth. And Christianity's primary sacred document, the Bible, is suffused with rich, ecological imagery that stretches from the Cosmic Potter in Genesis who fashions Adam from the dust of the ground and puts him in a garden, to the river of life in Revelation that flows from the throne of God, bright as crystal, vivifying the tree of life that yields its fruit to all of earth's inhabitants. Christianity is a fleshly, earthly, material religion.

In this chapter, I take up the question of Christianity's earthen identity by way of a nature-based retrieval of the Holy Spirit as the green face of God in the world. I suggest that the Spirit reveals herself in the biblical literature as a physical, earthly being who labors to create and sustain humankind and otherkind in solidarity with one another.[4] Appropriating the provocative figure of the earth as the body of God, I maintain that the natural world is best understood as the primary mode of God's presence among us today. To make this point, I develop a case study of the Crum Creek watershed (a local watershed near my home and workplace) as a Spirit-filled, sacred place because it continues to function as a vital habitat for a wide variety of native species and their young. But this is a controversial point, and so I ask, Is it appropriate in Christian terms to describe God's Spirit as the enfleshed presence of God in all things—and who thereby renders the earth we inhabit as sacred, holy ground? Is such a theology genuinely Christian, or surreptitiously animist or pagan? My hope in this essay is to explore the promise of biblical faith as a nature-centered, body-loving religion to help heal the human race's exploitative environmental habits. Throughout, I will invoke Christianity's central belief that the Spirit of God imbues all things.

THE CONTEST BETWEEN SPIRIT AND FLESH

Christianity's green identity is often at war, however, with a residual Platonist tendency within Christian theology to valorize "spirit" or "mind" as superior to "matter" or "body." Many of the church's most gifted and influential early thinkers were enamored with Plato's controlling philosophical metaphors of the body as the "prison house" or the "tomb" of the soul. The fulfillment of human existence, according to Plato, is to release oneself—one's soul—from bondage to involuntary, bodily appetites in order to cultivate a life in harmony with one's spiritual, intellectual nature.[5] Origen, the third-century Christian Platonist, interpreted literally Jesus' blessing regarding those who "have made themselves eunuchs for the sake of the kingdom of heaven" (Matt. 19:2) and at age twenty had himself castrated. As a virgin for Christ no longer dominated by his sexual and physical drives, Origen, in his mind, became a perfect vessel for the display of the power of Christ over bodily temptations.[6]

In the Christian West, Augustine is arguably most responsible for the hierarchical division between spirit and nature. Augustine maintains that human beings are ruled by carnal desire—*concupiscence*—as a result of Adam's fall from grace in the Garden of Eden. Adam's sin is transferred to his offspring—the human race—through erotic desire that leads to sexual intercourse and the birth of children. In their fleshly bodies, according to Augustine, infants are tainted with "original sin" communicated to them through their biological parents' sexual intercourse. Physical weakness and sexual desire are signs that the bodily, material world is under God's judgment. Thus, without the infusion of super-natural grace, all of creation—depraved and corrupted—is no longer amenable to the influence of the Spirit.[7] This long tradition of hierarchical and antago-nistic division between spirit and matter continues into our own time—an era, often in the name of religion, marked by deep anxiety about and hostility toward human sexuality, the body, and the natural world.

Nevertheless, the biblical descriptions of the Holy Spirit do not square with this oppositional understanding of spirit and flesh. Spirit language and imagery in scriptural sources and much of church history bring together God and the earth, the spiritual and the natural, mind and matter—but this mes-sage is often missed. Rather than prioritizing the spiritual over the earthly, the scriptural texts figure the Spirit as a carnal, creaturely life-form always already interpenetrated by the material world. Granted, the term "Spirit" does conjure the image of a ghostly, shadowy nonentity in both the popular and high thinking of the Christian West. In her earlier work, for example, McFague argued that the model of God as Spirit is not retrievable in an ecological age. She criticized tra-ditional descriptions of the Spirit as ethereal and vacant, and she concluded that Spirit-language is an inadequate resource for the task of earth-healing because such language is "amorphous, vague, and colorless."[8] Later, however, McFague performed the very retrieval of pneumatology she had earlier claimed to be impossible: a revisioning of God as Spirit in order to thematize the immanent and dynamic presence of the divine life within all creation.[9] McFague argues convincingly how the revival of the green Spirit tradition has the potential to energize humans' sense of kinship with other life-forms and relocate them within the cosmic story of the planet's evolutionary history:

> That tradition is of God as spirit—not the Holy Ghost, which suggests the unearthly and the disembodied, nor initially the Holy Spirit, which has been focused largely on human beings and especially the followers of Christ, but the spirit of God, the divine wind that "swept over the face of the waters" prior to creation, the life-giving breath given to all creatures, and the dynamic movement that creates, recreates, and transcreates throughout the universe. Spirit, as wind, breath, life is the most basic and most inclusive way to express centered embodiment. All living creatures, not just human ones, depend upon breath. Breath also knits together the life of animals and plants, for they are linked by the exchange of oxygen and carbon dioxide in each breath inhaled and exhaled. Breath is a more immediate and radically dependent way to speak of life than even food or water, for we literally live from breath to breath and

can survive only a few minutes without breathing. Our lives are enclosed by
two breaths—our first when we emerge from our mother's womb and our last
when we "give up the ghost" (spirit).[10]

McFague argues that God's Spirit is the founding and final breath of our
lives and the lives of all of our plant and animal relations. Her recovery of
scriptural Spirit-breath language underscores how the biblical texts stand as a
stunning countertestimony to the conventional mind-set that opposes spirit and
flesh. Indeed, the Bible is awash with rich imagery of the Spirit borrowed directly
from the natural world. The four traditional elements of natural, embodied
life—earth, air, water, and fire—are constitutive of the Spirit's biblical reality as
an enfleshed being who ministers to the whole creation God has made for the
refreshment and joy of all beings. In the Bible, the Spirit is not a wraithlike entity
separated from matter, but a living being, like all other created things, made up
of the four cardinal substances that compose the physical universe.[11]

EARTH, AIR, WATER, FIRE

Numerous biblical passages attest to the foundational role of the four basic elements regarding the earthen identity of the Spirit.

1. As *earth* the Spirit is both the *divine dove*, with an olive branch in its
   mouth, that brings peace and renewal to a broken and divided world
   (Gen. 8:11; Matt. 3:16; John 1:32), and a *fruit bearer*, such as a tree or
   vine, that yields the virtues of love, joy, and peace in the life of the dis-
   ciple (Gal. 5:15-26). Pictured as a bird on the wing or a flowering tree,
   the Spirit is a living being who shares a common physical reality with
   all other beings. Far from being the "immaterial substance" defined by
   the canonical theological lexicon, the Spirit is imagined in the Bible as
   a material, earthen life-form who mediates God's power to other earth
   creatures through her physical presence.
2. As *air* the Spirit is both the *vivifying breath* that animates all living things
   (Gen. 1:2; Ps. 104:29-30) and the *prophetic wind* that brings salvation
   and new life to those it indwells (Judges 6:34; John 3:6-8; Acts 2:1-
   4). The nouns for Spirit in the biblical texts—*rûach* in Hebrew and
   pneuma in Greek—mean "breath" or "air" or "wind." Literally, the Spirit
   is pneumatic, a powerful air-driven reality analogous to a pneumatic
   drill or pump. The Spirit is God's all-encompassing, aerial presence in
   the life-giving atmosphere that envelops and sustains the whole earth;
   as such, the Spirit escapes the horizon of human activity and cannot be

contained by human constraints. The Spirit is divine wind—the breath of God—that blows where it wills (John 3:8), driven by its own elemental power and independent from human attempts to control it, refreshing and renewing all broken members of the created order.

3. As the *living water* the Spirit quickens and refreshes all who drink from its eternal springs (John 3:1-15; 4:14; 7:37-38). As physical and spiritual sustenance, the Spirit is the liquid God who imbues all life-sustaining bodily fluids—blood, mucus, milk, sweat, urine—with flowing divine presence and power. Moreover, the Water God flows and circulates within the soaking rains, dewy mists, thermal springs, seeping mudholes, ancient headwaters, swampy wetlands, and teeming oceans that constitute the hydrospheric earth we all inhabit. The Spirit as water makes possible the wonderful juiciness and succulence of life as we experience it on a liquid planet sustained by nurturing flow patterns.

4. Finally, as *fire* the Spirit is the *bright flame* that alternately judges evildoers and ignites the prophetic mission of the early church (Matt. 3:11-12; Acts 2:1-4). Fire is an expression of God's austere power; on one level, it is biblically viewed as the element God uses to castigate human error. But it is also the symbol of God's unifying presence in the fledgling Christian community where the divine *pneuma*—the rushing, whooshing wind of God—is said to have filled the early church as its members became filled with the Spirit, symbolized by "tongues of fire [that were] distributed and resting on each one" of the early church members (Acts 2:3). Aberrant, subversive, and creatively destructive, God as fire scorches and roasts who and what it chooses, apart from human intervention and design—like the divine wind that blows where it wills. But like the other natural elements, fire should be understood as functioning in the service of maintaining healthy earth relations. Fire is necessary for the maintenance of planetary life: as furnace heat, fire makes food preparation possible; as wildfire in forested and rural areas, fire revivifies long-dormant seed cultures necessary for biodiverse ecosystems; and when harnessed in the form of solar power, fire from the sun makes possible safe energy production not dependent on fossil-fuel sources. The burning God is the God who has the power to incinerate and make alive the elements of the lifeweb essential for the sustenance of our gifted ecosystem.

God as Spirit is biblically defined according to the tropes of earth, wind, water, and fire. In these scriptural texts the Spirit is figured as a potency in nature who engenders life and healing throughout the biotic order. The earth's bodies of water, communities of plants and animals, and eruptions of fire and wind are not only *symbols* of the Spirit—as important as this nature symbolism is—but share in the Spirit's very *nature* as the Spirit is continually enfleshed and embodied through natural landscapes and biological populations. Neither ghostly nor bodiless, the Spirit is an earthly life-form, a living being, whose nature is the same as all other participants in the biotic and abiotic environments that make up our planet home. Running rivers, prairie fires, coral reefs, schools of blue whales, equatorial forests—the Spirit both shares the same nature of other life-forms and is the animating force that enlivens all members of the lifeweb. As the breath of life who moves over the face of the deep in Genesis, as the circling dove in the Gospels who seals Jesus' baptism, or as the Pentecostal tongues of fire in Acts, the Spirit does not exist apart from natural phenomena as a separate, heavenly reality externally related to the created order. Rather, *all* of nature in its fullness and variety is the realization of the Spirit's work in the world. The Spirit is an earthen reality—God's power in the land and sky that makes all things live and grow toward their natural ends. God is living in the ground, swimming through the oceans, circulating in the atmosphere; God is always afoot and underfoot as the quickening life force who yearns to bring all denizens of this sacred earth into fruition and well-being.

HILDEGARD'S GREEN PNEUMATOLOGY

There are numerous appropriations of the earthen God tradition within the history of theology that are important sources of the Spirit theology proposed here. One such source is the farsighted writings of Hildegard of Bingen. Similar to Joachim of Fiore—who taught that humankind had now entered the third period of history, the age of the Spirit—Hildegard was a twelfth-century monastic and mystical prophet who wrote trinitarian theologies with special attention to the role of the Spirit in the world. As did Joachim, Hildegard joined a religious order. But Hildegard did so at the behest of her parents at age nine. At this early age Hildegard became an anchoress and lived her life as a recluse, walled into a monastic cell by the local bishop for the rest of her life. Yet Hildegard emerged from her childhood cell to become a prolific writer, musician, artist, herbalist, abbess of her growing religious community, and even statesperson as she maintained influential relationships with bishops, kings, and emperors during the High Middle Ages. She was called the "Sibyl of the Rhine" for her wide-ranging impact on medieval culture through the power of her visionary writings.

In her major work entitled *Scivias* (that is, *Sci vias lucis*, "Know the Ways of Light"), Hildegard says she heard a voice from a living fire say to her, "O you who are wretched earth and, as a woman, untaught in all learning . . . Cry out and relate and write these my mysteries that you see and hear in mystical visions. So do not be timid, but say those things you understand in the Spirit as I speak them through you."[12] Hildegard, being commanded by God to "cry out and write," becomes an oracle of the Holy Spirit. Though women were forbidden to exercise public leadership roles in the teaching ministry of the medieval church, the Spirit cut loose Hildegard's hesitant tongue and enjoined her to preach. Many of Hildegard's contemporaries, including many male clerics, saw her as filled with the Spirit and able to exercise the biblical role of prophet in a culture that needed her special message. Still today, Hildegard is a Spirit-inspired trailblazer for women (and men) who look for God's call in their lives as a subversion of a male-dominated ecclesial and social order.

Resonant with the nature mysticism of biblical Spirit theology, the content of Hildegard's message was essentially ecological, as we understand that term today. Hearkening back to the earthen language of the Spirit in the biblical texts—the Spirit is breath, water, fire, and life-form such as a dove—Hildegard offers a nature-based model of the Spirit in relation to the other two members of the Godhead: "He who begets is the Father; he who is born is the Son; and he who in eager freshness proceeds from the Father and the Son, and sanctified the waters by moving over their face in the likeness of an innocent bird, and streamed with ardent heat over the apostles, is the Holy Spirit."[13] Hildegard's earthen spirituality was the source of her practice as a naturalist and plant-based healer. Keeper of the soil, she published extensive catalogs of the medicinal properties of the flora she cultivated and used for ailing visitors at the monastery in Bingen. She wrote and sang hymns of thanksgiving, praising God for the bounty of nature and the fertility of the earth. Spiritually and physically, the earth's rich vegetation has healing properties that can refresh and renew all of God's creatures. As medievalist Elizabeth Dreyer puts it,

> In addition to the Spirit's role as prophetic inspiration, Hildegard links the Holy Spirit with the term *viriditas* or "greening." She imagined the outpouring of the Spirit in natural rather than cultural metaphors. She combined images of planting, watering, and greening to speak of the presence of the Holy Spirit. Hildegard linked the flow of water on the crops with the love of God that renews the face of the earth, and by extension the souls of believers.[14]

For Hildegard, ecology and horticulture are religion because the Spirit lives in and through the natural world, bringing all things into health and fruition. Hildegard's explicit correlation between God as Spirit and the fecundity of creation is a significant source for my attempt to "green" theology in conversation with McFague's Christian environmental thought.

SOJOURNING IN THE CRUM CREEK

Developing a Spirit and land theology by way of the Bible, Hildegard, and McFague, I turn to an analysis of the Crum Creek watershed, at the edge of the Swarthmore College campus near my home and the place where I work, as a case study to illustrate my overall thesis concerning green pneumatology. Crum Creek winds through a thirty-eight-square-mile area of land that sits on the western edge of suburban Philadelphia. This area is a network of streams, wetlands, and aquifers that supplies two hundred thousand households and businesses with drinking water as well as being a discharge site for wastewater effluent and a natural floodway for stormwater events. The watershed is a scenic retreat for persons in the Philadelphia area who need a place of refuge from the strains and stresses of urban life. And it is an important habitat for many native plants and animals.

A variety of species of wildlife relies on the Crum Creek watershed for food and raising young. Scarlet tanagers migrate from Colombia and Bolivia to lay their eggs in the old-growth forests surrounding the creek area. Spotted and red-backed salamanders are two of the twelve or so species of amphibians that live within and along the banks of the creek and its tributaries. Monarch butterflies migrate from Mexico to the open meadows of the watershed area, where they roost to feed on milkweed plants and lay their eggs. Ancient southern red oaks survive in a section of the Crum Woods near the Swarthmore campus in an aboriginal forest relatively undisturbed by white settlement. American eels migrate downstream through the creek every fall to lay their eggs in the Sargasso Sea near Bermuda; in turn, their offspring then swim upstream to mature in the same creek area where their parents began their own journeys out to sea. And showy, large-flowered trillium wildflowers fade from white to pink each year in the deep, rich woods of the watershed.[15]

The section of Crum Creek near the Swarthmore campus is my favorite site for passive recreation and easy walking meditation. Living in a world awash in parking lots and strip malls, I find it healing and restorative to be able to take refuge in the dark quiet of the woods. Henry David Thoreau writes about the art of getting lost, the vertiginous pleasure of abandoning oneself to a natural place without the artificial supports of urban maps and street signs. "Not until we are lost do we begin to understand ourselves," says Thoreau. Today many of us travel with cell phones and global positioning devices so that no one need go missing and become confused. But in taming wild places and making them the quantifiable objects of our measurement and control, we have done harm to our basic humanity, our basic animal nature. We are animal beings at our core. Our need for sleep, hunger for food, drive for companionship, and desire for sex are telling signs of our carnal natures. To be sure, we are animals that are self-aware and self-conscious, animals whose conscience can burn with shame and guilt, animals who create art, engage in science, and produce grand mythologies that map the cosmos and set forth the roles each of us should play. But we are animals all the same.

To be divorced from our fleshly, bodily natures—not to see and hear the mad rush of a swollen river in the early spring or the smell of moist leaf litter in the autumn in the woods around us—is to be cut off from the vital tapsprings that make us who we are. We live and work in fixed-glass, temperature-controlled buildings sealed off from the natural world; we transport ourselves in fossil-fuel machines that require ever-widening incursions into undisturbed habitats; we eat processed food that has been genetically manipulated, irradiated, and then sealed in airtight packaging in order to preserve its interminable shelf life. We have replaced lives lived in sustainable harmony with the rhythms and vitalities of the natural order with soul-deadening, consumption-intensive lifestyles that leave us emotionally depleted and spiritually empty. We need untamed places to return us to our animal identities, and I am deeply grateful for the role the Crum Woods plays in my own return to the wildness within me.

Crum Creek is a celebration of the natural amity that characterizes the human and the more-than-human spheres of existence. It is a place of scenic beauty, sensual delight, and spiritual sustenance. Like the ancient groundwater aquifers in the woods that are recharged by winter snows and spring rains, the depths of my own inner life are recharged by regular sojourns along the forested banks of the streams and tributaries that make up the watershed.

But in spite of its natural beauty and seeming health, all is not well with the Crum Creek watershed. There are many threats to the biodiversity and well-being of the creek area. Overall development pressures pose the largest perils to the integrity of the watershed. In the upper portion of the creek area, housing construction, shopping centers, office parks, and parking lots have fragmented natural habitats and increased the amount of paved areas, leading to stormwater runoff problems. In the lower portion of the creek near Swarthmore College, continued institutional development by the college along the edges of the watershed has created the same sorts of problems. Ironically, while Swarthmore College has been a relatively benign caretaker of the woods near its campus for many generations, in recent years the college's growth pattern has made it a threat to the preservation of species and habitat in lower Crum Creek. This troubling growth pattern entails cutting down edges of the forest preserve to open up space for college facilities. Since the 1960s, new townhouses for faculty, expanded student dormitories, additions to existing academic buildings, new access roads, and construction of surface parking lots have shrunk the perimeter of the forest.

These past and future uses of forest near the college campus raise troubling questions about the long-term health of the Crum Creek watershed. Within Delaware County, the suburban area that includes Swarthmore College just west of Philadelphia, the Crum Woods includes the last remaining old-growth forest in the county, with remaining stands of native trees and deep-woods habitat for threatened and endangered species of plants and animals. This wealth of wildlife habitat—including, as I have noted, a southern red oak forest, spotted salamander breeding ponds, scarlet tanager nesting grounds, and migrating American eel populations, among others—relies on the protected forest interior to survive. Historically a good neighbor of the forest, Swarthmore College's institutional growth trajectory may further shrink the rich heartland of the forest that supports these and other plant and animal populations. By cutting into the woods, the college makes more compact the woodland core and thereby diminishes its strength and vitality. The shrinking of this deep-woods core makes forest-interior plant and animal life more vulnerable to temperature and weather changes and the invasion of exotic species.

CRUM CREEK AS THE WOUNDED SACRED

Degraded but still robust, wounded but still alive, the Crum Creek watershed is an impaired wildlife area that continues to supply water, food, and other basic elements to the many communities, human and nonhuman, that flourish alongside and within its banks and streams. Crum Creek suffers regular abuse from suburban storm-water runoff; sewage discharges; dams and other stream impediments that create low flow conditions; and the cutting down of perimeter forest that supports interior habitat networks for threatened plants and animals. But to me the Crum Woods is a sacred place, a place where I am nourished and affirmed in my religious quest, a place where I find God.

Does it make sense to say that the Crum Creek watershed is a *sacred place*?

Today our common discourse has expanded to make almost anything we do and believe in sacred. Special periods spent with family is sacred time. The important responsibilities assumed by law-enforcement officers or child-care workers is a sacred trust. And almost anyplace one might venture—from a graveyard to a churchyard, from a memorable site in one's childhood to a battlefield or even a football stadium—can be a candidate for a sacred place. But if anything or any place can be sacred, then what is not sacred? If the term is so elastic as to include virtually any activity or place we might imagine, then does the term any longer carry any meaningful significance?

I grant that to honor the Crum Creek watershed as a sacred place appears, at first glance, to continue to expand the use of this term to include locales that might not obviously appear to be sacred sites. The watershed is not a built religious structure like a church or a temple. It is not a time-honored legacy site such as a war memorial or historic battleground. It is not even a widely recognized natural place of extraordinary beauty and grandeur, such as the Grand Canyon or Yellowstone National Park. Nevertheless, the Crum Creek watershed is a living system that supports an astonishing wealth of native wildlife, and insofar as it continues to function as a vital habitat for a variety of species and their young, it is a sacred place. Health and vitality are the highest ideals that make life on Mother Earth possible and worth living. Plant and animal well-being in harmony with natural systems is the supreme value that supports human and nonhuman flourishing on our fragile planet. A place where God especially dwells, a place that is sacred, is a place where nature subsists in harmony with diverse ecosystems. God as Spirit inhabits the biotic support systems on which all life depends, invigorating these systems with divine energy and compassion. The Crum Creek is not a pristine watershed; it will not win any virgin forest or clean water awards. But it is a site for the landed sacred, a place that God inhabits because it is a small and increasingly rare patch of earth and river in harmony with itself that supports the well-being of its living inhabitants.

Wherever there are places left on Earth where natural ecosystems are in balance with their surroundings, there is God's presence. God is the giver of life, the sustainer of all that is good, the benevolent power in the universe who ensures the health and vitality of all living things. The Crum Creek watershed—battered and degraded though it may be—continues to function as a balanced and self-sustaining network of life-giving habitat for plant, animal, and human well-being. The life-giving role the Crum Creek performs is divine in the truest sense of the word because it describes precisely the role God performs in and through the earth: to give life, to make all beings come into fruition, to sustain the zest and vigor of creation. In this sense, the Crum Creek watershed and God are one because they are both sources of life and health for earthen beings. To say, then, that the watershed is a sacred place does not debase the meaning of the word "sacred" by designating just any such place as sacred or religious based on personal whim or fancy. On the contrary, to celebrate the Crum Woods as a sacred place is to drop to one's knees on the ground and extends one's arms to the sky, to honor this place of God's indwelling as one of the remaining life-giving habitats on our planet that make our existence, indeed the existence of all of us, possible at all.

The Crum Creek watershed is sacred, indeed, but it survives today as the *wounded sacred*.

Envisioning the unity of the Spirit and the Crum habitat opposes the classical theological idea of God as unchangeable and apathetic in the face of the suffering and turmoil within the creation that God birthed into existence. God's Spirit is not a distant abstraction but a living being who subsists in and through the natural world. Because God as Earth Spirit lives in the ground and circulates in water and wind, God suffers deeply the loss and abuse of our biological heritage through our continued assaults on our planet home. God as Spirit is pained by ongoing eco-squalor; God as Spirit undergoes deprivation and trauma through the stripping away of earth's bounty. As the earth heats up and melting polar ice fields flood shore communities and indigenous habitats, God suffers; as global economic imbalance imperils family stability and intensifies the quest for arable land in native forests, God suffers; as coral reefs bleach into decay and whole ecosystems of fish and marine life die off, God suffers; and as stream quality and wildlife habitats endure further degradation in the Crum watershed, God suffers. When we plunder and lay waste to the earth, the Spirit suffers as God's presence on a planet that is enduring degradation of natural resources and rapid species extinction. The Spirit is the injured sacred, the enfleshed reality of the divine life who grieves over what may become a lost planet, at least for human habitation. As the Spirit is the suffering God, so also is the body, so to speak, of the Spirit's worldly presence, the earth itself, the wounded sacred. Together in a common passion and common destiny, the Spirit of God and an earth scarred by human greed exemplify the wounded sacred in our time.

MCFAGUE'S PANENTHEISM

A primary source for a theology of the wounded Spirit is the agential-organic model of God in Sallie McFague's biocentric theology. For McFague, God as agent is relatively free and independent from Earth while God as organic life-form is the "embodied spirit" of the universe. As the radically immanent reality within which we "live and move and have our being" (Acts 17:28), God, organically understood, is the "body of the universe." In this model of the natural world as God's body, all forms of life, from the smallest microorganisms to the great whales of the ocean deep, are embodiments of God. All creation enfleshes the divine life in McFague's pan-*en*-theistic model of God: God is in every living thing and all living things are interanimated by the divine life-source. This model affords theology with a new planetary agenda, because once the Christian community can learn to reconceive of the world as God's body, it will understand that the health of the planet and the well-being of God are coterminous values that are achievable only on the basis of Earth-friendly lifestyles. But does this model also subject God to fundamental loss, perhaps even destruction, in a manner that the classical model of God fully divorced from earthly determination does not? As McFague writes, while "God is not reduced to the world, the metaphor of the world as God's body puts God 'at risk.' If we follow out the implications of the metaphor, we see that God becomes dependent through being bodily, in a way that a totally invisible, distant God would never be."[16]

On an initial reading of McFague's work, God appears to be fundamentally immanent to the world: the world, as God's body, is the primary medium of God's presence, and God is "at risk" in a world suffering from acute environmental degradation. But on a further reading we find that God, agentially understood, is not dependent on the world in the same way, for example, that we are dependent on our own bodies, in spite of what might appear to be the logical force of McFague's panentheistic model of God. "Everything that is, is *in* God and God is *in* all things and yet God is not identical with the universe, for the universe is dependent on God in a way that God is not dependent on the universe."[17] God is *in* all life-forms, but the reality of God is neither *identical* with nor *exhausted* by God's embodied participation in the well-being of the planet. In my mind, McFague appears to equivocate on the critical issue about whether God is fully enfleshed within Earth community or not. That is, if the world *is* God's body, and if "being embodied" (as opposed to simply "having a body") entails that a being is fundamentally dependent on its body for its life and sustenance, then in what sense is God *both* bodily and yet *not* dependent on God's body, the universe, for the divine life's health and maintenance? Does McFague want to have it both ways? Does she want to maintain both God's identity *with* and autonomy *from* the universe, God's body?

In McFague's agential-organic formulation, does God remain "up in heaven," as it were, ultimately secure and insulated from the environmental squalor suffered on the earth "here below"? In the end, it appears that God is not vulnerable to final loss and destruction in the event that God's Earth-body is destroyed—in spite of the fact that if we were to lose our bodies, meaningful personal identity as we know it would be lost as well. God is at risk in McFague's paradigm, but not in any terminal sense. But reimagining God as Spirit as *thoroughly* incarnated within the natural world—a move initially advanced by McFague but not fully embraced in her final analysis—entails the disturbing conclusion that God's fate and the world's future are fundamentally bound up with one another. By deciding in freedom, and not by any internal necessity, to indwell all things, including the Crum Creek ecosystem, God places God's self at risk just insofar as the modes of God's presence suffer environmental degradation. God, then, is so internally related to the universe that the specter of ecocide raises the risk of deicide: to wreak environmental havoc on the earth is to run the risk that we will do irreparable, even fatal harm to the Mystery we call God. The wager of this model is that while God and world are not identical to one another (so McFague), their basic unity and common destiny raises the possibility that continual degradation of the earth's biotic communities may result in the attenuation and eventual destruction of the divine life itself (*pace* McFague).

In the green Spirit perspective suggested here, God's vulnerability as one of us and damage to the Crum watershed are one and the same reality. Even today, the Crum Woods, a small fragment of aboriginal forest still functioning as a relatively hearty ecosystem on the edge of urban Philadelphia, is one of many surviving networks of life-giving habitat that show forth God's bounty and compassion in the earth. But the Crum Creek watershed also displays the Spirit of God's deep and abiding suffering in our present time as well. As toxins from ruptured sewer lines and storm water leech into the creek, as the edges of the forest are cut down to make way for more suburban sprawl and commercial and institutional growth, God as Spirit experiences the loss and depredation of this delicate watershed in the depths of Godself. God is harmed by what we do. God is injured by the ways in which we despoil the natural systems that have supported life in many bioregions, including the Crum Woods, for tens of thousands of years. Spirit in love with the land—God in friendship with this small strip of Pennsylvania greenway—are codetermined, fellow sufferers in a unified effort to bring sustainable well-being to the Earth community. Crum Creek is a small but important member of the Spirit's earthen body; as is all of creation, this forest fragment is part of the body of God's material presence. When the Crum Creek suffers, God suffers as well, reminding all of us to travel lightly on the earth as we participate in the evolution of particular ecosystems, including the evolution of this particular watershed.

COBB'S CRITIQUE OF SACRED LAND THEOLOGY

In traditional Christian thought only God is sacred. God alone is supremely absolute and sovereign over the whole created order. All other beings, while valuable as products of God's creative love and bearers of God's image, only have value and worth relative to God. The author and arbiter of life and death itself, God is the principal power in the universe who rules with authority, judgment, and compassion over all of the human and nonhuman subjects in God's care and domain. In this classically feudal picture of God's relationship to his creaturely vassals, sacredness belongs to God and God alone.

McFague has consistently challenged this feudal model as bad theology and bad ecology. She argues that the kingly model of God and the world has led to a hierarchical understanding of human beings as God's special image-bearers who are given the responsibility to exercise lordship and dominion over the earth. In the Great Chain of Being, God, as the disembodied source of all life, places humankind in between the highest order of being (heaven) and the lowest order (earth) so that human beings can be God's vice-regents over the created order. Since in the monarchical model neither God nor humankind is understood as intrinsically related to the world, it follows that the earth can be used—and sometimes abused—to serve human ends. Traditional Christian thought is indicted by McFague as partly responsible for the environmental crisis just insofar as it has sacralized this monarchical model of God and humankind as standing over against the earth—which, in turn, is relegated to the status of a lower order of being that needs human control and oversight.[18]

In most respects, this feudal view of God and the world is rejected by theologian John B. Cobb Jr. Cobb laments Christianity's myopic focus on the salvation of human beings to the exclusion of concern for the well-being of nonhuman plant and animal communities. This anthropocentric bias has blinded Christianity to the degradation of the biosphere and the cry of animal suffering that defines human history. A new vision of Christianity in harmony with nature is the demand of our time. Cobb's move to a thoroughgoing green Christianity in harmony with ascribing sacred value to the Earth community would seem to be the natural trajectory of his thought. And in certain important respects, Cobb does share basic assumptions with this orientation. All beings, including and especially human beings, are radically and mutually interdependent on natural systems: to destroy plant and animal life wantonly is to threaten and diminish the life quality and well-being of all of us, human and nonhuman alike.

But in spite of these core areas of agreement, Cobb also carefully distinguishes his project from that of the religious ecology suggested here. In particular, Cobb, while investing nature with spiritual power and sacramental meaning, disagrees with the tendency in nature-based religion to honor the natural world as sacred in itself. While God is in the world and benevolent toward creation, God alone is sacred. It is a dangerous misnomer, even blasphemous, to confuse the Creator and the creation and to venerate the earth as sacred along with God. In a word, God alone is holy. Cobb writes:

> Nevertheless, [the sacredness of all creatures] language is, from a historic Protestant perspective, dangerously misleading. Speaking rigorously, the line between the sacred and the profane is better drawn between God and creatures. To place any creatures on the sacred side of the line is to be in danger of idolatry. For many Protestants . . . the right way to speak is incarnational, immanental, or sacramental. God is present in the world—in every creature. But no creature is divine. Every creature has intrinsic value, but to call it sacred is in danger of attributing to it absolute value. That is wrong.[19]

Cobb's case against radical religious ecology is that it wrongly blurs the line of distinction needed to separate beings of relative value from the divine being itself, the bearer of absolute value. Unless theology polices the borderland that divides creation and Creator, there is the danger that religious faith will slip into the worship of a false divinity, an idol, and degenerate into an animist belief-system that regards all beings as holy—Spirit-filled bearers of divinity. Idolatry for Cobb is the confusion of realms of reality that need to be kept apart. Cobb's theology operates within a binary, either-or logical field: one worships either God or nature, but not both. Since Christianity is not an animist religion that invests all things with sacred presence, one should worship God alone as sacred. While nature *is* charged with God's presence, according to Cobb, it does not follow that nature *itself* is a divine reality alongside or internal to God and thereby an object worthy of our devotion and worship. To call the created order sacred, therefore, is dangerous and idolatrous: it is to deify and revere the earth as equal in worth and value to God. To do this is to displace God's unique role as humankind's proper object of worship.

From the perspective of classical theology, I understand Cobb's concern. But the witness of Scripture and tradition is to the world as the abode of divinity, the home of life-giving Spirit, God's dwelling place where the warp and woof of everyday life is sacred. As McFague writes, nature is a "divine habitation" and the place where "we see the presence of God in the world."[20] All life is sacred because the earth is a natural system alive with God's presence that supports the well-being of all created things. McFague's point is that God is not a dispassionate and distant potentate who exercises dominion over the universe from some far-removed place. Rather, in and through this planet that is our common home, God is earnestly working with us to heal the earth, but God also suffers deeply from the agony of this unlifted burden. Building on McFague's nature theology, I have said that the *earthen* Spirit who infuses all things with her benevolent presence is also the *wounded* Spirit who implores us, in groans too deep for words, to practice heartfelt sustainable living in harmony with the natural world around us. In the warmth of the sun, the shelter of the encircling sky, the strength of the great oceans, and the fecundity of the good land, we have everything we need to recover our kinship with Spirit and Earth and develop green lifestyles in response to this kinship.

It is not blasphemous, therefore, to say that nature is sacred. It is not mistaken to find God's presence in all things. To speak in animistic terms, it is not wrong to re-envision Christianity as continuous with the worldviews of traditional peoples who bore witness to and experienced divinity everywhere—who saw and felt the Spirit alive in every rock, tree, animal, and body of water they encountered. For me it is not idolatry to enjoy Crum Creek, degraded though it may be, as a sacred place that plays a crucial role in maintaining the health and well-being of humankind and otherkind in eastern Pennsylvania. God as Spirit is the gift of life to all creation, and where life is birthed and cared for, there God is present, and there God is to be celebrated. God is holy, and by extension, all that God has made participates in that holiness. Thus, when we labor to protect and nurture the good creation God has made, we invest all things with inherent, supreme value as a loving extension of God's bounty and compassion.

Sacred, then, is the ground we stand on; holy is the earth where we are planted.

Crum Creek spirituality envisions God as present in all things and the source of our attempt to develop caring relationships with other life-forms. This perspective signals a biophilic revaluation *and* continuation of characteristic Christian themes. Christians speak of the embodiment of God in Jesus two thousand years ago, but now *all life* is the incarnation of God's presence through the Spirit on a daily basis. Christians speak of the miracle of the Eucharist, in which bread and wine become Christ's flesh and blood, but now the *whole earth* is a living sacrament full of the divine life through the agency of the Spirit who animates and unifies all things. Christians speak of the power of the written Word of God, in which God's voice can be heard by the discerning reader, but now *all of nature* is the book of God through which one can see God's face and listen to God's speech in the laughter of a bubbling stream, the rush of an icy wind on a winter's day, the scream of a red-tailed hawk as it seizes its prey, and the silent movement of a monarch butterfly flitting from one milkweed plant to another.

PART THREE

ECONOMY

9
THE GLOBALIZATION OF NOTHING AND *CREATIO EX NIHILO*

Marcia Y. Riggs

It is an odd kind of privation, loss in the midst of monumental abundance, *but it is an apt description of a major problem of the age in the developed world.... This diagnosis of a central problem of the contemporary world—loss amid unprecedented affluence—means that even though we find ourselves surrounded by a plethora of (non)-places, -things, -people, and –services, we nevertheless are deprived of the distinctive content that always characterized places, things, people, and services. We could be said to be dying of thirst even though we are surrounded by water.*
—GEORGE RITZER[1]

Imagining the world creatively fosters a perception of the depth of goodness beyond the anxieties of the age.
—WILLIAM SCHWEIKER[2]

I believe in God's Spirit as the source of all life and love. Life in the Spirit is the only place where human beings can live fulfilled lives. This is the case because God is reality and in God we live and move and have our being. God is not an 'extra' added on to life, but life itself—and as we learn from Jesus as the Christ—God's intention is that all life should flourish. Life takes place in love and for love.
—SALLIE MCFAGUE[3]

And God stepped out on space,
And he looked around and said:
I'm lonely—
I'll make me a world.
—JAMES WELDON JOHNSON[4]

CONSUMPTION AND CREATION: MEDIATING THE TENSIONS

What is the connection between globalization, consumerism, and the doctrine of creation? This is the question that is explored in this chapter. Each concept evokes notions of power, desire, and relationship, and yet a creative mediation among the three invites us to consider the ways in which the latter concept of creation summons both globalization and consumerism into new relationships of critique and accountability. Framed by the theological concept of creation, both globalization and consumerism are called to account for their life-diminishing dynamics and invited to be transformed toward mutuality and responsibility. In the process, the tension among the three concepts is not so much resolved as it is creatively and humanely embraced.

This is an exercise in what I call *mediating theological ethical reflection*. Mediating theological ethical reflection is Christian ethical reflection for the twenty-first century. In the twenty-first century, Christian ethical reflection should emerge from a process whereby social issues and theological ideas are defined and interpreted through the interaction of a variety of texts, readers, and the contemporary context. The process is mediating because the interaction of texts, readers, and context is best understood as bringing "voices" into a dialogue with the express purpose of hearing each voice as well as exposing and engaging creatively the tensions between them. It is by hearing the voices on their own terms and exposing and engaging the tensions between them that the process of mediating theological ethical reflection occurs.

The voices in this dialogue about globalization, consumerism, and the doctrine of creation are represented in the four quotations that open this essay. These voices are (1) George Ritzer, a EuroAmerican sociologist, (2) William Schweiker, a EuroAmerian theological ethicist, (3) Sallie McFague, a EuroAmerican theologian, and (4) James Weldon Johnson, an African American poet. Of course, there is a fifth voice: mine. However, I have two roles to play here. First, I am the mediator guiding the process of explication, exposure, and engagement among the four voices. Second, I am an African American womanist Christian liberation ethicist[5] responding to these voices—not as one who resolves the tensions among them but as one who proposes a way of *living into* the tensions creatively so that the dialogue between the voices initiates responsive moral agency, that is, a way of being and doing for positive social change in our lives and world.

The chapter has three sections. In the first section I designate an ethical tension that derives from an explication of the sociological voice of George Ritzer. In the second section I propose another tension and discuss it through an explication of the theological voices of Schweiker, McFague, and Johnson. In the third section, with the explication of the voices in hand, I engage the tensions *between* the voices so as to suggest what is at stake as we seek to live *into* the tensions of globalization, consumerism, and creation as people of faith in the twenty-first century.

A SOMETHING-NOTHING TENSION

In his book, *The Globalization of Nothing,* Ritzer offers an unapologetic (in the face of critiques by postmodern sociologists and feminists) modern sociological analysis of globalization in the realm of consumption. His analysis is both descriptive and analytical of what he considers a general historical and global trend (with its origin and center in the United States) toward nothingness in the realm of consumption. In his words: "The social world, particularly in the realm of consumption, is increasingly characterized by nothing. In this case, 'nothing' refers to *a social form that is generally centrally conceived, controlled, and comparatively devoid of distinctive substantive content.* This definition carries with it *no judgment* about the desirability or undesirability of such a social form or about its increasing prevalence."[6] Among the forms of nothing that Ritzer describes are the credit card, fast-food restaurants, shopping malls, name brands, and the Internet, particularly large-scale consumption sites such as Amazon.com.

Ritzer places his understanding of nothing on a continuum with something: "[A] preliminary orienting definition of something [is that it is] *a social form that is generally indigenously conceived, controlled, and comparatively rich in distinctive substantive content*; a form that is to a large degree substantively unique" (7). Some of the forms of something to which Ritzer points are personally negotiated loans, crafts created by local artists, and gourmet meals. According to Ritzer, there are four major subtypes of the something-nothing continuum: (*a*) place (community bank)/nonplace (credit-card company), (*b*) thing (personal loan)/nonthing (credit-card loan), (*c*) person (personal banker)/nonperson (telemarketer), and (*d*) service (individualized assistance)/nonservice (automated, dial-up aid) (10, 39–65). Likewise, there are five subcontinua of the something-nothing continuum: (*a*) unique (one-of-a-kind)/generic (interchangeable), (*b*) local geographic ties/lack of local ties, (*c*) specific to the time/timeless, (*d*) humanized/dehumanized, and (*e*) enchanted/disenchanted (20–36). Although Ritzer notes in his argument the contradictions and self-reinforcing processes of the subtypes and subcontinua, he posits that what falls on the nothing end of the something-nothing continuum is proliferating. The contemporary context, then, is characterized by a movement toward nothing.

Ritzer situates this complex conceptualization of a something-nothing continuum at the heart of his analysis of globalization. He defines globalization as "the worldwide diffusion of practices, expansion of relations across continents, organization of social life on a global scale, and growth of a shared global consciousness."[7] In conversation with sociologist Roland Robertson, Ritzer asserts the need to nuance the understanding of globalization in terms of two concepts: "glocalization" and "grobalization." Glocalization refers to the way that the

144 THEOLOGY THAT MATTERS

global and the local become interrelated in a way that creates unique outcomes in different geographic areas. Grobalization, by contrast, refers to the imperialistic imposition of nations, corporations, and organizations on geographic areas to foster the growth of their power, influence, and/or profits in those areas throughout the world. The engines that drive grobalization are capitalism, Americanization (the propagation of American ideas, customs, social patterns, industry, and capital around the world), and McDonaldization (the growing power of the principles of the fast-food model for other sectors of social life, such as the university, criminal justice, and religion) (73, 80–91).

Although Ritzer agrees that glocalization does occur, it is the grobalization of nothing that is of overriding significance to him. The predatory growth of capitalism, Americanization, and McDonaldization is occurring at an alarming pace in today's world, he contends, threatening to undermine long-held values, traditions, institutions, and ways of relating. The grobalization of nothing occurs because nothing tends to be less expensive to produce (thus more money is spent on advertising and marketing). In addition, its simplicity and lack of distinctiveness make nothing relatively easy to appreciate and thus more transferable across cultures. Ritzer suggests that there is an economics of nothingness that drives grobalization. In this economy, the affluent can afford forms of something while those with less money are largely restricted to nothing. Because some minimal level of affluence and prosperity in a society overall must be reached before the people in that society can afford nothing, those below a certain income level (for example, near or below the poverty line in the United States) cannot even afford nothing. Ironically, even the wealthiest people often consume nothing. They are drawn to many of the same low-priced forms of nothing that cater to the mass population (160–62).

Glocalization and grobalization thus constitute for Ritzer a final set of binary, yet interrelated, concepts. Where glocalization is associated with something and with heterogeneity, grobalization correlates with nothing and with homogeneity. Indeed, there is a sense in which the two terms signify two worldviews. The glocalized worldview envisions a world "more diverse, effervescent, and free," while the grobalized worldview purports a world "more capitalistic, Americanized, rationalized, codified, and restricted" (80).

The something-nothing tension deriving from Ritzer's argument begins with the assumption that the social world consists of arenas of consumption. We find ourselves consuming not only products in shopping malls or on Internet sites; we are also consumers of services vital to human life such as health care and education. The economics of nothingness suggests an ambiguous relationship between the haves and the have-nots. Both, after all, participate in the consumption and hence valorization of nothing. Yet, it is clear that those who do the labor to produce nothing around the globe are by and large the have-nots of the world. There is, then, an overarching socioethical dilemma that character-izes the contemporary world: loss amid monumental abundance. The reality of loss amid monumental abundance constitutes a socioethical dilemma because, despite the apparent moral superiority of something over nothing, "nothing" is not necessarily bad (for example, cell phones), and "something" is not inevitably good (such as the existence of an exclusive country club).

As I listen to Ritzer's voice, I notice that this something-nothing tension and its overarching dilemma point toward socioeconomic, religious, and ethical dynamics deserving of further reflection. The socioeconomic dynamic is shaped by producers' need to create nothing so as to increase profitability. In response, consumers (feeling bereft of that which is unique and distinctive, or feeling unable to afford something) seek to turn nothing into something. Religiously, the something-nothing tension results in the loss of long-term cultural traditions in favor of more expedient notions of meaning and value. Since such cultural traditions are a source of myths and values that provide ultimate meaning (the religious), people find their sense of that which grounds them as individuals and communities eroding. The ethical dynamic produced by the interplay of something and nothing is comprised of competing needs in the arenas of con-sumption. This competition creates a heightened ambiguity between what is good and what is bad.

All told, Ritzer's sociological voice gives us a thick description of globaliza-tion as the context of our consumerism. It challenges us to become aware of the deep, systemic tensions between two very different worldviews and econo-mies—what he calls grocalization and grobalization. Such awareness confronts us with the fact that our own world and lives are increasingly (and ineluctably?) characterized by grobalization. For those who desire to engage this context as persons of Christian faith, there is the need to listen to additional voices. We turn, then, to the voices of Schweiker, McFague, and Johnson for what insights the doctrine of creation brings to bear upon this complex situation of globaliza-tion and consumerism.

A COMPLICITY-INTEGRITY TENSION

In *Theological Ethics and Global Dynamics in the Time of Many Worlds*, William Schweiker offers "the time of many worlds" as a metaphor to describe globaliza-tion as a phenomenon earmarked on one hand by a "collision and confusion of cultural forms" and on the other hand by an ability to communicate glob-ally in a "shared, universally present 'real time.'"[8] According to Schweiker, such a pluralistic context creates tremendous moral challenges with regard to how we come to know and respond to one another around the globe. This is the case because as we come to know the other through the social systems of the economy, media, and politics, we respond to one another according to the ways these systems shape our societies and our identities. Advertising is a poignant means through which this moral challenge is manifest. For market capitalism to use this medium to sell its products globally, traditional identities must be lost, or at least packaged to promote sales of these products to anyone.

Accordingly, for Schweiker, there is a need for the moral imagination to act as a counterforce to the distorted images of ourselves and to the insidious link between imagination and consumption that advertising effects. His way to foster the moral imagination as a counterforce is to draw from and reinterpret inherited religious myths. Ultimately, he argues that valuing all of the created order (both things and beings) in a way that diminishes human power and enhances the integrity of life is the most promising counterforce to capitalism's dynamics of distortion. Schweiker turns to the creation myth in the Genesis story in the Christian and Jewish Bibles as a point of departure. He reads this myth of creation from two angles, asserting that (1) creation is about the interaction of nature and sociocultural processes and time (*chronos*)—all as creations of God; and (2) creation, recognized by God as good, means that worth is written into the nature of things and that blessing is the key to world construction, to understanding reality (16–17).

Schweiker's reading of the Christian and Jewish traditions about creation also helps us to see a connection between creation as good and the valuing of all others, even those we call the enemy. Importantly, he insists that the story of creation be interpreted through the love command. He posits three insights from an explicative reading of the creation story:

1. The creation narrative explicates life as a realm of goods in and through the interworking of multiple forces and realities (heaven/earth, light/dark, and so forth). Genuine pluralism is not anarchy loosed on the earth. It is a complex, interacting reality affirmed as good but also marked by the ever-present possibility of conflict and violence.
2. By reading the love command within creation, the principle of reciprocity is seen to specify the moral meaning of God's creative abundance in the face of conflict. To seek justice is not to live by some generalized principle. It is, rather, to live in accord with creation amid the structures of sin but under the power of new creation.
3. When creation is conceived on the model of reciprocity within the integrity of life rather than on the model of metaphysical dependence, when God's abundant dealing with the enemy through the goods of life

grounds the principle of justice, then justice and creation are transvalued. [This means that justice no longer simply means to claim one's due or to treat others fairly; justice means] the merciful establishment of right relations among persons and social and natural processes. [Likewise, creation is now perceived as] a way of living out restorative justice and redemption. Through the creation narrative, morality and reality are thus connected in the moral imagination, deepening one's perception of what is important (33–36).

The moral meaning of creation, concludes Schweiker, is the integrity of life. Integrity of life means acknowledging that intrinsic worth is found in the right relations among complex goods (just as God declared creation to be good in the biblical story). It means, furthermore, that as moral agents we must be committed to that which maintains the wholeness of life. In sum, the moral imperative, an imperative of responsibility, is this: *"in all actions and relations, respect and enhance the integrity of life before God"* (37–38).

A PLANETARY THEOLOGY

Theologian Sallie McFague joins Schweiker's line of thought from the perspective of a planetary theology. In *Life Abundant: Rethinking Theology and Economy for a Planet in Peril,* McFague debunks neoclassical economics and its worldview as one that has given birth to its own form of religion: consumerism. From this point of departure, she offers her own construction of planetary theology.

Importantly, McFague points out that the neoclassical economic model inherited its fundamental ideas from religion (the sacredness of the individual and the sinfulness of all before God) and political science ("the rights of man"—life, liberty, and the pursuit of happiness). However, once those ideas were appropriated by economics (the individual free to pursue his or her own economic interests) beyond the eighteenth century (when individuals understood themselves within religious and political communities) into the twenty-first century (where individuals no longer have strong communal connections), neoclassical economics gives birth to its own form of religion, which is consumerism.

We humans have become consumers in search of the good life—a good life that is premised upon how much we can acquire without regard to whether or not this pursuit makes us authentically happy or whether or not what we pursue is good for everyone or the planet Earth. Indeed, although consumption is necessary to living, it is the excessive consumption of the North American middle class over and against the majority of the world's population who cannot consume the minimal necessities of living that concerns McFague. She is concerned with the way that, for the North American middle class, issues of distributive justice get subsumed by notions of charitable giving. Moreover, as the North American middle class overconsumes, we treat the planet Earth as if what is good for humans is good for the planet. This way of relating to the earth creates negative synergisms such as global warming.[9] McFague sums up the effect of the religion of consumerism this way: "We have allowed the economy not just to produce things, but people—the people we have become at the beginning of the twenty-first century. We have become consumers—not citizens, or children of God, or lovers of the world, but *consumers*" (96).

By contrast, McFague's planetary theology endorses an ecological economic model and worldview. Central to this model is community, understood comprehensively as the household of the planet Earth. Two critical features of such community are sustainability (the idea that the community must be able to survive over time) and distributive justice (all members have the use of the community's resources). The worldview of ecological economics requires that we reconceive ourselves to acknowledge "our inalienable membership in the earth community," striving "to balance individual freedom with the community's integrity" (102–3). As members of nature's household, we humans must see ourselves "living within a circle composed of networks of interrelationships and interdependence with all other beings, human and otherwise" (106). Within this worldview, the good life means the good of the community—that is, corporate good. Corporate good requires wise use of all nature's and humanity's capital so that the earth and future generations survive and thrive now and into the future. In other words, corporate good requires sustainability. The means toward sustainability is the sharing of resources—that is, distributive justice. Distributive justice means that all have the basics to survive and flourish.

Within this model and worldview, humans are still consumers. However, we are no longer consuming to amass luxury items or unnecessary amounts of goods. Instead, our consumption is based on maintaining quality of life for all (109–11). Moreover, this understanding of who we are holds globally: "globalization is not the opening of markets to free trade so that the six people who possess 59 percent of the world's wealth can get even more. Globalization in the ecological model means a decent life on a sustainable planet for all human beings" (122).

Finally, McFague proposes a planetary theology for twenty-first-century, middle-class North Americans. Using ecological economics as her interpretative context, McFague asserts a theology premised upon "an earthly God, an incarnate God, and an immanental God" (131). Portraying an earthly God entails seeing the world as the "body of God." It maintains that "God is not reduced to the body of the world but is also and primarily, the life and power, the breath and love, that makes the universe what it is" (140). An incarnate and immanental God points to a prophetic and sacramental Christology that derives from an understanding of the historical Jesus as a social revolutionary. This is the case because the ministry of the historical Jesus was driven by a vision of an egalitarian community. In other words, "we are invited into communion with God and partnership with Jesus to bring about a social transformation of life on earth for all creatures" (178). Consequently, from an ecological economic Christology a different understanding of abundant life emerges—"not the abundance of consumer goods but the possibility, the promise, of a new life in God for all" (179). Overall, it is life in the Spirit that signifies this understanding of abundant life.

For middle-class North American Christians, life in the Spirit means adopting a sacrificial, cruciform lifestyle. It also means churches must teach an alternative view of abundance. In McFague's final words we find the source for living life in the Spirit: "We were created in God's image, in the image of life, and our goal is to grow more fully into that image by loving each other and the world in concrete, practical, daily ways; in other words, in just and sustainable ways" (202).

OUT OF THE VOID

In "The Creation," James Weldon Johnson's poetic rendering of the biblical account of creation, McFague's discussion of abundant life is extended through the poem's interplay of earthy images of nature's abundance and God's abundant (creative) nature described as expressions of psycho-spiritual-emotional human needs.[10] Johnson opens the poem with a traditional theological doctrine of *creatio ex nihilo*, creation out of nothing.[11] However, unlike the mystery associated with the traditional doctrine, in the opening verse (quoted at the beginning of this essay), Johnson attributes a specific psycho-spiritual-emotional need to God as motivation for creating the world: "I'm lonely." The void, Johnson suggests, is not metaphysical but relational.

The following verses of the poem elaborate thus upon the opening verse by continuing to draw for us a picture of God with human needs, qualities, and behaviors. In the first half of the poem, God's creative acts are these: God sees the darkness, smiles, and light breaks; reaches out and takes the light and rolls it into the sun, moon, and stars; steps and walks on the earth to create valleys and mountains; spits out the seven seas; bats his eyes and claps his hands for lightning and thunder respectively; smiles again and the rainbow appears curled around his shoulder; and raises his arm and waves his hand over the sea and land so that the world can bring forth all species of fishes, fowls, beasts, birds, and vegetation. God admires and sanctifies these creative acts by saying: "That's good!"[12] One interpreter of the poem notes that Johnson's account of creation renders God's movements and physical presence, God's body (similar to McFague), as central to creation. Indeed, there is both God's power in relation to creating and God's intimacy with nature.[13]

In the second half of the poem, God stops and looks at the world thus far created, and says, "I'm still lonely." Thus, God sits down and thinks and finally exclaims: "I'll make me a man!"[14] So, God scoops up clay from the bed of the river, and

> Like a mammy bending over her baby,
> Kneeled down in the dust
> Toiling over a lump of clay
> Till he shaped it in his own image;
> Then into it he blew the breath of life,
> And man became a living soul.
> Amen. Amen.[15]

Importantly, Johnson understands the creation (nature and humanity) to be the work of God acting humanly yet divinely to make a world that is a response to God's deepest quest for relationship (in response to being lonely). The message is thus surely that we (*all* of creation) are God's companions and therefore responsible for one another and all of creation because of that relationship to God (compare with Schweiker).

The theological insights of Schweiker, McFague, and Johnson thus point to a complicity-integrity tension when one struggles with issues of globalization and consumerism from the perspective of the doctrine of creation. In the case of Schweiker, the nature of this tension resides in the quest to break our complicity with a commercially driven imagination that produces images of ourselves that hinder our ability to recognize one another and the wholeness (the integrity) of our global reality. We must accept our responsibility to and for one another and all of creation in that reality as a moral imperative intrinsic to God's creation. From McFague's point of view, this tension is about complicity in terms of our captivity to ideas about abundance that have distorted both our self-understandings (we are consumers) as well as the nature of the good life (the acquisition of many things). Integrity is the reclamation of the meaning of the good life as abundant life (as life in the Spirit) that emanates from knowing that we are created in the image of God and called to do justice daily. From Johnson, we are reminded that we must become complicit in the humanity of

God, because therein lies the integrity of our humanity. The integrity of our humanity in the face of globalization and consumerism will have much to do with advocacy for just labor and trade practices around the world, as well as what we buy, because as producers and consumers we must honor the goodness of God's creation (natural and human).

LIVING INTO THE TENSIONS OF GLOBALIZATION, CONSUMERISM, AND CREATION

With the explication of the voices of Ritzer, Schweiker, McFague, and Johnson in hand, the final move in this process of mediating theological ethical reflection is to engage the voices in relation to one another and the tensions between them. This move to engage the tensions should not, however, be perceived as primarily critical or analytical. Rather, here, engaging tensions is about searching for points of intersection and/or disjunction, agreement and/or disagreement for the purpose of expanding or enlarging our thinking and responses to globalization, consumerism, and the doctrine of creation. This process of mediating theological ethical reflection is about *living into tensions* rather than *resolving tensions*. Resolving tensions often means losing an opportunity for enlarging our collective wisdom, whereas *living into tensions* means opening up the space whereby creative responsive moral agency emerges.

The most obvious point of intersection—of living into the tensions— among the voices of Ritzer, Schweiker, and McFague is their acceptance of the complexity of the times in which we live. Ritzer describes the complexity in terms of glocalization-grobalization; Schweiker in terms of issues of pluralism and communication; and McFague in terms of competing economic models and worldviews (neoclassical and ecological) and the values each supports. All of the voices thus push us to resist the urge to simplify the nature and effects of globalization or to fear the challenges of being responsible consumers and global citizens.

Although Ritzer insists that the proliferation of nothing is an historical trend, he does not simply yearn for some former time when something predominated. Instead, he acknowledges the ambiguous relationship between something and nothing. Likewise, Schweiker does not revisit the myth of creation because it is the "right" story, but he does so in order to query the depths of its meaning for this particular moment, the time of many worlds. Equally, McFague theologizes constructively within the Christian tradition by deconstructing the world that neoclassical economics and the religion of consumerism have built. All these voices call on us to become agents (deconstructing, reconstructing, creating) rather than pawns of our present and future destiny.

Yet, because Ritzer remains more a sociological analyst than a social critic, it is Schweiker, McFague, and Johnson who propose alternative ways of seeing and engaging the complexity of our social context because for each of them the world is God's creation. Although all of these voices speak from Christian heritage, Schweiker and McFague do recognize that other religions can and must also speak to the times, and Johnson's poetic voice surely reminds us that scholarly insights in many forms must be heard if we are to reawaken the moral imagination.

Amid Ritzer's globalization and the creation of nothing, Schweiker sees justice as a creation event that radically alters who we are to love (the enemy) and what counts as meaningful (the pluralism that is the heart of creation). McFague tells us that by allowing ourselves to be defined as consumers, we have betrayed the image of God in which we were created. Thus, the activity of consuming nothing that Ritzer discloses can now be reframed as a need to reclaim our humanity. The stakes are high indeed. Johnson awakens the imagination in just the countercultural way that Schweiker and McFague and Ritzer are pushing for in their differing yet complementary ways. As Johnson insists that we see God through our own ways of being, doing, and needing, we are drawn into such relationship with God that to deny the relationship would be to deny ourselves and the world created by God. It would, in the final analysis, make Ritzer's nothing truly all that there is.

How, then, are we to live into the tensions of globalization, consumerism, and creation as people of faith in the twenty-first century? I propose that we live as religious ethical mediators. Whether we speak of globalization as grobalization (Ritzer) or as a moral space (Schweiker) or as an issue of planetary living (McFague), we must adopt mediating postures as we encounter the many religions (theologies and ideologies that claim something to be of ultimate concern) and the ethical pluralism (values and practices deriving from those many religions) of a world that must either listen and learn from a diversity of voices or not survive. As religious ethical mediators, we are always aware of the particular religion and ethics that ground us, but we will always expect the encounter with voices of different religions and ethics to be an opportunity for self-criticism and mutual criticism. Such twofold criticism must surely be the point of departure for the kind of responsive moral agency needed to navigate the complexities of globalization.

Responsive moral agency means, therefore, that we acknowledge that creation is the context of our being and doing as consumers in global reality. We must understand that creation refers both to physical places and spiritual spaces of encounter (places and spaces of globalization and consumerism) where relationship with the planet Earth and relationships with all beings must be earmarked by processes of acknowledging seemingly diametrically opposing positions (needs, interests, justice claims, and so forth) so that an ethical response that emerges will be one that interposes and communicates between the differing positions. This moral agency is responsive because it seeks to open the place and space of encounter creatively to engender the surviving and thriving of all concerned. The norms guiding this moral agency are receptivity, empathy, nonviolence, and life affirmation. How are we to live into the tensions of globalization, consumerism, and creation as people of faith in the twenty-first century? Responsively.

10
IT'S ABOUT TIME
Reflections on a Theology of Rest

Darby Kathleen Ray

I am tired. Not just "need a nap" tired or even "need a good vacation" tired but deep down, long-time-in-the-making weary. The kind of fatigue that is so deep down it is relatively imperceptible, even to its host. I am not depressed, am not lacking energy, passion, or satisfying relationships, and am not particularly cranky. Still, I find myself just barely out of my thirties and fantasizing about retirement! Too on-task and activist in orientation to be much of a daydreamer, my subconscious nevertheless snatches the occasional spare moment to entice me with visions of a garden I have time to tend, a book I am reading just for fun, or a social-justice effort I am able to follow from start to finish. Don't get me wrong: I treasure the life I am blessed to be living. It is undeservedly full of meaning and love. But it is also over-full in many ways—stuffed with responsibilities and commitments, bloated with to-do lists, gagging on worthy causes and projects. Deep in my soul and in the marrow of my bones, I crave permission to slow down, be less productive, be quiet and still. But my family, my job, and the world's needs and sufferings cry out for action, for stubborn commitment and audacious imagination. Clearly, it is my time to serve, and there is no time to lose.

I am not alone. The lives of most North Americans are beset by busyness. We scurry here and there, trying our best to remain purposeful and humane while juggling a dizzying array of tasks and commitments. We tell ourselves that if we can just make it through this phase of life, things will slow down, become sane: "Once I get that promotion . . ."; "When my children aren't so young . . ."; "After I pay off my credit-card bills . . ."; "Once we buy a house . . ."; "When this project is finished or that goal achieved. . . ." But the pace never seems to slow.

Despite the fact that everyone else we know is running as ragged as we are, we tend to think of the problem as a private matter, a personal challenge rather than a symptom of systemic or cultural dysfunction. We got ourselves into this mess and we'll get ourselves out, by golly. And so we resolve to slow down, to reprioritize and dedicate more time to the things that really matter. While well-intentioned, our efforts are usually short lived and unsuccessful because they are fundamentally at odds with our culture's reigning values: unfettered individualism, unlimited growth, and incessant reinvention. These values pervade our economics, our politics, even our religion, and they deal a fatal blow to the basic human need for rest—for a humane, healthy, and sustainable pace through life. Indeed, the ascendancy of these values over the past two centuries has led not only to new political, economic, social, and religious forms, but also to a new kind of human being—what Sallie McFague calls *homo economicus*, human being as consumer—as well as to a new concept of time: 24/7.[1] In today's world, the quintessentially human act is not thinking, caring, or creating, but buying. And like everything else in consumer culture, our humanity must be continually updated, constantly secured anew. Three cheers for around-the-clock shopping channels and Web sites.

A NEW ATHEISM?

According to McFague, the gradual privatization of politics and religion in the West has allowed neoclassical economics to emerge as the lone public discourse, the only shared vocabulary we have for describing our world, identifying our goals, and evaluating our actions. Most of us embrace other values as well, of course, but it is increasingly the economic values of individualism, growth, mobility, and novelty that we hold in common and view as authoritative, rendering everything else a matter of personal preference. The behavior that is culturally sanctioned above all others is buying, spending, consuming. It is the ritual that binds us together—young and old, rich and poor, black, white, brown, and yellow. It is the therapy of choice for more and more of us. It is, moreover, our civic duty. On this point Democrats and Republicans in Washington declare common cause: our main job as citizens is to help the economy grow. In times of national crisis, we serve our country best by going to the mall.[2] Clearly, it is not love but shopping/spending/buying/consuming that make our world go 'round.

While we might expect religion to provide a potent critique of and alternative praxis to the cultural valuation of consumerism, we find too often religion's own hijacking by economic forces and aims. Indeed, as theologian Harvey Cox suggests, the world's great religions are fast being eclipsed by "the religion of The Market," which boasts its own compelling theology, myths of origin, rituals, and high priests. Far from challenging the idolatry and doctrines of the new religion, traditional religions "seem content to become its acolytes or to be absorbed into its pantheon, much as the old Nordic deities, after putting up a game fight, eventually settled for a diminished but secure status as Christian saints."[3] Jeremy Carrette and Richard King, authors of *Selling Spirituality: The Silent Takeover of*

Religion, offer a slightly more sanguine appraisal of the situation. They propose that while religious traditions may well capitulate to the religion of the Market, settling for a supporting role by "offering succour and relief to an alienated and dehumanised congregation of individualised consumers," or retreating "into a siege mentality and [praying] that the predicted Armageddon will not happen," it is also possible they might mount a serious challenge to the new religion. Traditional religions might, that is, take back the realm of "the spiritual" from the capitalist discourse of commodification and convert it into "a site of resistance" to the God of the Market. By refusing to bend to the materialist, desacralizing demands of capitalism—that is, by refusing to grant ultimacy to the market—traditional religions have the potential to become genuine, albeit "unorthodox," alternatives to the religion of consumerism. As such, ironically, religions would become "the new atheisms" of our time:

> In the brave new world of the twenty-first century those perspectives that are classified as 'religious' in the modern consciousness provide the best hope we have as philosophical, social and cultural resources for this struggle . . . What a supreme irony indeed if we come to realize that the significance of Nietzsche and Marx's critique of the 'opiate of the masses' is that it is the religions themselves that provide the best hope for humanity in challenging the God of Money and providing the basic foundations on which to build alternative ideologies to the dominant religion of the early twenty-first century—corporate capitalism.[4]

Given the pace at which "the spiritual" is being turned into one of today's hottest commodities, from feng shui to WWJD paraphernalia, we might wonder what specific practices of resistance traditional religions have to offer and how those practices could possibly function as effective counterforce to the sophisticated and powerfully proliferating energies of the global marketplace.

For her part, McFague suggests that Christianity has important resources with which to meet the challenge. One such resource is the notion of "the world as God's body"—a startling metaphor that awakens us to the marvelously interconnected character of all that is and moves us to bring our own human identity and practices into line with God's desire for the flourishing of *all* creation.[5] Another Christian antidote to the poison of consumerism is what McFague identifies as a "cruciform" theology and ethic for today's context, according to which we attempt to sacrifice our consumptive ways of being and our market idolatry so we may take our proper place within "the Great Economy, the household of planet Earth."[6] A key conviction running through McFague's theological corpus is that if we humans are to have life abundant, then we must relinquish the false idea that we are the center of things. We must give up the idea that we are the sole or primary object and knower of God's being, creativity, and affection; that we are the apex and measure of creation; that we are the rightful recipient and exploiter of the world's resources and riches. When placed within truly ultimate contexts—such as the Infinite, the body of God, and the planetary household—our human claims to heroic knowledge, power, authority, space, and resources are profoundly relativized by the awareness that despite our best efforts, *God* is the source, center, and proper aim of reality.

IT'S ABOUT TIME

Where McFague's theological project has worked primarily with space—the space between the human and the divine (*Metaphorical Theology* and *Models of God*), the world as the space embodied by God (*The Body of God* and *Super, Natural Christians*), the space of the marketplace and the household of God (*Life Abundant*)—I am intrigued by the question of how time is also a critical dimension of our reality and, perhaps, one key to faithful living in the shadow of global capitalism. In a 24/7 world, time is constantly on the move, always ticking, perennially disappearing. There is urgency in the air: if we don't act now, we might miss a great deal. The natural, circadian rhythms of the body, the Earth, and the seasons are less and less noticeable, less and less relevant. Our grocery store's produce section reflects few seasonal variations—cantaloupes and strawberries can be had in any month. Entertainment and communication technologies do not differentiate between night and day, leisure and work, but invite us to stay connected and geared up around the clock. Daycares welcome children at midnight. Breasts, faces, necks, and thighs need not age. We have babies when we're sixty. Are we finally overcoming the limitations of time? Is the sweet taste of eternity on the tips of our tongues?

Let us pause (for a quick moment!) to consider the causes and costs of our 24/7 conveniences. The driving force behind twenty-first-century temporality is undeniably the capitalist economic system with its assumption that the good life is the life of consumption. The mantra of this system is "more." Adam Smith's eighteenth-century logic is basically still intact today: if we want to reduce human misery (or, put differently, increase human happiness), then we must produce more wealth—more goods and services for consumption. More production requires more work, which presumably stimulates the creation of more jobs, which produces more consumers and, eventually, more wealth. What we have learned since Smith is that once consumers' basic needs are met, the cycle of more cannot be allowed simply to stop. Thus, consumers must be provoked to desire more than we need. Indeed, our desire for more must be never ending. It must burn 24/7. The faster, the better. Neither rich nor poor is exempt from this dynamic. While for the affluent consumption is often a game, for the poor it is a more serious matter. "It is not simply a matter of keeping up with the Joneses or mimicking refined tastes," argues author William Greider. "The consumption is required to keep up with American life itself. To avoid experiencing public shame in this society a family needs far more than food and shelter." For *homo economicus*, one's humanity depends upon one's ability to consume ceaselessly. As a result, even those in poverty "are trying—struggling heroically, one might say—to remain good consumers and thus avoid public shame."[7]

To support the consumption habit of the masses and the profit habit of the capitalists, we must have a system of "free" markets motivated and regulated by competition and the survival of the fittest. We must have an industry (advertising/marketing) dedicated to the constant cultivation of desire. We must produce commodities that are viewed as desirable but that either wear out quickly or else go quickly out of fashion, so that consumer desire is not allowed to languish. We must train ourselves to focus only on short-term aims and outcomes. And of course we must all work long and hard—some of us to produce all those desirable but short-lived goods and all of us to make the money to buy those goods.

Despite labor-reducing technologies and record-breaking material wealth and abundance, most Americans spend increasing amounts of time at work. In fact, the average American spends 300 to 400 more hours at work per year than those in other leading industrial economies.[8] When we aren't at work, Americans spend the bulk of our waking hours with advertisers via television and the Internet.[9] We tend to think of time off of work as rest, but that time is usually far from restful as we scramble to accomplish the myriad chores, errands, and relationship maintenance tasks squeezed out by increased time at work. When it is finally time to "slow down," our vacations tend to be over-programmed and goal oriented, an extension of our multitasking work lives. Those of us who manage to carve out time to serve God or neighbor instead of simply our own bottom line or our nuclear family's immediate interests find ourselves weakening under what theologian Wayne Muller calls "the corrosive pressure of frantic overactivity."[10] Our good intentions are frequently undermined by exhaustion, disillusionment, and burnout.[11] "As we drive forward without stopping," Muller writes, "even our generosity takes on the characteristics of a high-speed train, forcing compassion, wanted or not, right prescription or not, on everything unlucky enough to get in our path."[12]

Whatever our intentions, says Muller, for most of us life is "a violent enterprise":

We make war on our own bodies, pushing them beyond their limits; war on
our children, because we cannot find enough time to be with them when they
are hurt or afraid, and need our company; war on our spirit, because we are
too preoccupied to listen to the quiet voices that seek to nourish and refresh
us; war on our communities, because we are fearfully protecting what we have,
and do not feel safe enough to be kind and generous; war on the earth, because
we cannot take the time to place our feet on the ground and allow it to feed
us, to taste its blessings and give thanks.[13]

Muller suggests we are addicted not only to destructive habits of consumption
and profit but to the busyness they demand: "The busier we are, the more
important we seem to ourselves and, we imagine, to others."[14] But the pace of
our living is simply not sustainable. Or if it is, we are moving only on life's surface, missing out on the profound challenge and satisfaction of deep living.

GIVE IT A REST

To live deeply requires rest and reflection. Occasional binges of inactivity or
vacation—mere crisis management—will not suffice. The truth is, challenging the soul-diminishing, community-destroying, Earth-ravaging dynamics of
24/7 temporality will take time: time to develop new habits to counteract the
addictive lure of the marketplace; time to create and institutionalize practices
of resistance that are intellectually, physically, and emotionally compelling and
sustainable. However, lest we fall prey to the mythology of perpetual novelty
that undergirds Market time, we will want to avoid the assumption that we
must necessarily create these habits and practices anew. We might begin, then,
by plumbing the old traditions for wisdom for our age.

This is precisely what Wayne Muller achieves in *Sabbath: Finding Rest,
Renewal, and Delight in Our Busy Lives.* Diving deep into the waters of Jewish
sacred texts and practices, Muller surfaces with jewels of insight for twenty-
first-century men and women of all faiths and none at all. His explication and
invocation of sabbath time is a powerful antidote to the frenetic pace, short-term
aims, and joyless dynamics of capitalism's 24/7 temporality. "While Sabbath
can refer to a single day of the week," says Muller, it "can also be a far-reaching,
revolutionary tool for cultivating those precious human qualities that grow only
in time."[15] Sabbath time is time out of the rat race; time spent not on producing,
consuming, or desiring more but on cherishing what we already have—time
spent deepening relationships and cultivating nonmarket values such as gratitude, mercy, mutuality, humility, and joy. Above all, sabbath time is rest, intentional and deep. "When we consecrate a time to listen to the still, small voices"

that are normally drowned out by the din of busyness, "we remember the root of inner wisdom that makes work fruitful. We remember from where we are most deeply nourished, and see more clearly the shape and texture of the people and things before us."[16] Where Market time is fragmented and fleeting, encouraging the proliferation of desires while undermining real bonds of affection, sabbath time bespeaks eternity and celebrates timeless bonds of connection. Our regular, 24/7 time is characterized largely by grasping and acquiring—what scholar Abraham Heschel calls "the tyranny of things of space." Sabbath practices, by contrast, summon us "to become attuned to *holiness in time*." Sabbath, says Heschel, connects us to "what is eternal in time." It summons us "to turn from the results of creation to the mystery of creation."[17]

Contrary to Market time, sabbath time is not outcome oriented. It is not linear, teleological, or recognizably productive. Rather, it meanders, lingers, and spirals. Sabbath time dillydallies, as my mother would say. Where the speed, novelty, and mobility of 24/7 temporality keep us in a state of perpetual amnesia and disorientation, sabbath time invites us to "remember who we are, remember what we know . . . Like a path through the forest," says Muller, "Sabbath creates a marker for ourselves so, if we are lost, we can find our way back to our center."[18]

A sabbath practice is any act of "sacred rest," anything that gives us refuge from the dehumanizing pace and aims of consumer culture: "Spend a day napping and eating what is left over in the refrigerator; play a game with your children, take a walk, have a cup of tea, make love, do nothing of any consequence or importance. Then, at the end of the day, where is the desperate yearning to consume, to shop, to buy what we do not need? It dissolves. Little by little, it falls away." Sabbath time is not merely a day off; it is not an absence. Rather, "it is the presence of something that arises when we consecrate a period of time to listen to what is most deeply beautiful, nourishing, or true. It is time consecrated with our attention, our mindfulness, honoring those quiet forces of grace or spirit that sustain and heal us."[19] Sabbath practices consecrate time for the kind of deep Listening advocated by Jay McDaniel.[20]

In addition to the sabbath practices Muller suggests above, any number of others could be added, from the personal and intimate (a daily time for centering prayer, meditation, or creative writing; a weekly habit of a real, lie-down-and-soak-awhile bath!), to the interpersonal (daily "nothing" time with a partner or child; a monthly potluck group with no official agenda), to the systemic and institutional (joining the Slow Food movement; participating in national Buy Nothing Day; embracing an "unplugged" Christmas).[21] Through the patient, persistent cultivation of sabbath practices, "the world becomes a place of rest."[22] If only for a while, the clock stops ticking, the debt stops accumulating, and

24/7 temporality loses its authority. In those blessed moments, we find renewal, reorientation, and reconnection. We marinate in the sweet juices of tranquility and eternity. Resting there, we find our petty self-absorptions beginning to dilute, our individual and social arrogances dissolving just a bit, our fears, resentments, and defenses giving way. We find, says Heschel, that "a beautifying surplus of soul visits our mortal bones and lingers on."[23] Gradually, under the gentle pressure of patiently held sabbath practices, we experience a grace-full decentering and recentering of the self in relation to God, our human neighbors, and the Earth.

When the nourishing rest of sabbath time becomes the foundation for our work in the world, that work holds new promise. It is not that the daily grind disappears or that systems of injustice are suddenly transformed. The desire for work that is personally meaningful, socially valued, and adequately compensated remains unfulfilled for most people, which means the struggle to rethink work and its defining systems must go on. And yet, despite these sad realities, rested work—work as it is viewed from the standpoint of rest, and work that is nourished by deep rest—gestures in significant ways toward transformation. Before turning to these gestures, let us consider the disfiguring impact of 24/7 temporality and market values on workers and work.

WORK AS DAILY DIMINISHMENT

Under corporate capitalism, work for most people is drudgery and shame. Typically, workers must check their identity, creativity, autonomy, and often dignity at the workplace door. They work for someone else—often someone they never even see or meet—and that someone else dictates their activities down to the smallest detail: what they wear, whether and where they sit or stand, what they say or do not say, who they relate to, when they go to the bathroom. William Greider notes that despite the suspension of basic rights such as freedom of speech and assembly, most workers' "loss of freedom goes largely unnoticed because it is so routinely part of their lives."[24] Those of us lucky enough to enjoy relative freedom at work may assume this is an outdated picture, a snapshot of the early 1900s, perhaps, but it is not. As Greider says, with confirmation from any number of scholars and untold contemporary workers, "despite the great leaps forward in technological invention and productive efficiency, despite the rising abundance and various civil protections, the economic realm of work continues to function in distinctly premodern terms—master and servant." The truth is, the vast majority of today's workers spend three-fourths of their waking hours in almost total subjection to another person's vision and authority. Their socialized powerlessness takes its toll not only on personal lives, where bruised egos become self-destructive or lash out at those with even less power, but also on the larger society. "Where," asks Greider, "did citizens learn the resignation and cynicism that leads them to withdraw as active citizens? They learned it at the office; they learned it on the shop floor. This real-life education in who has power and who doesn't creates a formidable barrier to ever establishing an authentic democracy in which [citizens] are genuinely represented and engaged."[25]

In the context of a society like the United States, where individual freedom is a sacred pillar of national identity, the correlation between autonomy and self-respect tends to be strong. Workplace curtailments of individual freedom surely take a toll, challenging workers' sense of worth and causing us to question the value of our own work. Far from being a font of self-expression, work becomes a force of daily self-diminution. The problem is compounded by the fact that those whose workplace freedom is most constrained tend to be those who are paid the least. When money and consumption are the markers of humanity (*homo economicus*) and work's sole or primary objective is a paycheck, then undercompensated work stands as a continual reminder of one's inadequacy as a human being. In the face of the persistent assaults on workers' dignity and self-worth perpetrated by an economics that systematically strips workers of autonomy, full participation, and just compensation, what solace can a sabbath praxis of deep rest and reflection possibly offer?

In addition to its negative impact on most workers, 24/7 temporality and the larger economic system it quickens is producing in the United States and across the globe a dramatic revaluation that threatens to remake, or unmake, human community as we have known it. The problem is not only the specific values embraced by corporate capitalism but also the totalizing force of that embrace and, consequently, the power and exclusivity those values then claim.

24/7 VALUES

The reigning values of capitalism are growth, productivity, efficiency, competition, innovation, and profit. The latter, it is often argued, is not intended as the sole or even primary end of work but is, rather, the carrot that motivates work toward productivity and efficiency and that motivates growth and investment in innovation. Similarly, it is typically alleged that competition is not an end in itself, but merely supports the development of good work—that is, work that is efficient, productive, and innovative. While it is certainly possible that capitalism in theory does not promote ruthless competitiveness and crass profiteering, in reality it often has such effects. However, even if we assume that the morally contentious values of profit and competition are not the leading actors in the drama of capitalist economics but instead play small supporting roles, we should still worry about the impact of the values of growth, efficiency, productivity, and novelty on human lives and communities and on the earth. In particular, we might wonder about their effect on our ability to live humane and sustainable—that is, rested—lives.

Consider efficiency. In service of this value, thinkers as august as Plato and Adam Smith advocate the division of labor.[26] Without a doubt, it is a smart convention. I for one have no desire to try to produce for myself everything I need for living; I am happy to share the work with others. But it is one thing to recognize that not everyone can or should make their own shoes or grind their own wheat, and another thing altogether to parlay that common sense insight into the kind of hyper-differentiated, ultra-hierarchical task structure we have today. Frederick Taylor's early-twentieth-century proposals for enhancing efficiency are often depicted today as relics of a bygone extremism, but they have actually carried the day in most work arenas, albeit with contemporary modifications. According to Taylor, good work is efficient work, and efficient work requires that workers be systematically "trained" not to waste time with "awkward, inefficient, or ill-directed movements."[27] Thus, Taylor advocated the creation of a class of managers who would study workers' movements, determine and notate scientifically the most efficient sequence and execution of movements, and then train workers to execute their work in precisely the manner delineated by management. This process of "scientific management" revolutionized work. Taylor's *Principles of Scientific Management* was translated into several languages and its ideas adopted around the world.

The new system was motivated by a desire to reduce "wasted" time—that is, time spent completing a task in a way that suits one's own intellectual and physical inclinations and limitations rather than someone else's definition of efficiency or "fast enough." A related and more sinister motive was also powerfully in play, and it, too, had to do with "waste." Rather than allow the knowledge of work to be "wasted" on mere laborers, it was to become the property and entitlement of the new management class. Where once there were master craftsmen whose time-honored knowledge and skill were bequeathed to the next generation via the patient practices of oral tradition and apprenticeships, the new system of work wrested knowledge and skill away from workers and gave it to management. Thus, for the sake of the value of efficiency—one of capitalism's much-heralded achievements—time is no longer the midwife of embodied self-expression, communal wisdom, or self-possessed workmanship. It has become, rather, the goad of the powerful and the bane of the worker. What a waste. At least Frederick Taylor had the courage in 1911 to acknowledge the cost of what was then the new value of efficiency: "In the past the man has been first; in the future the system must be first."[28] Today we are so accustomed to thinking of efficiency as an uncontestable good that we hardly notice its impoverishing effects on our understanding and experience of time, nor on the meaning of work for most of the world's laborers.

Productivity is another of capitalism's key virtues. Like efficiency, it is on its face a sensible thing to aim for in work, both individually and systemically. When workers are productive, they sometimes receive positive affirmation in the form of higher pay or expanded responsibility. They may also gain a sense of personal satisfaction in having met a challenge or pleased a superior. Higher productivity usually means increased profit for the owners of (or investors in) production, which at least occasionally gets reinvested in future innovations or trickles down to workers in the form of higher pay, better benefits, or safer working conditions. Thus, it would seem that workers and owners alike benefit when the virtue of productivity is enacted. However, there are significant losses to consider as well. In service of the goal of increased productivity, worker well-being is routinely compromised. Workers are pushed to work faster and faster, harder and harder in order to meet quotas for strawberries picked, patients seen, sales completed, or hours billed. The unrelenting pace often takes its toll on workers' physical, mental, and spiritual health. In addition, productivity goals and requirements often pit workers against each other, undermining worker solidarity, which is often a vital humanizing factor in contemporary workplaces. The pressures of increased productivity can also prompt workers to act unethically, if not illegally. For example, in order to log her firm's required number of billable hours, a lawyer bills a client for the time she spent in the shower because the client's case happened to cross her mind while shampooing; in order to see the expected thirty-two patients a day, a doctor orders an expensive barrage of tests for a patient because he doesn't have time for an extended diagnostic conversation; to make quota, a grove worker in Florida routinely includes vermin-infested or overripe oranges in his crates.

In addition to negatively affecting workers' individual well-being, relationships with each other, and moral compass, the specter of productivity routinely turns time spent at work into nothing but Market time. Time becomes the enemy. Whether the clock is moving too quickly to permit one to reach one's production goal/quota, or too slowly to let one escape productivity's tyranny, time is one's personal nemesis. Even when the card is punched, the board room dark, the workday over, the struggle with time does not end. For some, the frenetic pace, the pressure to be productive, the goal-oriented mentality that mark the workday hours characterize nonwork time as well, so that it becomes impossible to slow down, relax, be fully present with a child, a partner, or a good book. The mind is always racing, the knee bouncing, the teeth grinding.

Rest is what unproductive people get to enjoy. Others of us respond to the day's productivity pressures not by staying revved up but by shutting down. With the help of a remote control, computer mouse, six-pack, or some other tranquilizer, we make our escape, moving beyond the reach of oppressive time at last—or so we imagine. But without the rejuvenating energies of sabbath time, this "alternative" time is no match for Market time; it is anesthesia, not resistance. In sum, we see that productivity, while heralded along with efficiency as a key virtue of capitalism, functions far too often to undermine the well-being of workers. One of its more subtle deleterious effects is its corruption of our relationship to time, its undermining of our ability to experience deep rest and reflection—vital ingredients of humane and sustainable living.

Among capitalism's widely praised virtues, it is innovation that is likely to receive the least critique, the most cultural affirmation. Who could possibly take issue with the motivating and rewarding of human creativity? If the market's emphasis on efficiency, productivity, competition, and profit functions to reduce workers' esteem and autonomy, then the heralding of innovation is surely the answer to the problem. Indeed, it is capitalism's robust embrace of the value of innovation that is routinely identified as the main reason for the system's purported moral and practical triumph over socialist economies. Capitalism, it is argued, not only does not stifle workers' individuality but raises it to new levels, encouraging and rewarding creativity, risk, ingenuity, and self-expression. Once again we must acknowledge the significant kernel of truth here: opportunity for creative self-expression *is* a key ingredient of human flourishing. No one would dispute this. However, we might very well contest the claim that in practice capitalism actually supports workers' genuine self-expression. The fact is that for the vast majority of workers, invitations to be creative, to contribute their own ideas or inventions to the workplace, occur rarely, if ever. Sure, workers can and do find ways of expressing themselves at work—personalizing their work station, developing signature hairstyles or ways of greeting the customer—but these innovations are developed *in spite of* the work and workplace. As the system is currently configured, it is the privileged few whose work includes genuine and substantive opportunity for creative self-expression.

Still, most workers certainly feel the impact of capitalism's emphasis on innovation. While it is the few whose creativity is solicited and affirmed, all of us feel the impact of a systemwide glorification of novelty. The dynamic of "more" that drives the capitalist economy demands the constant creation of new and "improved" fashions and products, as well as the concomitant production of consumers' desire for novelty. Were we all to be content with last year's style of shoe or car or PDA, the entire system would be threatened. Its "health" depends upon our perennial dissatisfaction with what we already have, with the way things currently are. Satisfaction or happiness must be always on the horizon but never quite attainable; we need to see it (on TV, in magazines) and imagine it, but we must not be allowed to experience it. After all, it is the incessant grasping for what we do not have that turns the wheels of the system. To stop, to rest, to say "enough" or even "time out" is heresy, treason—a rejection of *homo economicus.*

Sociologist Richard Sennett argues that capitalism's enthronement of novelty, its demand for incessant reinvention, contributes to a "corrosion of character."[29] Trained by the dynamics of "more" to be constantly dissatisfied with what we have, we find ourselves perennially on the move, always on the lookout for new and better products or opportunities. Loyalty to the "old"—last season's products, our employer of any number of years, the house or neighborhood we live in, the religion of our upbringing—is a liability. For good living in the world of 24/7 temporality, loyalty must be replaced by flexibility and mobility. The consequence of the economic and cultural coronation of novelty, says Sennett, is the correlative institutionalization of contingency. Long-term commitment is largely a thing of the past. When we move to a new city or neighborhood, fewer and fewer of us attempt to put down roots—meet our neighbors, learn the rhythms of the bioregion, become active citizens. The relationships we develop tend to be functional and superficial. We may know lots of people—from work, church, the gym, or our toddler's playgroup—but there are precious few to whom we can turn in times of deep joy or pain, precious few who know our unique history, our vulnerabilities and dreams. The truth is that in a world governed by market values, "fleeting forms of association are more useful to people than long-term connections."[30]

In addition to undermining the development of authentic connections to place, people, and the past, Sennett argues that our culture's embrace of novelty is changing the way we relate to our work as well. Gone are the days of workers' lifelong and even intergenerational family loyalty to one employer or line of work, and with it the time and care spent developing one's workmanship as part of one's obligation to "the company." Gone, too, are the pride and social status that once attended those long-term relationships—the satisfaction and social regard that came from rendering good and faithful service over the long haul. Today's younger generation of workers can expect to change jobs numerous times in their lifetime and to develop a new skill set several times as well. They must be flexible, mobile, ready to reinvent themselves again and again. Their loyalty is to themselves and their dependents, not to the company, community, ecosystem, or neighborhood school to which they are momentarily connected. In a 24/7 economy, the chief aim of work is not the company's success or excellent workmanship but self-promotion. If company objectives, the common good, the guild's ethics guidelines, or the law of the land conflicts with that self-advancement, it is increasingly the latter that wins the day.

Precipitating and aggravating the erosion of worker loyalty and long-term commitment is the dramatic dissipation of "the company's" regard for and loyalty to workers. In a 24/7 culture of novelty and contingency, workers are more interchangeable than ever. Global communication and transportation technologies allow corporations to move jobs to cheaper labor markets (with fewer environmental restrictions) almost overnight. Outsourcing, downsizing, and "flexible production" are positive goals of the emerging business regime, with institutional commitment to workers as the main casualty. When a corporation gets into trouble in today's flexible economy, commitment to employee well-being is jettisoned as workers' insurance and pension funds are reduced or eliminated altogether. In the flexible economy invigorated by 24/7 temporality and the virtue of innovation, workers must function in a state of constant unpredictability and instability.

All in all, each of the reigning values of capitalism—productivity, efficiency, competition, growth, innovation, and profit—has its merits, its contribution to make. But taken together and allowed to gain such cultural authority that other values *lose* their authority, these capitalist values are troubling indeed. Together in their current constellation of power, these values undermine individual character and mitigate against the common good and ecological sustainability. As Sennett says, "the qualities of good work" as defined by corporate capitalism simply "are not the qualities of good character."[31] Loyalty, mutuality, long-term connection and commitment, workmanship, patience, honesty . . . these virtues are "outdated" according to today's market paradigm. They are relics of the past. Out with the old, in with the new; the faster the better—that is capitalism's message.

SOMETHING FROM NOTHING?

One important contemporary voice characterizes this trend as a cultural shift from "something" to "nothing."[32] In *The Globalization of Nothing*, sociologist George Ritzer argues that thanks to the value set promoted so effectively by capitalism, societies today are less and less likely to embrace local products, small businesses, and distinctive indigenous practices and social forms—what Ritzer calls "something." Instead, what we see happening at an astounding rate is the proliferation of globalized products, international chain stores, and other highly centralized and impersonal economic entities—what Ritzer terms "nothing" because they are "devoid of distinctive substantive content."[33] Using Ritzer's terminology to inform our own discussion of capitalism's dynamics of "more," we might say that capitalism encourages the production of nothing—products created not because of any genuine need but simply to keep the wheels of production and the flames of desire turning and burning; products intentionally created to wear out or obsolesce quickly; products whose main value is nothing more than being part of the latest trend, one of the new consumables. But of course, all of this nothing is presented as if it were really *something*—something altogether new and useful and wonderful; something that will make our life easier or happier; something to make us feel better about ourselves or look better in the eyes of others; something we really need.

What we have here is a claim to a kind of economic *creatio ex nihilo*—the creation of something out of nothing. Perhaps part of the allure of capitalism—the reason it is so successful in turning us all into willing consumers—is the appeal of its heroic mythology. According to theologian Catherine Keller, it took a couple of centuries for Christian tradition to settle on *creatio ex nihilo* as the trope for divine creativity.[34] After all, Genesis 1:2 clearly implies that the world was created out of "a formless void," "a primal chaos," "a bottomless Deep," a "matrix of possibilities"—rather than an absolute vacuum of mere absence—a fact about which, says Hebrew Bible scholar Jon Levenson, there has been among biblical scholars "a near, if nervous, consensus for decades."[35] In spite of this, the doctrine of creation out of nothing has reigned supreme since about the third century—most likely, argues Keller, because of the appeal of the idea of mastery. How better to secure and buttress a claim for one's God's omnipotence (and, by extension, for the superiority of one's religion, one's community, one's gender, oneself) than to insist that "He" found a way to create something out of absolutely nothing, that He is a God of heroic creativity and unparalleled power? Says Keller: "The Father needs nothing but his own logos to create. This is a rhetoric of sheer power."[36] When Christian tradition does not simply ignore the watery chaos of Genesis 1.2, it demonizes it as an unruly monstrosity that is heroically vanquished by a warrior God. Creation is not simply out of nothing, but against it as well.

If Christian tradition has privileged the heroic, mastering novelty of *creatio ex nihilo* theologies, then post-industrial Western culture and its capitalist economic system have apparently followed suit. We have already seen that according to this system, what is worth having is the new. The old, the past, the out-of-fashion is worthless—nothing. If we are to be stylish/happy/fulfilled, this nothing must be vanquished. Thanks to the wonders of commodity capitalism and the 24/7 marketplace, we can always find something with which to conquer the nothing. Even those of us with limited resources will nevertheless go to heroic lengths to buy something, to assert our power as consumers; otherwise, we fear, we are nothing. We try not to notice or admit to ourselves that the something we consume with such ferocity is constantly becoming nothing—wearing out or going out of style and hence demanding a new vanquishing, a new creation, a new heroic act.

It is heroic work that the market tends to value and society to esteem. Physicians conquer disease and even death; movie stars and models defy age; successful entrepreneurs make something from nothing; lawyers vanquish untruth; business beats the competition, as do professional athletes; real estate developers triumph over nature. Work that merely sustains, or that traffics in chaos without conquering it, is far less valued: housekeeping, child care, teaching, social work, service-sector work. As Muller notes, the 24/7 economy rewards those who are fast, whose busyness yields quick or dramatic results. By contrast, "people who work with those precious things that grow only in time—caring for children, making peace in troubled communities, harvesting crops that feed us—these people are invisible, necessary but easily replaced, 'a dime a dozen.' If they were smarter, luckier, more motivated, they could be out there making real money."[37]

Despite the powerful allure of a theology or an economics of mastery, the reality is that we don't create *ex nihilo*. The "nothing," the "always already there" that is the precondition of our work is constituted by vast but usually overlooked networks of care, support, and responsibility: the Earth; the unpaid labor of our parents, family, and mentors; the underpaid labor of our teachers and coaches; the unseen labor of those who buff the floors and clean the toilets of schools, hospitals, and businesses; the undeserved and unearned gifts and graces with which we find ourselves blessed; the generations who have gone before us, clearing a path that we might walk with confidence into the future. Whatever "something" we are able to make through our own work stands on these shoulders, is indebted to these and other connections and contributions. Contrary to the mythology of the market, we do not create out of nothing.

Moreover, and in contrast to the assumptions of Market time, we would do well to realize that genuinely creative work—life-giving, life-nourishing work—takes time. Good work has the wisdom of rest in it. It does not compromise its integrity under the pressures of 24/7 temporality. While good work can be ambitious, take risks, and turn a profit, it is not done at the expense of self-care, care for others and the earth, and care for future generations. Good work is not too hurried to care. Neither is good work too self-important to rest. The world will get along just fine without me for a short time, and when I return rested, my work will be better, more energized and sustainable, more authentic and connected to larger goods than survival or self-promotion.

If we can see through the heroics and pretensions to mastery of the *creatio ex nihilo* doctrine, we can appreciate the more subtle but also deeply profound portrayal of creativity, of good work, suggested by the Genesis creation narratives. We may notice, for example, that God does not plunge frenetically into the task at hand but, rather, takes time to "hover" or "move" over "the face of the deep" before getting to work. God's work begins, it appears, with lingering reflection, thoughtful consideration of the possibilities. Once the work begins, God is not a workaholic. In fact, God pauses periodically, predictably, habitually to survey and enjoy God's work: "And God saw that it was good." The pace of work is by no means hurried or frantic; in fact, despite its grandiose results, it feels quite modest: "And there was evening and there was morning, one day." "And there was evening and there was morning, the second [third, fourth, fifth . . .] day." Here we notice that God's work, good work, occurs in harmony with the circadian rhythms of the universe. God is not, it appears, burning the midnight oil, pushing the Divine Self to extremes in order to make a buck, meet a quota, make partner, or earn tenure. When the job is finished and the work of creation completed, God does not collapse into exhaustion or head for some escapist relief. Instead, God takes the time to reflect back on what has been accomplished, to take pleasure in the workmanship, the beauty of a job well done: "And God saw everything that God had made, and behold, it was very good. And there was evening and there was morning, a sixth day" (1:31).

Thus, we see that well before the seventh day, the day "blessed and hallowed" by God as a day of rest, God's work was already punctuated by pauses for reflection and renewal. As Heschel notes, "The Sabbath preceded creation and the Sabbath completed creation."[38] Nevertheless, in spite of the clear integration of sabbath practices throughout God's work, there seems to be a concern that the valuation of sabbath time might be missed, that we might overlook its critical importance to good work. And so on the seventh day, God does one more bit of work: God creates the Sabbath. We often assume the work of creation ended on the sixth day, but the biblical text is clear that "on the seventh day God *finished the work* that God had begun" (2:2). God took special effort to create and consecrate rest, *menuha*. It was only then, says Heschel, that "the universe was complete."[39]

Just as the universe is not complete without rest, neither are we. Our work, our lives, our relationships must include rest—deep rest. Without genuine and habitual times of renewal, even our most well-intended work falls short of what it could be. Without rest, we are merely *homo economicus*—beings defined by the market and the demands of its 24/7 temporality for unceasing work and consumption. Without opportunities for rest and renewal, the earth is nothing more than raw material for human exploitation.

I am learning that humane and sustainable living depends upon deep rest and reflection. In the final analysis, our striving for justice, our efforts at transformation, our desire to participate in the ushering in of God's kingdom—all this good work suffers when it is not inspired, punctuated, and reinvigorated by sabbath time and practices. Sabbath time generates practices of self-care, simple acts of rest and refreshment that defy and counteract the daily diminutions of self that are part and parcel of work for most people these days. Dwelling in sabbath time reminds us that the Market is not our only measure, that there are grander, more authentic scales of worth in whose estimation we are unquestionably valuable, intrinsically worthy. Sabbath time encourages us to connect with others in modes of mutuality and caring, to engage others and be engaged by them thoughtfully and imaginatively, to allow the self to be touched and enriched by authentic relationships. Thus, a sabbath praxis invites experiences of authentic self-expression and self–affirmation that function as antidotes to the superficialities, alienations, and indignities of the workaday world under global capitalism. Moreover, sabbath experiences of self-care and self-worth, of deep rest and sustained reflection, support the development of a critical consciousness in relation to the dehumanizing dynamics of corporate capitalism and 24/7 temporality.

Sabbath time stands as a clear alternative to these dynamics—a quiet indictment of their soullessness. It prepares the deeply rested one not merely to return to and endure the tyranny of the market but to resist it, to work patiently at its dismantling. Thus, when we engage in sabbath practices—lying dormant by the world's standards—we find ourselves paradoxically awakened. Freshly aware of our own dignity and worth and of our authentic connectedness to God, neighbor, and the earth, we find that our work, no matter how modest, now aims not merely at material survival or even prosperity but at bolder objectives like self-actualization, economic justice, environmental sustainability, and mutual flourishing. When all is said and done, a sabbath praxis will not turn back the clock on 24/7 temporality or vanquish the market's values. It will not save us from having to navigate our way through a complex maze of economic and technological realities, or relieve us of our myriad responsibilities. But it does hold out the promise of rest along the way—time to recover old wisdoms for humane living, time to listen to and learn from the wisdom of our own bodies and the rhythms of the earth, time to be still and know that God is God.

THE CHURCH AS A HOUSEHOLD OF LIFE ABUNDANT
Reimagining the Church in the Context of Global Economics

Eleazar S. Fernandez

How do we reimagine the church in the face of today's ecological and economic challenges? What image of the church would be adequate and responsive to our globalized context? What would discipleship and ministry look like in an age of predatory global capitalism that destroys both human beings and the ecosystem? Although the church is not alone in responding to the ecological economic challenge, it plays a crucial role. This role is to become an active participant in reenvisioning an alternative economic paradigm, one that promotes life abundant for all members of God's body.[1] If theology is about constructing a worldview for people to inhabit, and the church is about the "good life" for all, then it must be an advocate of an alternative economic model, or of new "table manners" for a household (*oikos*) characterized by just (right) relations. In this regard, I agree with Sallie McFague that the church must be an advocate of alternative economics (ecological economics); however, the church can only effectively perform such a role if it embodies in its own life and ministries the new economic paradigm. In this chapter I take up McFague's call by reimagining or reenvisioning the church as an entity that embodies and advocates an alternative economy—an economy of life abundant for all members of God's household. The overarching metaphor in my task of reimagining the church in the era of capitalist globalism is the church as "household of life abundant."[2]

KNOWING GOD, KNOWING THE WORLD: THE CONTEXT OF PREDATORY GLOBALISM

Reinhold Niebuhr declared that "there is nothing more irrelevant than the answer to an unasked question."[3] This point is extended by fellow theologian Robert McAfee Brown, who contends that "confusing the question one has been asked with the question one is prepared to answer is equally irrelevant."[4] Understanding the questions that are posed by our context is crucial for our engagement with the world. A faith that seeks to engage and, more so, to transform the world needs an accurate reading of the world. But an accurate reading of the world is not only crucial politically. It is also crucial theologically, for an error in understanding the world, as Thomas Aquinas puts it, leads to an error in understanding God.[5] If God is revealed (paradoxically also hidden) through the world, then we have no way of knowing God apart from the world.[6] If we misread the world, we misread God.

The world I would like us to read is characterized by the phenomenon of heightened globalization.[7] It is not my intention to write more about this phenomenon because there is abundant literature on this topic, but to use it as a context for reimagining the church. Central to this phenomenon is the formation of a unified global economy, or what is commonly known as global capitalism.[8] Global capitalism has been presented to us not only as the trend of the time and the wave of the future but also with an air of inevitability. Mainstream media have promoted global capitalism without ceasing: they continually show the lives of the successful and the winners.

There is, however, an underside perspective to the story of global capitalism that mainstream media do not care to show. There is no doubt that global capitalism has brought more wealth than the world has ever known. But this enormous wealth has not benefited the largest and the poorest segment of the world's population. On the contrary, recent empirical evidence suggests an increasing disparity and the concentration of power in the hands of the global elites. Metaphorically speaking, contrary to the belief that "a rising tide raises all boats," the reality has been that "a rising tide raises all yachts."[9] Capitalist globalism has created and promoted "asymmetries, conflict, and a sense of no alternatives for those not included in the flow of its information, technology, capital, and goods."[10] Thousands of people die every day around the world because of this system of global inequality. As Mohandas Gandhi starkly puts it: "The earth provides enough for everyone's need, but not for everyone's greed."[11]

The havoc wrought by global capitalism is not limited to the economy; it has spiraled to other dimensions as well. Instead of the promised "global village," the world has experienced "global pillage" or fragmentation. Villages and whole societies have experienced fragmentation and anomie when traditional values are eroded by alien market values. Economic downturns, war for control of resources, and ecological devastation brought by the forces of capitalist globalism uproot and divide communities. Families suffer separation as members participate in the wave of migrant workers.[12] Host communities often react to the presence of newcomers with alarm. In the face of various threats, society usually scapegoats its weakest members. We are familiar with the following sequence: "A man gets chewed out by his boss at work, goes home and yells at his wife, and she scolds her child, and the child kicks the dog."[13]

It is significant to note that as the homogenizing effects of capitalist global-ism spread, movements of various motivations—ethnic, religious, nationalistic, cultural—also rise.[14] As new boundaries are redefined, and artificially imposed divisions of Cold War politics vanish, ethnic conflicts and culture wars inten-sify.[15] Cynicism and other forms of anti-globalist sentiments, many of which have religious motivation, have emerged thanks to the erosion of religiously based traditional life by modernist, secularist, market-driven worldview and values; the collusion of Western-educated global South leaders with foreign powers; and massive violation of human rights. The most desperate and disas-trous expression of these anti-globalist sentiments is terrorism—a terrorism intertwined with the terrorism of the global market and the imperial projects of some countries in the global North.[16]

It is not only the human population that suffers (though unevenly) from the effects of global capitalism, but also the ecosystem.[17] One consequence of rapid global economic activity and increased consumption is the devastation of the natural environment and the pollution of whole ecosystems. Liberalized trade conditions have increased the volume of trade, thereby accelerating the deple-tion of natural resources and the destruction of ecosystems. Also, in an effort to amass more profit and monopolize the food supply, transnational agribusinesses have introduced genetically modified organisms (GMOs) and terminator genes (Frankenstein genes). Cattle have been fed with animal byproducts; one result of this practice is the infamous "mad cow disease." In this context, Indian activist Vandana Shiva has made the right choice, saying: "I would rather be a sacred cow than a mad one."[18]

REORIENTING THE CHURCH

Global capitalism affects the whole of our lives and the plight of the Earth. It is destructive of human communities and ecosystems. Perhaps its insidious power lies in its ability to gobble our minds and define who we are. Global capitalism is more than a mechanism of control or a network of relations driven by profit; it creates a global culture that shapes the way we think, dwell, and act. "The architects of McWorld," as theologian Tom Sine reminds us, "are not simply trying to increase global free trade and free enterprise; they are . . . working to redefine what is important and what is of value in people's lives all over the planet, to sell their wares."[19] We not only live in a "market economy," we live in a "market society" in which "market-based values define the atmosphere in which we live and move and have our being."[20]

The global market's claim on our lives is thorough and pervasive. It has colonized the way we think and act. As an omnipresent phenomenon, there seems to be no place to hide from the power and reach of the global market. Even those who resist it are not outside of its influence. Certainly, the church is not exempt from its influence. While common discourse on the church puts the global market as a context to which the church needs to respond, what requires response is not totally outside of its own life. The church may claim to be the "christified portion" of the world, but this "christified portion" of the world is not outside the pale of the global market.[21]

The global market's most insidious impact on the life of the church appears in theology, organizational life, liturgy and worship, and spirituality. In response to the demands of "church shoppers," the church's primary identity has been transformed into a vendor of individual salvation or a service provider (entertainment center, therapy clinic, hospice, funeral parlor, welfare office, and so forth), and less as a community with a distinct identity experiencing God's transforming power and seeking to transform the world. "Call us when you need us" is the motto of a market-driven congregation. "In our desire to attract people," says Keith Russell, author of *In Search of the Church: New Testament Images for Tomorrow's Congregations*, "we have offered a variety of services or experiences that might please them, but we have not expected much back in return or asked for more than a minimal commitment."[22]

One of the most visible impacts of the market on congregational life is the adoption of a marketing strategy for church shoppers. I do not suggest that we completely disregard marketing issues, for we live in a world in which people are presented with a plethora of choices, including various forms of religiosity and worship.[23] But let us not allow worship to be used as a marketing ploy. The marketing ploy takes the upper hand when worship becomes entertainment rather than a means for connecting worshipers to God for the sake of transforming their lives. Worship is entertainment when it fails to challenge the worshipers to live differently and to carry out the ministry of the church in the world.

The church has experienced many confusing turns and distractions from its desired course as it has navigated through history. An image that has remained vital to the church throughout the years has been that of a boat. This boat continues to sail, sometimes when the sea is calm and at other times in gusty winds and soaring seas. The church is no stranger to those times when it has been in the eye of a perfect storm. Those who are familiar with ship travel across the ocean, especially in stormy weather, will agree with authors Clark Williamson and Ronald Allen's advice: find a spot where you can see out, such as on a deck with a view or through a porthole. Extend your sight to the horizon to get a wider perspective and a sense of balance.[24]

I contend that the church can only experience a sense of balance and right perspective when it reorients itself toward God's *basileia* (kingdom or reign).[25]

Without an orientation toward God's *basileia,* the church is without a compass and becomes vulnerable to the sway of the various idols of death. God's *basileia* counters the sway of the god of mammon and provides the compass for the church to reorient itself toward what it is and what it is called to be. It helps the church stay focused and remain true to itself. Amid the world of mammon, Jesus is saying: "But strive first for the [*basileia*] of God and his righteousness, and these things will be given to you as well" (Matt. 6:33).

CHANGING THE WIND: AN ALTERNATIVE ECONOMICS

It is true that the church has a mixed history. On the one hand, we can say that in many ways it has been swallowed by the global market. On the other hand, its little light has continued to be a beacon of hope. The church and other faith-based organizations have been at the forefront in responding to the challenge of poverty and hunger and other social issues. They have been among the most effective organizations in responding to the needs of the poor, the sick, and the lonely. Faith-based programs in the United States provide some of the most effective work on low-income housing, job training, health care, hunger, and neighborhood violence. The government and other nongovernmental organizations (NGOs) have lauded the work of faith-based organizations. However, while political leaders welcome the churches' social services, most often they do not welcome their prophetic witness.

The phenomenon of massive poverty in the context of organized social inequality and the destruction of the ecosystem calls churches to work beyond being service providers and caregivers. It calls for solutions beyond piecemeal pragmatic interventions or changes in government leadership, important as they are. As evangelical theologian and activist Jim Wallis reminds us, trying to solve systemic problems such as poverty by starting at the top can be a wasted effort. Wallis asks: how do you distinguish a Senator or a Congressperson in a crowd? They are the ones, says Wallis, "who are always licking their fingers and putting them in the air to see which way the wind is blowing."[26] We often make the mistake of thinking the solution is to replace one wet-fingered politician with another one. When no significant change happens, we are disappointed. If we really desire change, continues Wallis, "we must change the wind about fundamental issues like poverty," not just change the guardians of our current political-economic system. So, let us work to change the direction of the wind. This means changing our fundamental understanding of the world, particularly of the political economy.

A significant contribution the church can offer in changing the direction of the wind is through its prophetic critique and moral imagination. Advocating a political economy that promotes greater well-being for all is not advocating something foreign to the church's mission or reason for being. Economy is not outside the pale of God, hence not outside the concern of the church. God, says theologian M. Douglas Meeks, is an economist in a deeper sense of *oikonomia,* in which God takes care of the whole household, making sure the needs of all are met while sustaining the ecosystem's well-being.[27] The church's mission is to participate with God the economist in maintaining a household in which all creatures are adequately nourished and sustained.

The church is not alone in advocating a just and sustainable world, but it occupies a strategic place because of the pivotal role religion plays—in spite of its mixed history—in society.[28] When the forces of global capitalism crush various communities, push many into diaspora, distort priorities, leave families fragmented and alienated, drive the multitude into cynicism and despair, and consume the lives even of the winners, religion provides transcendent orientation and "antisystemic" force.[29] Religion's transformative energies can push back against alienating, death-dealing systems, providing an alternative set of values, commitments, and aims that are fundamentally life affirming. "The prospects of creating some form of human global governance in the twenty-first century seem likely to depend," says international law expert Richard Falk, "on whether the religious resurgence is able to provide the basis for a more socially and politically responsible form of globalization than what currently exists."[30] Religious communities are called to an enormous and challenging task of acting as midwives in giving birth to the "antisystemic" force of religion.

SUBVERSIVE COHABITATION

Without a doubt, global capitalism is a pervasive phenomenon. There is no place to hide outside of the reach and influence of the global market. The challenge is to devise ways of faithfulness and resistance while living in the space occupied by global capitalism. Instead of escape or conquest as guiding metaphors for this task, biblical scholar Marianne Sawicki appropriates the metaphors of salt and leaven. Like salt, the church must be a corrosive and preservative presence, and it must be "infectious, expansive, and profane like leaven." Both salt and leaven, suggests Sawicki, express a theology of "digging in and staying put"; they both express an "ecclesiology of infiltration" or a stance of "subversive cohabitation."[31]

A New Testament concept that corresponds to the posture of subversive cohabitation is *paroikoi* ("resident aliens"). The New Testament Christians adopted the term *paroikoi* to speak of their identity in relation to the world (Acts 7:6; 1 Peter 2:11). As resident aliens, they not only have a specific identity,

task, and burden, but also a specific promise and destiny. They are expected
to behave in accordance with their identity. Following the Johannine rendering of the otherworldly identity of Jesus ("not of this world"), resident aliens
know that they are "in" the world, but not "of" this world. They do not escape
from this world but affirm both being in the world and not letting the world
define them.[32]

Being "in" but not "of" this world is a challenge to the church that seeks to
be faithful. Perhaps, in the effort to make Christianity acceptable to the world,
liberal Christians tend to minimize or polish the tension between Christianity
and the world.[33] Such a posture exacts a high price by blurring the salvific message of the Crucified One, which is a stumbling block to its "cultured despisers."
As a "culture-religion" of mainstream America, liberal Christianity has lost its
power to disturb middle-class values and its ability to articulate a strong Christian vision of who we are and what God calls us to do.

When there is no difference in being a church member and not being one,
then what is the point of staying in the church? William McKinney and Wade
Clark Roof suggest in their sociological study of congregations that people
drop out of church life altogether because the mainline churches have become
"something of a 'culture religion,' captive to middle-class values, and somewhat
lacking in their ability to sustain a strong transcendent vision."[34] Because mainline churches are closely identified with mainstream culture, this means that
church members can "drift off into that culture without the sense of having
suffered any serious loss."[35]

In a world globalized by the forces of the market, there is no doubt that the
church is called to be a "contrast society" or a "countercultural community."[36]
However, the church can be a contrast society without being a fortified colony
of resident aliens. The apocryphal Gospel of Thomas offers a different image:
"Whoever is near me is near the fire, and whoever is far from me is far from
the kingdom."[37] The image of the church as a "burning center" with "porous
borders" conveys a posture or stance of faithfulness without being closed off. It
is also a stance that witnesses to the world but refuses to be swallowed by the
world. "Without a burning center and a closeness to Christ and his vision of
the kingdom," theologian John Fuellenbach rightly argues, "such a community
will be swallowed up by the values and standards of the society that surrounds
it."[38] Mainline churches need to learn how to be open without loss of identity
and how to be centered without being closed off to the great issues and questions and human suffering of this present destructive age.

PROPHETIC ATHEISM AND EXORCISM

The global market is not devoid of religiosity, but its religiosity runs counter to the central tenets of major world religions. Even at the level of semantics, there are obvious correlations: both fields regularly employ such words as trust, fidelity, bond, confidence, fiduciary, debt, redemption, saving, and security.[39] The total market operates, according to theologian Franz Hinkelammert, on an "entrepreneurial metaphysics."[40] Devotees to this metaphysics speak of "commodities, money, marketing, and capital as the great object of their devotion; a pseudo-divine world towers over human beings, and dictates their laws to them."[41]

Theologian Harvey Cox offers a sharp and cogent critique of the religious claims of the global market.[42] Cox argues that the global capitalist market has usurped the traditional attributes of God: omnipotent, omniscient, and omnipresent. Like the omnipotent God of the Hebrew Scripture, it does not tolerate any other divinities and demands undivided devotion and worship. And, as an omniscient one (all-knowing), it claims to know all and know best; thus, every intellect in this world must bow down before it. It seems, contends Cox, that the real venue of *sacrificium intellectum* today is not the church but the shopping mall. In the face of the god of the market, devoted consumers crucify their intellect and accept the absurd, saying: *"Credo quia absurdum est"* (I believe because it is absurd).[43]

Moreover, the market-god is omnipresent; it is pervasive and ubiquitous. Wherever we go, the market-god is there. How can we flee from its presence? If we ascend to the heavens, the market-god is there. If we make our bed in Sheol, it is there. And "if we take the wings of the morning and settle at the farthest limits of the sea," even there the hand of the global market is present (Ps. 139:7-10). The global market has become the god "in whom we live and move and have our being." So it claims: "Outside of the market there is no salvation."

Global capitalism has created an idol—an idol that sucks the blood of people around the world, though unevenly and differently. True to its name, consumerism consumes and capitalist globalism gobbles the consumers and the gobblers. Theologian John Cobb Jr. offers a critique of the religious metaphysics of this global market. "Economism" is the name of this religion, and its god is endless economic growth. The priests are the economists; evangelists are the advertisers; and the laity are the consumers. The shopping mall is the cathedral; virtue is competitive spirit; and sin is inefficiency. "Shop till you drop" is the only way to salvation.[44]

Confronting the idols of the global market is a daunting task for the church. Religious believers are called to the task of exposing and smashing the religious icons of the global market. In the face of these global market idols we need to affirm with political philosopher Ernst Bloch: "Only an atheist can be a good Christian."[45] This is no mere atheism of the modern secular person, but religious prophetic atheism. In the face of the idols of death of our time, prophetic atheism is a mark of religious faithfulness.

Along with our stance of religious prophetic atheism, we must engage in the task of exorcism. Demon possession has taken various forms in our contemporary context. We can see its forms in personal acts, but its most diabolic expression is in the principalities and powers of our time, such as unrestrained global capitalism. Exorcising demons is a risky undertaking, but it is a risk that we must assume. It is an indispensable task in the birthing of a new and better tomorrow.[46] God's *basileia* can only be established by exorcising the demonic power of global capitalism.

A HOUSEHOLD OF MORAL IMAGINATION

The Christian tradition offers an alternative economy that is symbolized by the eucharist. The eucharist encapsulates a vision of a new humanity in the new heaven and the new earth. It points to the direction and shape of God's economy (God's household) and the demands of living in the present. It discloses the character of the reign of God or the *basileia tou theou*, the place of human beings, and the quality of relationships that exist between beings. Even as the eucharist has been clouded by distorted interpretations, it continues to be a powerful symbol that invites us to imagine a different world of relationship.

There is no doubt that the eucharist points to the ugly reality of our world. The broken bread and the cup of wine symbolize what the forces of death can do. Bread broken and cup poured point to the reality of the breaking of the web of life; they point to the broken relations brought about by interlocking forms of oppression. Nevertheless, while pointing to the world in need of healing, the eucharist also offers a vision of a healed world. Out of a broken body has emerged a vision of a mended body. The broken body of Jesus, symbolized in the broken bread of the eucharistic celebration, is broken open for the many that all may experience healing and liberation. The body is broken open as a symbol of openness, service, and hospitality. Out of the broken body, ritualized in the eucharistic celebration, comes the invitation to dine at a common table.

The common table, particularly the meal table, is an important direction. As a symbol, the eucharistic table points to the common meal table of the household. "Like all households," as Meeks accurately puts it, "God's household is structured around a table."[47] The meal table is central to the household. It is here that the members of the household are served, fed, and nourished. Important household conversations happen around the meal table. Instead of limiting our image to one of a single family sharing, serving, and feeding each other, we imagine a meal to which all are invited. Theologian C. S. Song renames the Last Supper a "people supper." It is a people supper prepared by the community for the whole community.[48] The community prepares and shares the meal. The people supper is a communal event. I suggest that we interpret the eucharistic celebration in this way.

Following the New Testament background, I suggest that we see the eucharist through the lens of the egalitarian meals Jesus offered throughout his ministry (Matt. 14:13-21; Luke 9:10-17; John 6:1-14).[49] It was through one of these egalitarian meals that the people recognized the resurrected Jesus, as in the Emmaus story (Luke 24:13-35). It was in the breaking of bread that he was recognized by his sorrowful followers. Likewise, we recognize Jesus and recognize God wherever egalitarian meals happen. In egalitarian meals the crucified Jesus is resurrected, and in shared meals God's power is alive. As Jesus' presence is known in the breaking and sharing of bread, so we are known as disciples of Jesus and children of God whenever and wherever we celebrate egalitarian meals. "Were such an understanding of the eucharist to infiltrate Christian churches today," notes McFague, "it could be mind changing—in fact, perhaps world changing."[50]

Inasmuch as God's household is beyond individual human households, it is fitting, as McFague reminds us, to speak of a meal table for the whole world (cosmic table). The egalitarian meals, in McFague's words, point to the "prospective" phase of Jesus' life and ministry. This prospective phase cannot be divorced from the "deconstructive" (parables) and "reconstructive" (healing) phases of Jesus' ministry. The egalitarian meals (prospective phase) point to the radical vision of Jesus in which all are invited into the banquet. It offers both what she calls "minimal and maximal vision": the exhortation that even when there is little food at the table, every one must receive their proper share, and the hope of abundance—a feast that satisfies the needs of all.[51]

Deepening the symbol of the eucharistic meal, Song suggests that the egalitarian people supper happened at a "round table."[52] The round table signifies the egalitarian power dynamics, the positioning of all in relation to the food, the sharing of the meal, the communication that transpires among those around the meal table, and other related "table manners." In relation to ministry, author Chuck Latrop has this to say: "Concerning the why and how and what and who of ministry, one image keeps surfacing: A table that is round."[53]

The people supper at a round table manifests not just the presence of food, but the miracle of sharing. The food is located at the center of the table, within reach of each member. The round table shows us the positioning of persons in relation to the food: everyone is located at a spot that has direct access to the food. With each having direct access to the meal, the structure or system is already organized in such a way that sharing becomes possible. The giving and receiving of food circulates around the table. In the round table people supper, communion becomes a reality.

Hospitality is another direction toward which the people supper at a round table points. The round table is a "welcome table" to which those who have long been unwelcomed are welcomed. At the welcome table we can discern the longing that those who have long been excluded will some day sit at the round table. At the round table those once excluded can dine, enjoy the banquet, and participate in the table talk. The African American church tradition gives us a glimpse of this passionate longing for the welcoming round table:

> We're gonna sit at the welcome table!
> We're gonna sit at the welcome table one of these days;
> Alleluia![54]

In the context of the interdependent web of life, the people supper at a round table needs to be extended into a cosmic round table. Hospitality within the framework of ecological sensibility means allowing others to have spaces where they can live with integrity in relation to the overall harmony. It involves creating a home for each one to feel at home and flourish in the cosmos. This is in consonance with God's economy, in which God intends to make this world into a home for all.

Moreover, the people supper at a round table is a proleptic celebration, or a foretaste of the promised future. It is a rich and deep symbol of what we are called to be and to do. The bread and wine, produce of God's Earth and products of human work, come together in an act of communal liturgical celebration to reveal the interdependence and communion of God, humanity, and nature. The elements of bread and wine truly re-present the broken body of Jesus because Jesus' broken body is one with the produce of the Earth. In partaking of the elements we truly re-member the broken bodies throughout the ages because they live in us—the living—and are one with us in our experience of re-memberment (being made whole). Through the eucharistic/egalitarian meals we experience a foretaste of the richness of a liberated and healed community of interdependent beings in a cosmic body. The whole sacred celebration points to God's incarnation in the fullness of history and nature in which "God may be all in all" (1 Cor. 15:28) and human beings will truly embody the image of God.

LIBERATION FROM COMMODITY ADDICTION

The vision of an alternative economics must find embodiment in the life of the congregations, informing how they do Christian formation (discipleship) and various forms of ministry. There should be congruence between the vision and discipleship training that church members receive in their respective congregations. If money, property, and various forms of commodities exercise a powerful influence on a person's life, then there should be an economic component in every discipleship training and practice. Members must learn the right relationship between stewardship and the meaning of wealth. In a world tyrannized by the god of the global market, Christian formation (discipleship) must prepare members for an evangelism that confronts the idols of the market and helps people in society develop a liberating understanding of wealth. Since these are issues at the heart of Christian identity, they cannot be left to the individual to sort out alone. Church members need communal help to sort out priorities, establish a table of values, and make decisions with regard to these crucial matters.

CHRISTIAN IDENTITY AND SPIRITUALITY FOR HOUSEHOLD MEMBERS

There is no doubt that the global market is a powerful shaper of self-identity—an identity defined by possession and consumption. The "endless acts of consumption provoked by the *danse macabre* of capitalism," says author Peter McLaren, "organizes subjectivity in specific ways around the general maxim: I purchase, therefore I am."[55] Possession and consumption define who one is or how one is perceived and given value by others. That which we consume and possess are not, however, limited to the use value of something: we are consumers of image value. We buy things for the purpose of enhancing our self-image. When image value becomes the object of fixation, we can say that the individual's desire finds no limit and, consequently, no satisfaction.

Consumerism not only involves the consumption of an image value that an individual desperately needs to elevate his or her status, it is also an expression of a deep psychological alienation. Greater conspicuous consumption provides greater psychological compensation for the rote meaninglessness of one's life. More than an expression of a deep psychological alienation, consumerism is a spiritual matter. I say spiritual because consumer goods and commodities have been spiritualized or have been equated with the presence of the spirit. The world of capitalist consumerism considers increased consumption of commodities a sign of the spirit's presence in one's life. At the heart of this claim is a spirituality—more particularly, a distorted spirituality.

If consumerism is a distorted spirituality, then it must be addressed spiritually. Addressing consumerism spiritually requires not only that the spirituality of consumerism be exposed and opposed. It also requires that we expose and oppose the consumerising of spirituality. Beyond exposing and opposing distorted spiritualities, the church must articulate what spirituality means in response to commoditization and consumerism. Spirituality is not simply the acquisition of meditation techniques to ward off unpleasant thoughts, but liberation from commodity addiction for the sake of life abundant.[56] Spiritual direction must lead household members to see their self-worth beyond the worth given by the market. The church must provide opportunities and support for members who are struggling to develop a lifestyle not defined by consumerism. When members find life's meaning not in what they possess and consume, they become more open to the various gifts of the Spirit. Instead of loading themselves with things, which only "thingify" people, they seek to be filled with the Spirit. And when they are filled with the Spirit, they bear "fruits of the Spirit," such as "love, joy, peace, patience, kindness, generosity, faithfulness, gentleness, and self-control" (Gal. 5:22-23).

EDUCATING THE HOUSEHOLD

Money is a taboo topic of conversation in contemporary life. "Does your mom or dad make a lot of money?" is a much more awkward question to ask at a Thanksgiving dinner conversation than the innocent question of a young child: "Where do babies come from?" It does not mean, however, that just because we are silent about money it has ceased to play a powerful and pervasive role in our lives. In fact, our silence suggests the opposite: money is so central to our very identity that we do not want others to know about it. We want to claim it as our sole domain. James Hudnut-Beumler's words are on target: "When people have but one central operative value, they guard it carefully and surround it with mystery and taboo, lest that one value be taken away."[57] The money taboo "stems from money's central role as an expression and index of worth."[58] My encounter with this ugly truth came as a shock when someone asked me: "What is your net worth?" Our value as an individual in a consumer-and-market-oriented society is measured in terms of our net worth. Since in a market-consumer society we are what we do and what we consume (possess), we are loath to have our worth compared with others lest we fall short of other's expectations, much less our own measurement of success.

There are, of course, a few places where we disclose our finances, but we do so only because there is no choice. The church is certainly not one of those places where people share their money matters openly. The car dealer may get financial information from a church member in fifteen minutes, but not the beloved pastor—not even after several years as a pastor of a congregation. Why do we not talk about money and its place in our lives and in our churches? Why should we leave the money matter outside the church? Are we not in the business of dealing with the whole person—head, heart, and checkbook?

It is difficult to talk about money in churches, but it should be a topic of study because it has direct bearing on our ultimate commitments and Christian discipleship. Our relationship to money is an expression of our inner self. How we make our money and what we spend it on is a witness to others about who we are as persons. The choices we make about how we use our money reveals much about ourselves and what we value. These are matters that are properly theological and moral; hence, they are at the heart of the church's concern. If the church does not talk about money and its place in our lives, we are likely to confess verbally that we are following God's way, while in practice we leave money in a protected private space. Ironically, this protected private space is wide open to the god of the market and to Visa and MasterCard.

The Christian tradition offers insights about our proper relationship to material goods in general and money in particular. It is important that churches study its tradition, for it offers guidance concerning proper attitude and relationship toward money and possessions. There are writings ranging from the early church communities to the founders of contemporary denominations that provide a compass with which members may examine themselves in relation to the issue of possession and consumption. These writings need to be exhumed and appropriated in a market-driven culture that has lost its proper orientation with regard to material possessions.[59]

FORMATION OF COUNTERNARRATIVE

Without a powerful narrative to define its life, there is no doubt that the church will be swallowed by consumer capitalism's ferocious appetite. Instructions regarding our relationship to money and spirituality must be complemented with the formation of a counternarrative. Unless the church articulates a powerful narrative that shapes the lives of its members, it will be swayed and tossed in various directions until it is lost in the globalized world. Without a powerful narrative, the church will be controlled by the narrative of the global market. Narrative provides a religio-moral direction for the people of God as they navigate the world of competing loyalties and expectations.

The church must recover and articulate clearly its own narrative, for it is a community defined by a unique narrative. This narrative is not only a guide for its life; it is also a form of witness to the world. We can find this narrative by rediscovering what is at the heart (*coeur*, French; *cor*, Latin) of its tradition. The church must rediscover its central story if it is to regain "the courage to be itself," as Paul Tillich would put it.[60] I say that the church can claim itself as a Christian church only in relation to what God has done in Christ through the life and witness of Jesus of Nazareth, which, following McFague's categories, is characterized by acts of deconstruction (parables), reconstruction (healing ministries), and a radical vision of life abundant (prospectively egalitarian meals). This is our narrative as much as it is the narrative of God. It is a narrative of God's liberating and reconciling love in Jesus, which has found embodiment in the life of the church throughout the ages. The church must articulate and inculcate this narrative to its members through sermons, Christian education, worship and liturgical celebrations, and the like.

ECUMENISM

The task of reimagining the church and the wider society is immensely difficult. It does not arise simply by the wave of a magic wand, nor does it arise simply by sitting in a meditation center and imagining a better world. A crisis may provide the impetus for imagination, but it may also lead to its opposite: imagination shrinks when fear dominates. Rather than creativity, defense of the status-quo becomes the posture. This, unfortunately, is the posture of many churches of our time. They may put on the appearance of business as usual, but deep inside they are churches, says theologian Douglas John Hall, that are "trying very hard to keep Christendom alive—to put that Humpty Dumpty together again."[61] It is only in the sprouting and flowering of creative imagination that we can move from the posture of defenders of the status-quo to harbingers of *fluxus quo*—toward new ways of thinking, dwelling, and acting.[62] But fertile soil and right conditions must be in place for creative imagination to sprout. I agree with R. B. J. Walker that the challenge of social imagination or cultural creativity is: "not only a matter of creating visions of a better world but of reconstructing the conditions under which the future may be imagined. Cultural creativity does not occur in abstraction. It arises from concrete everyday practices, from people able to make connections with each other and engaging in dialogue about the meaning of their experiences."[63]

Truly, the task of social imagination, or more particularly, ecclesial imagination, requires creating the conditions under which the "once and future church" may be imagined.[64] These conditions include putting ourselves in uncomfortable places: in the betwixt and between, in the liminal spaces, in the interweaving of the local and the global, and at the intersections of many worlds. Imagination demands living between memory and hope: it requires the retrieval of muted dangerous memories and the giving of oneself fully to the demands of the future through active involvement in transforming actions in the present. Imagination is an orphan without memory, and *vice versa*. Imagination has no roots without memory, and without roots it does not have wings to fly.

The conditions under which the new world and the new church may be reimagined cannot be created by a few gifted individuals. Creating the conditions under which the new world may be reimagined is at its heart an ecumenical enterprise. Beyond the pragmatic demands of politics, at stake in the ecumenical enterprise is the issue of the limits of our perception and the expansion of our theological and moral imagination. As embodied knowers, our views are limited, but through the aid of a community of interpreters our limited views are exposed to the possibility of expansion.[65]

With the understanding that reimagination demands an ecumenical approach, I suggest that our orientation and work must be open not only to those within the Christian fold but to other religious groups as well. The task of reimagination cannot be done monoculturally or mono-religiously. Like Christianity, other major world religions offer rich resources for countering the god of the global market and reimagining a new ecological economics. They are very clear on their stance against various forms of idolatry. Yahweh is a jealous God who has zero tolerance for idols. No idols can stand before Allah. A Muslim will render submission only to Allah, never to the market-god.[66] Thich Nhat Hanh, a well-known Buddhist monk, warns of absolutizing the Buddha and his teachings, for to do so is like mistaking the finger pointing to the moon with the moon itself. Likewise, "the raft is not the shore. If we cling to the raft, if we cling to the finger, we miss everything."[67]

Ecumenical openness must, however, be converted into concerted action for the sake of transforming the world. I call this concerted action an act of conspiracy, literally "to breathe together."[68] To "con-spire" is to share breath: share life-affirming and liberating ways of thinking, dwelling, and acting. It means establishing life-affirming communities or social movements and networking with similar movements both locally and globally. We must engage in a conspiracy of imagination and transformation, for it is only through our concerted efforts that our voices and vision gain the power for liberating change. No business-as-usual realism, piecemeal pragmatism, nor couch-potato optimism can take us out of sick bay. A realistic hope for our society and churches today does not lie in some miraculous intervention, whether supernatural or techno-capitalist, but in the groaning and greening of socially conscious and active people who have conspired to make a difference in various locations and stations in life.[69]

Conspiracy (breathing together) is also necessary if we are to endure in the long and arduous struggle. Without the life-giving and nourishing breath (spirit) of our companions, we easily fall into compassion fatigue and cynicism. Detached from the company of breath-sharers, we easily dry up and wither under the scorching heat of the noonday sun. "If we are a drop of water and we try to get to the ocean as only an individual drop, we will surely evaporate along the way," says Thich Nhat Hanh. "To arrive at the ocean, [we] must go as a river."[70] The community is our river. This community includes those in close proximity to us in terms of time and space, as well as those who have gone before us and even those who are still to come, especially if we think along with the ecologist that "we no longer inherit the earth from our parents; we borrow it from our children."[71]

Only through our conspiracy are we able to withstand the forces of global capitalism that seek to stifle our imagination and crush our hopes. We have to believe it: *Otro Mundo es Posible!* "Another world is not only possible, she is on her way. On a quiet day, I can hear her breathing," said writer-activist Arundhati Roy at the 2005 World Social Forum in Porto Alegre, Brazil.[72] Likewise, a new church is possible, she is on her way. On a quiet day we can hear her breathing. There are signs around us. The new church is visible and audible for those who have the eyes to see and ears to hear. And this new church is not outside of us; we carry it in our hearts. That church is growing this minute. It is emerging out of the old. It will not come, however, by itself, but only through our concerted efforts. Let our politically engaged spirituality usher its coming! Let our conspiracy of social imagination and transformation be a midwife for its birthing!

ARTISANS 12 OF HOPE, ARTISANS OF WONDER

Sharon D. Welch

Shortly after the presidential elections of 2004, a group of young people, artists, and activists from the Kerry campaign, Moveon.org, and other progressive organizations met outside New York City at the farm of the recording artist Moby. They explored what had worked during the presidential campaign: young people voting in record numbers, for example, and what had not worked. There was a clear consensus that one of the major problems, not the only one of course, within the Kerry campaign was the lack of powerful rhetoric that communicated the depth, passion, and moral clarity and coherence of democratic policies. It is easy to despair over the pressures of a sound-bite society: how can profound, complex, real ideas be communicated in slogans and three-word phrases? The intellectual critique of metaphorical thinking has a venerable pedigree. Even Plato spoke of "the long quarrel between philosophy and poetry," adding to that quarrel his own denunciation of the epistemological and ethical deceptions of poetics.[1] For metaphors can be misleading—simplifying and distorting thought—yet metaphors can also open thought, can crystallize insights and visions, can function as complex symbols, rather than as one-dimensional signs. I have heard the following quote attributed to Hubert Humphrey: "We campaign in poetry and govern in prose."

These activists and artists agreed on the need for compelling political poetry and metaphors. MTV's Vote or Die campaign was quite successful, ironically and defiantly playing on a host of fears, from environmental collapse to the reinstatement of the draft. The group was evenly divided, however, on what sort of metaphors to use, and what type of rhetoric. Half argued for fighting fire with fire—sharpening and amplifying the polarities that currently exist and expressing powerfully the fear, anger, and outrage that many of us have in our current economic and political climate. The other half of the people were committed to the exploration of other forms of rhetoric—metaphors that not only bridge seemingly intractable polarities, but metaphors that build on hope, not fear, that evoke responsibility, irony, wonder, and imagination, not exclusion and self-righteous resolve.

Though I did not attend this meeting in New York, I have been involved in subsequent meetings in which we explore the latter challenges in regard to alternatives to militarism.[2] In these efforts, we have encountered several deeply puzzling conundrums. The first conundrum: we know that metaphors are powerful, that they can stop thought as much as elicit it. How, then, do we counter vivid metaphors that elicit thought-stopping prejudice?

Sallie McFague reminds us of the power of metaphors, their ability to "express [what] cannot be said directly." Not only do "our concepts derive from metaphors," but "a fresh metaphor . . . immediately sparks our imagination."[3] McFague also claims that metaphors are intrinsically temporary and partial. Once "reified or petrified," they are "no longer heard" and are interpreted as definitions of how things are, rather than as spurs to creative thought.[4] McFague finds this true of our metaphors for God, for the human self, and for our relationship to nature. She writes of metaphors for God: "All are inappropriate, partial, and inadequate; the most that can be said is that some aspect or aspects of the God-world relationship are illuminated by this or that model in a fashion relevant to a particular time and place."[5]

Not only may metaphors become reified and lose relevance (one of the examples she gives is "armchair"), but metaphors may distort our relationships and have ethically damaging consequences. McFague is critical, for example, of the subject-object model for imagining ourselves (the rational subjects who know) and our relationship to the physical world of bodies and of nature: "We have seen the results of the subject-object model: the objectification of other people (those who fall into the category of body—women, children, people of color, 'primitives,' the disabled, the poor, and the homeless, etc.) as well as the natural world (as a resource for our use.)"[6]

McFague challenges us to remember that "none of our many interpretations [of nature] are innocent, natural, or absolute."[7] Metaphors can distort as well as enliven perceptions and relationships. McFague is especially clear in her analysis of the deleterious ecological effects of the metaphor of the human as "the isolated, superior, individual self surveying the world": "The subject that set out to know the world as object, to colonize and control all others, ends by being itself destroyed . . . Human beings cannot live in the world this way because the world is not set up to accommodate the behavior that issues from such arrogance, as deterioration of the environment, for instance, is proving."[8]

While some people may recognize the danger of certain common metaphors, how do we counter those that are both alive and destructive? To return to the conundrum facing those seeking a vital, engaging, political vocabulary, how do we counter vivid metaphors that elicit thought-stopping prejudice? Recall, for example, President Clinton's nomination of Lani Guinier in 1993 to be the first black woman to head the civil rights division of the Department of Justice. Guinier had written articles examining alternative means of structuring voting to make the process more genuinely democratic than our winner-take-all system. Rather than a careful consideration of these positions, Guinier was characterized as "a quota queen," and serious debate was derailed.

To counter such metaphors, it is important to recognize their power. Karen McCarthy Brown, scholar of Haitian Vodou, described the characterization of Lani Guinier as a quota queen as a form of "word *wanga*," an incantation of deep-seated stereotypes and fears.[9] The current use of the term "axis of evil" by the Bush administration for the countries of North Korea, Iraq, and Iran offers a similar constellation of prejudice, clarity, and seeming security in the face of complex and manifold dangers.

Linguist George Lakoff has described the ways in which some religious and political conservatives in the United States have created a political and moral vocabulary that is concise, internally consistent, and easily replicated in sound bites and short phrases. Lakoff does not address the ways in which this rhetoric masks the internal complexity of conservatism, a topic well worth examining, nor the ways it stifles debate among conservatives. His focus is on the divisions between this particular variant of conservative thought and contemporary liberalism. He contrasts what he calls "Strict Father" morality and politics with "Nurturant parent" morality and politics. The gender specificity in the former is intentional. The Strict Father morality is a consistent worldview in which authority is clearly delineated: patriarchal in ideal, if not always in fact, a world in which legitimate authority provides protection and guidance in the face of a dangerous world. Competition and self-reliance are the mainstays of individual and social achievement. And, in this dangerous world, there are real enemies, and whether those enemies are other nations or democratic opponents, the task of the righteous is to defeat enemies, not to compromise with them or negotiate with them, much less *learn* from them.[10]

It is very difficult to challenge this metaphorical universe directly. Its well-documented failings (children from authoritarian homes are more likely to be aggressive and needing external controls; internationally, an aggressive war on terror that violates human rights has increased hostility and international instability) are taken by the adherents of this worldview as the signs of the recalcitrance of human nature and the need for more force and control, not less.[11]

Let me give one example of the effects of this rhetoric in preventing serious discussion. British Prime Minister Tony Blair was clearly outraged after the first exposure of torture at Abu Ghraib: "Let me make it quite clear that if these things have actually been done, they are completely and totally unacceptable. We went to Iraq to get rid of that sort of thing, not to do it."[12] This outrage has too quickly been eroded by a displacement of responsibility on what are seen as a few ill-trained and misguided soldiers ("bad apples"), and the policy decisions by government officials that not only allowed but fostered such abuse have yet to be thoroughly and independently investigated.[13] What has led to this erosion of concern, to the staying power of these metaphors?

Social psychologist Albert Bandura has described how easy it is for moral clarity and absolutism to lead to cruelty and violence. Bandura describes five dimensions of moral disengagement, the process by which genuinely decent human beings commit and justify behaviors that they would otherwise recognize as morally abhorrent. The first factor is being convinced that one is the bearer of a just cause and that there are no other ways of protecting or advancing that cause without some form of coercion. A second dimension is avoiding the negative consequences of one's behavior through the use of euphemistic language: for example, the term "collateral damage" for the death and injuries caused to civilians; the terms "professional interrogation techniques," or "softening up prisoners" for interrogation, for physical and psychological torture. The negative consequences of one's actions may then be disregarded or denied. Third, when the severity of the consequences can no longer be avoided, one dehumanizes and/or demonizes the victim. The victims somehow deserve the negative consequences: they are all terrorists; or, they all share an irrational hatred of us. The fourth step is disadvantageous comparison—our violence pales in comparison to theirs. Recall Alberto Gonzales's response when challenged by Senator Lindsey Graham to condemn decisively the use of torture by U.S. personnel: "While we are struggling to try to find out about Abu Ghraib, they're beheading people like Danny Pearl and Nick Berg. We are nothing like our enemy." The fifth step is a diffusion of responsibility: one was only following orders, or acting as can only be expected in "the chaos and fog of war."[14]

These processes of moral disengagement are pervasive and extremely hard to dislodge once in place. Let me give an example. Many of my students are convinced that President Bush is a faithful Christian, a man of God, and led by God. Evidence that his initial justifications for the war in Iraq have been demonstrated to be false is, to them, completely irrelevant. The fact that he may have thought there were weapons of mass destruction and there are not, does not discredit their belief that he is led by God. As humans, we often think that God is leading us to act for one reason, when there is really some deeper or larger purpose that we cannot fully grasp. If one is supremely confident in the rightness of one's goals, it is also easy to discredit or disregard the consequences of one's actions: thousands of U.S. and allied troops killed, possibly 100,000 Iraqi civilians killed in an increasingly brutal war.[15]

Let us return to our first conundrum: how do we find a way of bringing effective internal critique to such powerful metaphors, and to such a morally coherent and self-justifying worldview? We who are liberals and leftists can easily craft arguments exposing this Orwellian logic that *we* find persuasive. That is not the problem. How do we find the logic, the examples, the metaphors, and the stories that can engage others in self-critical reflection—affirming, and not denying, their capacities as moral agents?

The second conundrum. This challenge is exacerbated by a very effective inoculation by some conservative commentators against liberal and leftist political and social critique, another form of word *wanga*. Lest we think this is a simple matter of being outmaneuvered, or overwhelmed by a sort of conspiracy, I will soon discuss the ways in which these forms of inoculation are often effective because of common pedagogical and political strategies practiced by many of us on the Left.

First, let us explore the inoculation. A report in the *New York Times* by John Tierney on the resistance of many college students to liberal and progressive political analysis and critique is instructive. He cites a Berkeley undergraduate, Kelly Coyne, who makes a telling statement: "I'm glad to get the liberal perspective, but it would be nice to get the other side, too . . . I don't want to spend another semester listening to lectures about victims of American oppression."[16]

For some people, lectures about U.S. oppression are revealing and empowering. Others, however, either feel paralyzed by them or do not believe the critiques. Such disbelief is fostered when criticism is simply and boldly deflected, rather than addressed directly. For example, in response to Howard Dean's charges of unethical behavior by Tom DeLay, DeLay's spokesman, Dan Allen, dismissed these criticisms as the empty rhetoric of one who is "leading a party with no ideas, no solutions, and no agenda."[17] Lakoff also recounts the ways in which social critiques are dismissed by some commentators and politicians as asking for unwarranted rights without responsibilities, favoring "special interests" and not, as liberals see it, extending opportunities to all.[18]

How is it that we may contribute to these critiques? Let us go back to the first quote: "I don't want another lecture on American injustice." We find that most of our students do not respond positively to professorial critiques of American injustice at home or abroad. They do, however, respond positively to invitations to think together, critically and systematically, for themselves, exploring together the power structures, the opportunities and imbalances that shape their lives. Rather than simply declaring that there are negative consequences to avowed good ends, we ask people to examine for themselves the degree to which power is shared equitably in their communities. What are the most powerful institutions in their communities—banks, large businesses, the military, the media, schools, governmental agencies? Who has the most decision-making power in those institutions? Are all groups of people fairly represented at the top levels of decision making? If not, what are the results? Are some groups exploited, marginalized, powerless? Are others the victims of cultural imperialism and violence?[19]

Another dimension of what is needed, and oft ignored by many professors, was brought home quite clearly in the first class I taught at the University of Missouri, Feminism 101. I was thrilled to share with eighty young women and five young men the masked truths of our lives, the extent and depth of discrimination, exploitation, and violence against women throughout the world, and I was shocked that many students hated the class. Luckily, a brave few told me that things were not going well before the semester ended—in time for needed reflection on why my experience of discovering the depth of women's oppression was so different than theirs. I, and many others of my generation, found these discoveries empowering and exhilarating for two reasons. First, we were making the discoveries ourselves, and second, as we did so, we were surrounded by music that held our anguish, fear, joy, and pride. Recall the powerful healing music of Bernice Johnson Reagan and Sweet Honey in the Rock, Chris Williamson, and Holly Near. The feminist struggles of the 1970s and 1980s and the concurrent explosion of women's music was not, of course, unique. Recall as well the powerful transformation in the civil rights movement of gospels and spirituals into political anthems; the protest music that accompanied opposition to the war in Vietnam; and the healing and transformative use of music in the long struggle against apartheid in South Africa. What are the forms of new music that we can offer in our time—the combinations of rhythm and harmony that can hold our anger, our pain, and simultaneously celebrate our joy, wonder, and belonging to a larger whole, a community of people who live for justice and well-being for all?

There is a third, and final conundrum to explore. We have in the past found metaphors for justice work that, although partial, were evocative: "Sisterhood is powerful," "Workers of the world, unite, you have nothing to lose but your chains," "A dream deferred is a dream denied," "Let justice roll down like waters, and righteousness like a mighty stream."

How do we express most vividly our appeals *now*, not just to sisterhood and to workers, but to all humanity, for justice and for nurtured dreams? How do we metaphorically combine acknowledgment of the particularity of identities and community in a larger whole—a common good that genuinely sees and values the unique histories, needs, cultures of different social groups *and* of different dimensions of the natural world, human and other-than-human?

In his study of identity-based conflicts in South Africa, Eastern Europe, and Canada, Vern Redekop points to what is essential for healing and reconciliation: ways of framing collective and individual identity that provide a deep sense of the past (incorporating "memory, story, and coherence") and an equally evocative sense of the future (rich with "imagination, stimulation, and continuity").[20] The problem, however, is that such collective stories are often self-righteous and self-justifying narratives of exclusion, framing the past and the future in terms of "us against them," either innocent victims bravely resisting a demonic foe, or beneficent victors, the proud bearers of all humanity's destiny. How do we convey other stories, ones of blessing and abundance, vitality and honest self-critique?

We may find key components of this alternative sensibility in the work of McFague and Bandura. McFague describes a "common creation story" in which humans are "decentered as the point and goal of evolutionary history and recentered, in the words of biologist Stephen Jay Gould, as 'the stewards of life's continuity on earth.'" As a Christian theologian, she adds another dimension to this "new shape for humanity," emphasizing that we may see ourselves "*recentered* as God's partners in helping creation to grow and prosper in our tiny part of God's body."[21] While interpreting the implications of the "common creation story" that emerges from contemporary science in light of the Christian story, McFague is open both to the insights of other religious traditions and to the ongoing insights derived from further scientific exploration. She claims that we can both know and acknowledge the limits of our knowing: "nature is too complex, mysterious, vast, rich, and intricate to be circumscribed under any of our limited ways of knowing."[22]

From her particular location in time and place, McFague provides an evocative set of metaphors for the divine and for human work for justice. Rather than remain with the metaphor or model of God as king-redeemer, she explores the metaphor of God as mother-creator. Within this model, "the goal [of divine justice] is neither the condemnation nor the rescue of the guilty but the just ordering of the cosmic household in a fashion beneficial to all. God as mother-creator is primarily involved not in the negative business of judging wayward individuals but in the positive business of creating with our help a just ecological economy for the well-being of all her creatures. God as the mother-judge is the one who establishes justice, not the one who hands out sentences."[23]

McFague also explores the ethical implications of the metaphor of God as Lover, a God who seeks healing: a "balanced integration of all parts of the organism, the health (or salvation) of the body of the world involves redressing the imbalances that have occurred in part through inordinate human desire to devour the whole rather than be part of it."[24]

While we may craft compelling visions of a just world, Bandura reminds us that humans most often find moral rationales for what others see as immoral acts. We see ourselves as "fighting ruthless oppressors, protecting . . . cherished values, preserving world peace," but "condemn those [militant actions] of [our] antagonists as barbarity masquerading under a mask of outrageous moral reasoning."[25] This form of self-justification is so widespread that Bandura claims that "the massive threats to human welfare stem mainly from deliberate acts of principle rather than from unrestrained acts of impulse."[26]

How do we rationalize immoral behavior? It is easier to disregard and distort the negative consequences of our actions when we do not experience them directly. We may also develop an elaborate defense of our actions, denying the fact of negative consequences, dismissing the credibility of those who challenge us. Bandura describes this process of moral disengagement both in the justification of warfare and in the operations of industry: "For example, certain industries cause harmful effects on a large scale, either by the nature of their products or the environmental toxification and degradation their operations produce. Disregarding or minimizing injurious consequences. . . . For years the tobacco industry, whose products kill more than 400,000 Americans annually (McGinnis and Foege, 1993), disputed the view that nicotine is addictive and that smoking is a major contributor to lung cancer."[27]

While we need to open ourselves to critique and not isolate ourselves from it, such openness is painful and difficult to sustain. McFague's work may help us here as we explore more fully the necessity of, and the gift of, friendship—the necessity of, and the mandate for, hospitality toward the stranger. For what is it that friends, and especially strangers, may offer? A gift of companionship, new and old, is seeing the world through different eyes. Others may see what we disregard: the negative impact of our actions on other people and on the natural world.

Bandura argues that the most effective check on unethical behavior is the resolute humanization of those who could be perceived as "other." He writes of the "striking evidence that most people refuse to behave cruelly, even under unrelenting authoritarian commands, if the situation is personalized by having them inflict pain by direct personal action rather than remotely and they see the suffering they cause." He states that "the affirmation of common humanity can bring out the best in others."[28] Bandura gives as an example the story of the helicopter pilot, Thompson, who came upon the My Lai massacre in Vietnam and helped airlift surviving villagers to safety. In this massacre, villagers, women, children, and old men were killed by United States troops. Unlike those who saw only enemies, Thompson "was moved to proactive moral action by the sight of a terrified woman with a baby in her arms and a child clinging to her leg." Bandura cites Thompson's sense of common humanity: "These people were looking at me for help and there is no way I could turn my back on them." He was moved by the sight of a two-year-old boy, found holding his dead mother: "I had a son at home about the same age."[29]

Bandura highlights several elements that lead to moral engagement, rather than disengagement. It is possible for people to respond, to "take personal responsibility for the consequences of their actions; remain sensitive to the suffering of others; and see human commonalities rather than distance themselves from others or divest them of human qualities."[30]

McFague makes a similar claim in regard to ethical action in relationship to the natural world. "Over the years I have learned that the closer attention I pay to whatever piece of the world is before me . . . the more amazed I am by it. . . . It is the specialness, the difference, the intricacy of each creature, event, or aspect of nature that calls forth wonder. And that wonder helps sustain me; it helps me stay the course."[31]

Just as Bandura emphasizes connection with other human beings, McFague extols a "basic change in sensibility from the modern post-Enlightenment confidence in the individual who, as rational man, is set over against the world, which he can both know and control. The new sensibility understands human beings to be embedded in the world—indeed, in the earth: they are social beings to the core, and whatever they know of the world comes from interaction with it. The goal of knowledge is not control so much as it is healthy, humane existence for all parties concerned—not progress and profit but sustainability."[32] This model of relationship is "not oppositional but interactive," and it enables a recognition that "one's own well-being could not come about apart from the well-being of others."[33]

There is a further dimension to this ecological understanding of self and world. Rather than solving all problems forever, for all people, and for all times, our challenge is living fully now. This is the lesson of Esther: "for such a time as this" (4:14). We have the challenge of living with integrity now, and of teaching, mentoring, and nurturing future generations who will face unanticipated challenges, as well as the typical ones of growing in courage, justice, and fairness. What can hold all these strands of fallibility and interdependence, of companionship, unresolved tensions, and ongoing risk? This is a complex task, to be sure, but in conclusion I leave you with a metaphor: let us be artisans, artisans of hope, artisans of wonder, working with the clay of human longing—of our capacities for greed and indifference, for exclusion and fear, as well as our capacities for generosity, courage, forgiveness, and resilience. As artisans, let us craft together flourishing communities of honesty, inclusion, self-critique, and hope.

EPILOGUE
Human Dignity and the Integrity of Creation

Sallie McFague

For I am about to create new heavens and a new earth;
the former things shall not be remembered or come to mind.
But be glad and rejoice forever in what I am creating:
for I am about to create Jerusalem as a joy, and its people as a delight . . .
no more shall the sound of weeping be heard in it, or the cry of distress.
No more shall there be in it an infant that lives but a few days
or an old person who does not live out a lifetime; . . . .
for like the days of a tree shall the days of my people be,
and my chosen shall long enjoy the work of their hands.
They shall not labor in vain, or bear children for calamity;
for they shall be offspring blessed by the Lord . . . .
Before they call I will answer, while they are yet speaking I will hear.
The wolf and the lamb shall feed together, the lion shall eat straw like the ox . . .
They shall not hurt or destroy on all my holy mountain, says the Lord.
—ISAIAH 65

Reading this passage makes us weep—weep for our world, our poor, sorry world. The world we want, that we ache for, is a world where children get to grow up and live to old age, where people have food and houses and enjoyable work, where animals and plants and human beings live together on the earth in harmony, where none "shall hurt or destroy." This is our dream, our deepest desire, what we cannot let go of. This vision of the good life makes us unwilling to settle for the unjust, unsustainable, and indeed cruel and horrendous world we have. In the heart of each of us lies the wish and the hope that says: "Things are not supposed to be this way. A different world is possible." Isaiah's hymn to a new creation and Jesus' parables of the reign of God touch this deepest desire in each of us for a better, different world. It would be a world in which human dignity and the integrity of creation would be central, a world in which the intrinsic value of all human beings and of the creation itself would be recognized and appreciated. Hence, our topic—human dignity and the integrity of creation—lies at the heart of the biblical vision of the good life.

Do we have any hope for a different, better world? Given the situation we face at the beginning of the twenty-first century of war, violence, global warming, AIDS, and capitalist greed, as well as plain old human indifference and selfishness, it seems absurd to even bother with such a question. And yet, we read in the Isaiah passage that in the midst of painting this wonderful picture of life beyond our wildest dreams, God says, "Before they call I will answer, while they are yet speaking I will hear." "While they are yet speaking"—we have only to ask for God to answer! But we must ask with our whole being; it must become our deepest desire. And this means, of course, we must *work at it*, we must give our whole selves to it.

First, let us look at the kind of destruction that our world is presently undergoing—this will be an analysis of what is wrong. Then we will consider what we need to do to turn things around—in other words, our preliminary work, so that God may answer.

Since September 11, 2001, terrorism appears to many people to be the major kind of destruction that we face. Terrorist acts are sharp, clear, and horrible: we all react instinctively to them with fear and loathing. Terrorist acts encourage us to see ourselves as good and the destroyers as evil; they provide us with an enemy for our world's troubles that is not ourselves. Of course, if one digs deeper and looks at the roots of terrorism—things like poverty, racism, market greed, the struggle for arable land and clean water—then a whole different picture emerges of who is to blame. But our current popular analysis of acts of terror does not encourage this kind of thinking. Rather, it tells us that the terrorists are evil and we, on the other hand, are basically good, or at least okay.

But there is another kind of destruction that is slower and deeper, and it involves us more clearly. Two examples of this kind of destruction are climate change and AIDS. Here it is more difficult to escape the root analysis that, as with terrorism, we are somehow involved—our understanding of who we are and how we should be acting is part of the world we see before us. More people, including children, die in a world being destroyed by climate change and AIDS than from terrorist acts; the dying is slower and for the most part out of our sight. As such it allows for our denial and indifference—in other words, for sins of omission. Unlike those terrorists, we don't actually have to commit evil acts to participate in the evil of climate change and AIDS: our very existence as well-off North Americans living the good consumer life assures that we are involved. Even when we try to hide our heads, saying that we don't yet have all the facts about climate change or that those folks who get AIDS bring it upon themselves from their behavior, we know we are rationalizing. We know that we would rather focus on the terrorists and their blatant evil acts than on ourselves and our less obvious but more damaging acts of omission and indifference. More people and plant life die from our neglect and our overconsumption than from acts of terror.

So where does this leave us? Burdened with guilt, but helpless? Sorry for what we are doing but not knowing what else to do? Yes, all of these things, but something else also comes to mind: repentance. The first step in behaving differently is often admitting that we have not really and truly been asking God for a better world, not asking with our whole heart. Do we have the willingness to turn around, to change, to see ourselves and the world differently? This is an enormous question and would take a lifetime to answer, for we would have to live it, not just think it. But let us at least begin to think differently with the hope that we might also begin to live differently.

Our topic is human dignity and the integrity of creation, the most basic one we can imagine. I would like to suggest three movements toward a new picture of ourselves and our place: Who are we? Where do we fit on Planet Earth? And how do we get there?

WHO ARE WE?

The Earth Charter, a United Nations document that emerged from a decade-long, worldwide, cross-cultural conversation about common goals and shared values, suggests a picture of who we are. It is a statement of fundamental principles for building a just, sustainable, and peaceful global society. It has sixteen major principles, the first one being the most important: "Respect Earth and life in all its diversity." Spelled out in more detail it states: "Recognize that all beings are interdependent and every form of life has value regardless of its worth to human beings. Affirm faith in the inherent dignity of all human beings and in the intellectual, artistic, ethical, and spiritual potential of humanity." As I read these two sentences, they are a fleshing out of our topic of human dignity and the integrity of creation. They claim that all life, human and other Earth life, is valuable *as such*. There is here no separation of good and evil beings, nor the suggestion that some are worthwhile only because they are useful to others. The value of all life and the dignity of human beings is the first and most important principle in the Earth Charter.

This same insistence on the intrinsic value of all life is at the heart of the first creation story in the book of Genesis. What many remember from that story is that the text tells human beings to subdue and dominate the rest of creation, but while that is mentioned once, what is central to the story is the seven times that God says, "It is good." After each act of creation—the sun, moon, stars, ocean, plants, animals, and finally human beings—God says, "It is good." Not good for me, God, or good for human beings, but simply *good*. After finishing creation, God steps back as it were to view the whole panorama and announces, "It is very good." This is amazing—God appears to have an aesthetic appreciation for every scrap and tidbit of creation. God loves things for themselves, simply because they are. I think philosopher Iris Murdoch was trying to express something similar when she wrote: "Love is the extremely difficult realization that something other than oneself is real. Love . . . is the discovery of reality."[1]

What the Earth Charter, Genesis, and Iris Murdoch are suggesting is that the dignity of human beings and the integrity of creation rest on seeing everyone and everything as valuable, on seeing everything as "good" as God does. We want to see some people as good and some as bad, some parts of creation as useful to us and other parts as less useful. We want to think in dualisms, not continuities. But this new picture of who we are says that God loves—that is, recognizes the value of—each and every piece of creation.

If we were to begin to think this way about ourselves and other creatures, what might the consequences be? Recently, I have been reading and teaching about some of the people we call saints—people like the Dalai Lama, Jean Vanier, Dorothy Day, Nelson Mandela, and Bishop Tutu. One outstanding characteristic of these people is their universal love—love that seems to know no bounds. It does not stop with family, tribe, race, country, or even species. All life is honored just because it exists. John Woolman, an eighteenth-century American Quaker and early abolitionist, describes his conversion experience in these terms. He writes that true religion consists in loving God the creator and willing justice and goodness to all people and even to "brute creatures," for he claims, "to say we love God as unseen, and at the same time exercise cruelty toward the least creature moving by [God's] life . . . is a contradiction in itself."[2] In other words, one can't love God without loving all that God has made—to do otherwise is a contradiction. His conversion to what he calls "true religion" consists of a deepening love of God which results in the increase of "universal love to my fellow-creatures."

Another example is that of the Holocaust rescuers. Studies done on these people reveal that they did not hide and save Jews because they had any special preference for Jews; rather, they did so simply because they felt that every human being has the right to live.[3] Nor did they think they did anything special: they thought anyone in their position would have done the same thing. Of course, not everyone did. Not everyone does see themselves and all other human beings as well as creation itself as valuable in and of itself. Not everyone is truly a democrat when it comes to existence, as God is in Genesis.

The first movement that we need to make in our repentance to think and act differently, then, is at the most basic level of who we think we are. The dignity of human beings and the integrity of creation rests, first of all, on our willingness to affirm the value of all life, not just our own, or our own tribe or religion or country or class or species. Like the saints we need to practice developing a universal love that knows no bounds, a love that becomes more and more inclusive. How far can it go? Jesus suggests that the stretch must include the enemy—that is certainly an interesting proposal.

We have seen that human dignity and the integrity of creation rest on a sensibility that respects the "other," whether that other is a human being or a nonhuman aspect of creation. The most basic stance we must take in order to live differently in the world is appreciation for something other than ourselves and our own interests. Like God, we need to be able to look at the world and say, "It is good." Period.

WHERE DO WE FIT?

A second movement is equally important and is in fact part of the first: all things—whether they be human beings, tigers, mountains, dandelions, apples, slugs, elephants, water, or air—exist only because of other things. As the poet Wallace Stevens said, "Nothing is itself taken alone. Things are because of inter-relations and interconnections."[4] Unlike the Western, North American belief that human beings are individuals who live *on* the earth, we in fact live *in* it. Moreover, we do not decide *when* we want to form relationships with other people and the earth, for we are *in* the most intimate and complex relationships from before our birth until after our death. Hence, the appreciation for each and every creature in creation—for its particularity and specialness and difference—does not mean a doctrine of "individualism" such as we see in our present Western culture. Just the opposite: individuals only exist in networks of interrelationship and interdependence.

This is one of the most important shifts needed in our view of ourselves if we are to make some progress toward human dignity and the integrity of creation. Let us consider two insights about who we are and where we fit that come from the centrality of interrelationship. First, interrelationship says that everything is on a continuum. Since we and everything else in the universe evolved together from the Big Bang billions of years ago, we are all related—we are distant cousins to the stars, to oak leaves and to deer. This means that we are like and unlike these others in mysterious and interesting ways. We want to think that humans are totally different from animals and plants. By thinking in terms of dualisms we can use and misuse others. But nature operates in terms of continuities. Thinking on a continuum has profound implications for both human dignity and the integrity of creation: it means that all humans are inti-mately related to one another, whether they be male or female, black or white or brown, straight or gay, rich or poor, able bodied or physically challenged,

Muslim or Christian. The centrality of interrelationship means that regardless of whether other human beings are like us or not, and whether we like them or not, they *are* our relatives, our closest relatives, our nuclear family, if you will. It means that all other creatures are our relatives as well, even if distant cousins. The continuum also means that some people are not totally good while others are evil, some people entirely right while others are wrong, some people all healthy and others sick—we exist together in various shades and gradations. The edges are fuzzy that separate us one from the other, and it is at these fuzzy edges that we often stretch out and touch each other.

The second insight about ourselves that emerges from the centrality of relationship concerns how the individual fits into the whole. It is easy for this to go wrong—for an individual to dominate the whole (as in totalitarianism) or for the whole to suffocate the individual (as in some fundamentalist cults). How can genuine individuality and radical relationship exist together? In the United States, the image of the melting pot unites all individuals into a somewhat bland similarity, whereas in Canada the mosaic allows individuals to be nicely differentiated but not very united. Ecological unity—the unity in which individuals exist *in* relationships and only in relationships—says that the whole is made up from the differences among individuals. In other words, individuality and unity depend on one another: an old-growth forest consists of millions of different plants and trees, insects and animals, each doing its job, in order for the whole to be sustained. The whole is nothing but the healthy functioning of all the parts; hence, each and every part is valuable and necessary.

Needless to say, this understanding of the whole and the parts has important implications for global economics as well as environmental standards. Justice and sustainability belong together: all the parts must have the necessities of existence in order for the whole to survive. Justice to individuals—feeding people and sustaining plants—is not a choice that well-off people might make in a spirit of charity. On the contrary, justice at the level of the basics needed for the health of individuals, human and nonhuman, is a necessity. The whole cannot be sustained apart from the health of the parts. This is a sobering fact that calls for a radical change in the behavior of those of us presently taking more than our share, and hence causing other people and life-forms to deteriorate for lack of nourishment.

If we accept this picture of interrelationship and interdependence—the picture that puts us on a continuum with all other creatures and that claims that the whole can only be healthy if the parts are fed—then we have a very different understanding of ourselves than our consumer culture tells us. That culture basically says that each of us human individuals has the right to all we can legally acquire—in fact, we owe it to ourselves to have the very best.

Although no traditional religion has ever said, "Blessed are the greedy," the new religion of consumerism *is* telling us precisely that. We do not even have to feel embarrassed or ashamed of our level of comfort and convenience. But these two pictures of who we are in the scheme of things are radically different. Which will we choose? The philosopher Erich Heller warns us: "Be careful how you interpret the world. It *is* like that."[5] Indeed, it is.

Once again we turn to our saints for some insight. In his Christmas sermon in 1967, Martin Luther King Jr. wrote: "As nations and individuals, we are interdependent . . . all caught up in an inescapable network of mutuality, tied into a single garment of human destiny."[6] We do not want to admit this because acknowledging it demands too much of us. And yet, King's view is what contemporary science is also telling us about our world. It is not just Christian piety that claims relationships are central, as in the Great Commandment to love God and neighbor. Recall Iris Murdoch's way of putting it: "Love . . . is the discovery of reality." What a wonderful sentence that is! It tells us that loving others is not a sentimental religious teaching; rather, it is an objective statement about our world and where we fit into it. The individualistic view of capitalist consumerism is outmoded. It came from the eighteenth century, which discovered the importance of the individual (and we are all grateful for that) but did not realize that individuals exist only in relationship.

HOW DO WE GET THERE?

We are called to live in a different world, a world where the good of the individual and the good of the community are intrinsically and intimately related. But how do we get there? How do we even begin to live differently when our world is increasingly ordered around the greed of the individual and the decay of nature? Given what has happened since 9/11 in terms of hatred, violence, deception, war, imperialism, climate change, poverty, and AIDS, why even imagine such pictures, such visions of a different world? We return to verse 24 in Isaiah 65: "Before they call I will answer, while they are yet speaking I will hear." That is the only reason we dare to imagine a different world—because God is before us, God is there already. The world imagined by our biblical texts is not a fantasy; it is what the Jewish and Christian traditions tell us is God's will for us and promise to us. The One in whom we live and move and have our being assures us that this other world of appreciation for each and every individual creature living in networks of interrelationship and interdependence—that this is not a dream, but the way things should be, and will be, with God's help. To the degree we live in God, from God, and for God, this world will emerge.

Now, fantastic as it sounds, this *is* what Jews and Christians, and in fact many religious people of other faiths, believe. God is in charge and God wills a different world for all of us. As we turn now to the small steps we might take—what Isaiah says is our call to God—we listen to the wise words of Canadian activist Nellie McClung: "Let us do our little bit with cheerfulness and not take the responsibility that belongs to God. None of us can turn the earth around. All we can ever hope to do is to hit it a few whacks on the right side." We will now consider a few whacks on the right side that might help us get to a different world.

ASKING AND IMAGINING

The first whack on the right side is to imagine and ask for a different world. But how can we break out of our conventional world to even imagine a different one? Jesus' parables are helpful at this point. They tell of people who were living conventional lives, only to have things turned upside down, inviting them into a new way of living. One thinks of the parables of the Good Samaritan, the Prodigal Son, the Rich Ruler, the Great Dinner: in each of these stories, expectations about who is righteous, valuable, and important are abruptly derailed. The world each character knew is brought under sharp critique, and a different way of being in the world is presented—one in which foreigners, younger sons, poor people, and the marginalized are invited into God's favor. I think one of the most important things the parables suggest to us is that "a different world is possible." Mostly we don't believe this and why should we, given the horror we see all around us? Despair is the appropriate response for thoughtful, sensitive, good-hearted people.

But Jesus was not a despairing type, though surely his world was equally awful. Rather, he had what some anthropologists have called a lot of "wild space." "Wild space" is that part of each of us that doesn't quite fit into our conventional worlds; it is that part of our own personal world that does not completely overlap with the ordinary world—for us, this is the consumer- and market-oriented, individualistic, greedy world. Maybe we have some wild space because we are different in some way: poor, disabled, a person of color, a refugee, gay or lesbian, and so forth. Maybe we have some wild space because we have lived in an impoverished country and seen people without clean water or medicine, or maybe we have had a very rough childhood or recovered from a serious addiction. Whatever makes it possible to think outside the box, to think that things ought to be different—not just for oneself but for the world—is useful wild space. Jesus had a lot of wild space; in fact, we could say he was a *wild man.* He imagined what he called the kingdom of God where this new pattern for living would come about—the pattern that Isaiah sums up with the wonderful words, "they shall not hurt or destroy on all my holy mountain." We *want* this different world. Peter Short, the current moderator of the United Church of Canada, puts it this way: "the residual memory of paradise is still in you, lingering like a scent of jasmine on a breeze. You are a paradise-haunted creature. If it were not so, why would you expect so much of the world? Why would you expect so much of yourself? See how you rage when hatred and greed and the desecration of the good earth make clear again and again that this is no paradise?"[7] Our wild space is the memory of where we came from and the hope of where we are going: from paradise to the kingdom of God, from living with all other creatures within the love of God to living once again all together within God's love. Nothing short of this will satisfy us. We come from paradise and yearn for the reign of God.

In order to "see differently," to entertain the possibility of a different world, we must let our wild space come out from its hiding place. And then, in the wonderful words of Paul, we can begin to open ourselves to the glory of God whose power working in us can do more than we can ask or imagine. *But we must ask and we must imagine.* This is, I think, the first and most important step toward living differently.

The question then arises, if we see ourselves differently—not as isolated individuals, but as part of a vast network of valuable creatures who need and enjoy each other—will we begin to act that way? The Greeks said that to know the good is to do the good. If that were so, then our only problem would be knowing who we are and where we fit—correct action would follow. But Paul wasn't so optimistic. He called himself a wretched man because he knew the good, but he didn't necessarily do it. There is no direct connection between knowing the good and doing the good. This is what the Christian tradition has called "sin"—being conscious of a better way but not choosing it. Moving beyond this paralysis is terribly difficult, especially when our culture rewards us for staying with a very different picture of who we are and what we ought to do. We do not have to commit active sins in order to stay within the framework of the individualistic, greedy picture of human and planetary life. All that well-off North Americans have to do is live like everyone else around us is living. The tradition calls this the sin of "omission" rather than the sin of "commission," and in many ways it is more insidious because we don't feel we have done anything bad.

So, how to move out of this place of denial and indifference? One possibility is summed up in the phrase: "Just do it." This perspective is in some ways the reverse of belief and action: it says, start with the action and the belief will follow. Many religious traditions stress action over belief—what matters is what you do, more than what you think. Sometimes the most effective way of getting out of paralysis, of our denial and indifference, is simply to get on with it. The Jewish tradition is focused on people following the Torah, the law of God. Living the truth is of primary importance. The saints of the church seem to agree: Teresa of Avila, a sixteenth-century nun, suggested that if you are not certain about your relationship with God, stop worrying about it, focus on loving your neighbor, and the God-question will take care of itself. Present-day Latin American liberation theologians claim that theology needs a fundamental revolution, from its traditional focus on orthodoxy to a new focus on orthopraxy—from concern with right belief to right action. As they often say, "to know Jesus is to love Jesus." Or in the words of Gustavo Gutiérrez: "We find the Lord in our encounters with [human beings], especially the poor, marginalized, and exploited ones. An act of love toward them is an act of love toward God."[8]

In summary, following Nellie McClung's advice, our first good whack on the right side of the world is to imagine and ask for a different world, to dare go with our wild space about what is possible, and then to start to live differently, in whatever halting and limited ways we can.

MATERIAL WELL-BEING

A second whack on the right side of the world is for us to focus not on the spiritual but on the material well-being of others. Why should we do this? For two reasons: first, an incarnational religion demands that we pay attention to the flesh, the body, the most basic needs of others. Second, by focusing on the material needs of others, we begin to see how much our own level of material well-being keeps us from seeing differently. To expand on the first reason: Christianity claims that the divine became human and dwells among us—flesh of our flesh, in and of the earth. It seems like an outrageous claim: how could or should the transcendent God become one with us, with all flesh, with the earth itself? However, it is not an outrageous claim if one believes that God is not distant, supernatural, but the One in whom we live and move and have our being, the One from whom all life comes and to whom all life returns. It was not outrageous to Isaiah, whose God answers before we even call, who hears us before we have finished speaking. This God does not seem to care so much about our spiritual or religious needs as about our ordinary ones: long life, houses to live in, food to eat, enjoyable work, healthy children, peace and well-being among all creatures. How mundane! Indeed. An incarnate God is exactly that: mundane. I think this God cares about entire species of animals becoming extinct because humans grab all the land and about the 1,400 African children who die every day from AIDS; God cares about the fact that North Americans who make up 5 percent of the world's population use 25 percent of its energy resources; and

God cares about the women who have no protection against AIDS because they have no control over their sexual lives.

An incarnate religion demands an incarnate spirituality; one could call it "spirituality of the body." Hence, issues of distributive justice become religious issues: who has food, shelter, medical care, education, work, leisure—these become "works of the spirit." When life is seen as intrinsically valuable and all life exists in networks of interrelationship and interdependence, then there is no split between spirit and flesh, with religion concerned mainly with the spirit. An incarnate religion refuses to allow well-off people to pacify the poor with promises of eternal life while their ordinary lives lack the necessities for a decent existence. This is seen for what it is—an ingenious maneuver by those of us with ample material goods to deny them to other needy human beings and life-forms.

Turning to the saints again for insight, these folks appear to do exactly what most of us do not: they see the material condition of others as a spiritual matter. If we think of Francis of Assisi, Dorothy Day, John Woolman, Jean Vanier, Simone Weil, or Nelson Mandela, it is the body and its needs that are their central concern. These saints do not work to save the souls of the poor for the sweet-by-and-by. They put their own bodies on the line in order for the ordinary, mundane needs of other human beings to be met. Their universal love that knows no bounds is an earthly, bodily love. Issues like climate change and AIDS, which directly affect the health of bodies—human ones as well as other life-forms—become from this perspective heinous sins, much worse sins than our minor personal moral failures. What matters is how we live day by day, our ordinary lives, and whether the way we live helps the material condition of others. The winner of the Nobel Peace Prize for 2004, Wangari Maathai, has lived such a life. For three decades she has been instrumental in planting over 30 million trees in deforested parts of Africa. As the Nobel committee realized, "peace" is not just the cessation of wars; more basically, it is about providing the earth and its people with the basics of existence.

But *how* can we learn to see the material needs of others as a spiritual matter? John Woolman sold his profitable grocery business because he was making too much money. The money kept him from seeing clearly. He said that he wanted his eye to be single so he could see things as they really are, but he kept seeing double because his own material wealth was squarely in his line of sight. When he got himself and his money out of the center, he could see the relationship between slavery and wealth: in order for some people to live lavishly, they were willing to enslave others. Without the lavish lifestyle, might they have been able to see differently—perhaps with their "wild space"? There is a deep wisdom in most religious traditions that self-emptying, self-denial, allows us to see differently and hence to live differently. Self-denial is not principally for ascetic flagellation; rather, it is often the first step toward universal love of others, toward seeing all others as valuable and all as interrelated.

But looking at the lives of the saints, while highly instructive, can also lead to despair. St. Francis gave away *all* his possessions, not only to clothe and feed others, but also to attain spiritual poverty—the poverty of radical humility, of radical openness, to God and all other creatures. We are not likely to do this. In fact, stories like those of Woolman and Francis can turn us away: *we* can't be saints, so we might as well do nothing. Dorothee Soelle, the German theologian, writing about mysticism and resistance, said: "The retreat of a Thomas Merton to the solitude of a Trappist monastery is not that far removed from an annual intervention in a shareholder's meeting."[9] She notes that in the United States today more than $450 billion is invested in line with ethical criteria rather than maximum profit. The people who are insisting on the ethical investments are not St. Francises, nor are they engaged in a revolution, but they are *resisting*. "Resisters" engage in acts of self-denial, of limitation, of saying no, of standing firm, of resisting temptation for more, of refusing to join the crowd. Resisters can be as modest as a child who recycles or as bold as those who speak out at a stockbroker's meeting. What matters is the clarity of vision that comes from stepping out from the blinders that our consumer culture puts on us, so that we begin to see differently.

PERSEVERANCE

And this leads us to a third good whack on the right side: perseverance. Our small acts of resistance, of saying no to more, of refusing to just go with the crowd, will not save the world, but they can help us see the material needs of others as our spiritual task. We have suggested that a vision of all life as valuable and interdependent can come about for us if we open ourselves to seeing differently—to letting our wild side imagine such a world and to limiting our own material worth so we may see better and others may have more. Now we suggest that the important thing is to "hang in there." "Ecological despair" is one of the most difficult problems for us as we try to change—to see differently and to live differently. By "ecological despair" I mean the overwhelming sense of futility that comes over us the more we learn about the state of our world and its creatures. Every time we open a newspaper, we read more grim statistics: in fifty years the glaciers in the Rockies will be gone; a recent UNICEF report says that Iraq has lost more ground in child mortality rates than any other country due to two wars and a decade of sanctions; in the past fifty years Africa has had 186 coups and 26 major wars, killing over 7 million people. Moreover, in light of the present direction of the United States, mainline Christians and political liberals are being swept up into another level of despair. Even if we imagine a different world and want to work for it, how does one do so when the world's superpower has an agenda in which human dignity and the integrity of creation are distant, if not absent, values? At the very least, the churches should wake up to the importance of advocating a different paradigm for human beings and for the world than one sees in the union of Christian and political conservatism. A different gospel must be preached. The churches must imagine and work for a different world.

But it all seems so overwhelming. Why bother? When I want to turn away in despair and give up, I am brought up short by a remark by Dorothy Day, who spent forty years in one of the poorest areas of New York City. Of people who called her a saint, she said, "Don't dismiss me so easily." Meaning, don't let yourself off the hook so fast. She claimed that to live as she did does not require great talent or courage, but mostly hard work. "I have done nothing well," she said, "But I have done what I could."[10] Indeed. Those who study the lives of the saints emphasize the ordinariness of becoming a saint. As one says, "Goodness is banal as training for something is banal."[11] In other words, living differently from the world is a habit one develops. People are not born good—or saintly; they become so through small, daily, constant changes in behavior and insight. Seeing differently and behaving differently appear for those most successful at it to be a cyclical process of small but persevering decisions. Most of us do not want to consider the banality of goodness, just as we don't want to accept the banality of evil—that people like Hitler and Saddam Hussein are ordinary people, not demons. We would prefer to see the very good people or the very bad ones as saints or demons; then, when we read their stories, the finger does not point to us. We cannot be that good or that bad, we say, but we can be better or worse. I like the following bits of advice: Confucius said, "It does not matter how slow you go, as long as you don't stop"; T. S. Eliot adds, "Only those who risk going too far can possibly find out how far one can go."[12]

We have been reflecting on human dignity and the integrity of creation by asking the questions, Who are we? Where do we fit on Planet Earth? How do we get there? As we come to the end of our thoughts for now, I would like to put these reflections in perspective by suggesting two qualifications. The first qualification is that in focusing on questions of who we think we are in the scheme of things—the worldview we hold—we have only looked at one small, though I think important, issue. Our subject of human dignity and the integrity of creation is huge—it includes the entire planetary agenda, that is, what all people must do in every field of endeavor, every religion, every aspect of their daily lives so that things can get better. As people of faith, I believe one of our crucial tasks is to help people change at the level of their most basic assumptions about who we are and therefore how we should act in the world. This is one of the primary functions of religion: forming these profound and often unconscious beliefs. That is what we have focused on here, but it is just one thing that needs to be done.

The second qualification on our reflections is to return us to our Isaiah passage. The presumption of trying to think differently, let alone act differently, is only possible because our religious traditions tell us the marvelous news that God answers before we call, that God hears before we speak. We are not alone. The dream we have for a new world, a new earth, is not just our dream; it is the dream of God, and God has placed this dream within each one of us. The dream of paradise and the dream of the kingdom of God is, finally, why we keep going and how we keep going. We are paradise-haunted creatures who yearn for the kingdom of God. We hang in there because God hangs in there. Hallelujah!

Notes

PROLOGUE

1. Jeremy Carrette and Richard King, *Selling Spirituality: The Silent Takeover of Religion* (New York: Routledge, 2005).

1. WHOSE CONVERSATION?

1. Karl Barth, *Church Dogmatics,* ed. G. W. Bromiley and T. F. Torrance (Edinburgh: T. & T. Clark, 1957), II/1, 219.

2. Barth, *CD,* III/3, 293.

3. Barth, *CD,* I/1, 1.

4. Barth, *CD,* IV/1, 661.

5. Ibid., 689.

6. Ibid., 700.

7. Mary Ann Stenger and Ronald H. Stone, *Dialogues of Paul Tillich* (Macon, Ga.: Mercer University Press, 2002), 1.

8. Paul Tillich, *Systematic Theology,* vol. 1 (Chicago: University of Chicago Press, 1951), 3.

9. Ibid., 4.

10. Ibid., 6.

11. Paul Tillich, *Christianity and the Encounter of World Religions* (1963; repr., Minneapolis: Fortress Press, 1994), 78.

12. Ibid., 61.

13. Ibid, 61–62.

14. Ibid., 65.

15. Tillich, *Systematic Theology,* vol. 1, 14.

16. Ibid., 61.

17. Ibid., 10.

18. Paul Tillich, *Dynamics of Faith* (New York: Harper & Row, 1957), 97.

19. Ibid., 125.

20. See John Milbank, *Theology and Social Theory: Beyond Secular Reason* (Cambridge, Mass.: Basil Blackwell, 1990), 278–325. See also Mary Potter Engel, "Historical Theology and Violence against Women: Unearthing a Popular Tradition of Just Battery," in *Violence against Women and Children: A Christian Theological Sourcebook,* ed. Carol J. Adams and Marie M. Fortune (New York: Continuum, 1995), 242–61.

21. See Nancey Murphy and George F. R. Ellis, *On the Moral Nature of the Universe: Theology, Cosmology, and Ethics,* Theology and the Sciences (Minneapolis: Fortress Press, 1996), 115–72.

22. Sallie McFague, *Life Abundant: Rethinking Theology and Economy for a Planet in Peril* (Minneapolis: Fortress Press, 2001), xi.

23. Sallie McFague, *The Body of God: An Ecological Theology* (Minneapolis: Fortress Press, 1993), 164.

24. McFague, *Life Abundant,* 187.

25. Ibid., 195.

26. Dietrich Bonhoeffer, *Letters and Papers from Prison,* enlarged edition, ed. Eberhard Bethge (New York: Macmillan, 1972), 382.

27. McFague, *Body of God,* 162.

28. Sallie McFague, *Super, Natural Christians: How We Should Love Nature* (Minneapolis: Fortress Press, 1997), 174.

29. Shawn Copeland, "Body, Race, and Being," in *Constructive Theology: A Contemporary Approach to Classical Themes,* ed. Serene Jones and Paul Lakeland (Minneapolis: Fortress Press, 2005), 115.

30. McFague, *Life Abundant,* 14.

31. Ibid., 22–23.

32. Ibid., 183.

33. Sallie McFague, *Speaking in Parables: A Study in Metaphor and Theology* (London: SCM Press, 2002), 138–39.

34. Ibid., 156.

35. Ibid., 160–61.

36. George W. Bush, "President's Remarks at National Day of Prayer and Remembrance" (speech, The National Cathedral, Washington, D.C., September 14, 2001); http://www.whitehouse.gov/news/releases/2001/09/20010914-2.html.

37. One of the more demonic examples of this is a confession of the "German Christians" written in 1932: "We see in race, national character, and national orders of life given and entrusted to us by God, to maintain which is a law of God for us. Therefore, racial mixing is to be opposed." Cited in Shirley C. Guthrie, *Christian Doctrine*, rev. ed. (Louisville: Westminster John Knox Press, 1994), 21.

38. John Dominic Crossan, *Jesus: A Revolutionary Biography* (San Francisco: HarperSanFrancisco, 1994), 54.

2. IN THE BEGINNING IS THE LISTENING

1. Joan Chittister. *Wisdom Distilled from the Daily: Living the Rule of Saint Benedict Today* (San Francisco: HarperSanFrancisco, 1991), 24.

2. Sallie McFague. *Super, Natural Christians: How We Should Love Nature* (Minneapolis: Fortress Press, 1997), 111.

3. Thomas Oord, *Science of Love: The Wisdom of Well-Being* (Philadephia: Templeton Foundation Press, 2004), 9.

4. Earth Charter International, "The Earth Charter: Values and Principles for a Sustainable Future,"The Earth Charter Initiative, 2000; http://www.earthcharter.org.

5. McFague, *Super, Natural Christians*, 82.

6. Ibid., 94.

7. Here, too, I am following McFague. In *Super, Natural Christians* she suggests that listening no less than touch can ground us in healthier ways of seeing the world. When touch is seen as primary, she says, we come to take listening more seriously: "Hearing, another responsive sense, would gain higher status than it presently has" (94). She then indicates that attention to hearing can help us become more patient because hearing requires others to speak first. Our very thinking can then be anchored in listening just as it is anchored in touch. Such anchorage provides an antidote to what is all too characteristic of Western thinking: an impulse to speak before listening. As McFague explains: "The Western way of knowing is based on the distancing, objectifying, controlling eye. It has also been a thinking primarily anchored in saying-without-listening." The eye that objectifies and controls is based on the mouth that speaks: ours is a 'logocentric culture' anchored in 'assertive discourse' . . . When touch is seen as primary, listening and hearing gain in importance . . . Listening puts us immediately into a responsive relationship to others: in fact hearing depends on waiting until the other speaks or makes a noise" (94).

3. TOWARD AN ELEMENTAL THEOLOGY

Portions of this essay appeared in slightly different form in "Beyond Atheism and Theism," my contribution to the "Constructive Proposals" section of the chapter on "God" in *Constructive Theology: A Contemporary Approach to Classical Themes,* ed. Serene Jones and Paul Lakeland (Minneapolis: Fortress Press, 2005), 45–52.

1. Sallie McFague, *Metaphorical Theology: Models of God in Religious Language* (Philadelphia: Fortress Press, 1982); *Models of God: Theology for an Ecological, Nuclear Age* (Philadelphia: Fortress Press, 1987); *The Body of God: An Ecological Theology* (Minneapolis: Fortress Press, 1993).

2. Sallie McFague, *Super, Natural Christians: How We Should Love Nature* (Minneapolis: Fortress Press, 1997) and *Life Abundant: Rethinking Theology and Economy for a Planet in Peril* (Minneapolis: Fortress Press, 2000).

3. Friedrich Schleiermacher, introduction to part 1 of *The Christian Faith,* rev. ed., ed. H. R. Mackintosh and J. S. Stewart (1928; repr., London: T & T Clark, 1997), 131–41.

4. Excerpts from Anselm's *Proslogion,* trans. David Burr, http://www.fordham.edu/halsall/source/anselm.html, (accessed June 4, 2006).

5. Thomas Aquinas, *Summa Theologica,* trans. Fathers of the English Dominican Province (New York: Benzinger Bros., 1947), pt. 1, Q. 2, http://www.ccel.org/a/aquinas/summa/home.html (accessed June 4, 2006).

6. Aquinas, *ST,* pt. I, Q. 2, art. 2.

7. Aquinas, *ST,* pt. I, Q. 12, art. 1.

8. Thomas Aquinas, *Summa Contra Gentiles,* annotated and abridged, ed. and trans. Joseph Rickaby (London: Burns and Oates, 1905), bk. 1, chap. 37, 148–54, http://www.nd.edu/Departments/Maritain/etext/gc.htm, (accessed June 4, 2006). See also *ST,* pt. I, Q.12, art. 13.

9. See Dionysius the Aeropagite, *On the Divine Names and The Mystical Theology,* trans. and ed. C. E. Rolt (Missoula, Mont.: Kessinger Publications, 1920), http://www.ccel.org/ccel/rolt/dionysius.titlepage.html (accessed June 4, 2006).

10. The list of scholars who have taken up the topic of mysticism is too long to give here. For two intriguing books on the topic, see Françoise Meltzer, *For Fear of the Fire: Joan of Arc and the Limits of Subjectivity* (Chicago: University of Chicago Press, 2001), and Amy Hollywood, *Sensible Ecstasy: Mysticism, Sexual Difference, and the Demands of History* (Chicago: University of Chicago Press, 2002).

11. Mary Daly, *Beyond God the Father: Toward a Philosophy of Women's Liberation* (Boston: Beacon Press, 1973), 19.

12. Ludwig Feuerbach, *The Essence of Christianity,* trans. George Eliot (New York: Prometheus Books, 1987).

13. For information on the Project on Lived Theology (housed at the University of Virginia and run by Dr. Charles Marsh), see http://www.livedtheology.org/. For more on this point, see my "Interpreting Practices, Sustaining Differences: Deconstruction as Hermeneutical Praxis" in *Between the Human and the Divine: Philosophical and Theological Hermeneutics,* ed. Andrzej Wierciński (Toronto: The Hermeneutic Press, 2002), 573–80.

14. McFague, *Body of God,* 142.

15. Ibid., 140.

16. Ibid., 149.

17. A pun that is central to the second story would be interesting to pursue in connection to what will follow. Phyllis Trible, for example, argues for translating *'adam* as "earth creature" to capture the pun with *'adamah,* dust, the material out of which *'adam* is created. See Phyllis Trible, *God and the Rhetoric of Sexuality,* Overtures to Biblical Theology (Philadelphia: Fortress Press, 1978), 80.

18. McFague, *Body of God,* 143.

19. The term "French feminist" is an American appellation that refers to a set of theorists and activists located in France whose work found its way across the Atlantic in the 1980s. It is, as many have argued, a misnomer since these thinkers vary in their stance toward feminism and several of them are from countries other than France. See the introduction to *French Feminists on Religion: A Reader,* ed. Morny Joy, Kathleen O'Grady, and Judith L. Poxon (New York: Routledge, 2003), which is a good place to start to get acquainted with Irigaray's work on religion. See also the essays using Irigaray's work in its companion volume, *Religion in French Feminist Thought: Critical Perspectives,* ed. Joy et al. (New York: Routledge, 2003), and in *Transfigurations: Theology and the French Feminists,* ed. C. W. Maggie Kim, Susan M. St. Ville, and Susan M. Simonaitis (Minneapolis: Fortress Press, 1993), for a variety of perspectives on its promise and limits.

20. The degree to which Irigaray's approach can support other kinds of sexual difference (GLBT, for example) or racial/ethnic differences—all of which are also arguably caught up in the current sexual economy in unhelpful ways—is a matter of considerable debate. For a sample of the issues raised and answers given, see chapter 4 in my *Deconstruction, Feminist Theology, and the Problem of Difference: Subverting the Race/Gender Divide* (Chicago: University of Chicago Press, 1999), Mary Keller's contribution to Joy, et al., eds., *Religion in French Feminist Thought,* and Alison Stone, "The Sex of Nature: A Reinterpretation of Irigaray's Metaphysics and Political Thought," *Hypatia* 18, no. 3 (Summer 2003): 60–84.

21. Luce Irigaray, *This Sex Which Is Not One,* trans. Catherine Porter and Carolyn Burke (Ithaca, N.Y.: Cornell University Press, 1985), 76.

22. See Luce Irigaray, *Marine Lover of Friedrich Nietzsche,* trans. Gillian C. Gill (New York: Columbia University Press, 1991), and *The Forgetting of Air in Martin Heidegger,* trans. Mary Beth Mader (Austin: University of Texas Press, 1999).

23. Luce Irigaray, "Divine Women," *Sexes and Genealogies,* trans. Gillian C. Gill (New York: Columbia University Press, 1993), 57–72.

24. For other criticisms of Irigaray's reliance on projection, see Serene Jones, "Divining Women: Irigaray and Feminist Theologies," *Yale French Studies* 87 (1995): 42–67, and Amy Hollywood, "Deconstructing Belief: Irigaray and the Philosophy of Religion," *Journal of Religion* 78, no. 2 (1998): 230–246.

25. See my contribution to Joy, et al., eds., *Religion and French Feminist Thought* as well as those by Keller and Judith Poxon.

26. Luce Irigaray, *An Ethics of Sexual Difference,* trans. Carolyn Burke and Gillian C. Gill (Ithaca, N.Y.: Cornell University Press, 1993), 129; translation modified.

27. See Jones, "Divining Women," 63–65, "This God Which Is Not One: Irigaray and Barth on the Divine," in Kim, et al., *Transfigurations,* 109–42, and Grace Jantzen, "Feminism and Pantheism," *The Monist* 80 (April 1997): 266–85. For Jones, this is a problem; for Jantzen, it is not.

28. Irigaray, *Ethics,* 129.

29. Indeed, in "Feminism and Pantheism," Jantzen draws on Irigaray's notion of a sensible transcendental to argue for pantheism as a useful—perhaps even necessary—path toward reforming the masculinist religious symbolic in the West. While I agree with Jantzen that the West's religious symbolic needs a strong jolt (and pantheism can provide it), my own deployment of Irigaray's sensible transcendental does not go in that direction.

30. For more on air as figure for the divine vis-à-vis a reading of Irigaray's *The Forgetting of Air,* see my contribution to Joy, et al., eds., *Religion in French Feminist Thought.*

31. Michael Eric Dyson, *Come Hell or High Water: Hurricane Katrina and the Color of Disaster* (New York: Basic Books, 2006).

4. GOD AND POWER, PROPHETS, AND NATIVE LANDS

1. The Social Creed can be found online on the United Methodist General Board of Church and Society Web site at http://www.umc-gbcs.org/site/pp.asp?c=fsJNK0PKJrH&b=845453 (accessed June 14, 2006).

2 . This shift is so pronounced that many scholars assume that two different stories have been put together. See, for example, Ernst Würthwein, *Die Bücher der Könige, 1. Kön. 17—2. Kön. 25: Das Alte Testament Deutsch*, vol. 11, no.2 (Göttingen: Vandenhoeck & Ruprecht, 1984), 251.

3. See ibid., 248–51.

4. Ahab's report to Jezebel in 21:5 that he "spoke to Naboth" would better be translated as "spoke repeatedly to Naboth." See ibid., 249.

5. At first it does not occur to Ahab that he could claim this more absolute power. It is his wife Jezebel who promotes the new power. The daughter of the king of Tyrus, Jezebel presupposes a different, more absolute, understanding of the power of a king. See ibid., 251.

6. See Frank Crüsemann, *Der Widerstand gegen das Königtum* (NeukirchenVluyn: Neukirchener Verlag, 1978), 72, 112.

7. It is "our manifest destiny to overspread the continent allotted by Providence for the free development of our yearly multiplying millions." These words were written in 1845 by John O'Sullivan, a Democrat leader and editor of the newspaper *The Democratic Review*. See Howard Zinn, *A People's History of the United States* (New York: Harper Perennial, 1990), 147–66, for the context of this statement.

8. Sallie McFague, *Models of God: Theology for an Ecological, Nuclear Age* (Philadelphia: Fortress Press, 1987), 67. See also page 63, where McFague adds that neither are these images perceived as oppressive. I am not sure, however, whether a top-down image of God's power necessarily means that God is removed from the world, as McFague seems to imply.

9. See Ward Churchill, *Struggle for the Land: Native North American Resistance to Genocide, Ecocide, and Colonization* (San Francisco: City Lights, 2002), 374.

10. "Colonialism has now, by and large, officially come to an end," I wrote in the past. That was not entirely correct. See Joerg Rieger, "Theology and Mission in a Postcolonial World," *Mission Studies* 21, no. 2 (2002): 202. Nevertheless, Native American reality has informed my argument even in that essay. For the term "internal colonialism," see Churchill, *Struggle*, 25.

11. Churchill, *Struggle*, 26. The Native American arguments not only for their rights to the land but also for their national integrity are strong, indicating that Native Americans never renounced their own nationhood, that the U.S. Senate recognized Native American nations (demonstrated by the fact that it ratified approximately 400 treaties with Native American nations—treaties being instruments exclusively reserved for transactions between nations), and that international law affirms steps to be taken toward decolonization (for example, U.N. General Assembly Resolution 1514 [XV]). See Churchill, *Struggle*, 37–90. The Indian Claims Commission of the United States, created in 1946, found that the United States has no legal basis to one-third of the land within its borders, Ibid., 376.

12. See *Feminist Theory: A Reader*, ed. Wendy Kolmar and Frances Bartkowski (Mountain View, Calif.: Mayfield Pub. Co., 2000), 44.

13. Edward Said, *Culture and Imperialism* (New York: Vintage Books, 1994), xvii.

14. Michel Foucault, *Power/Knowledge: Selected Interviews and Other Writings 1972–1977*, ed. Colin Gordon (New York: Pantheon Books, 1980), 104–5.

15. Hardt and Negri, *Empire* (Cambridge, Mass.: Harvard University Press, 2000), 23.

16. Ibid., 24.

17. Even harmless-looking details have their effect. As John Stuart Mill pointed out, "the family is a school for despotism," as quoted inKolmar and Bartkowski, eds., *Feminist Theory*, 44.

18. This is the logic behind the proposed FTAA free trade agreement with Central and Latin America, the recently passed Central American Free Trade Agreement (CAFTA), and the already implemented North American Free Trade Agreement (NAFTA).

19. Hardt and Negri, *Empire*, 150–51.

20. This new slavery is more widespread and more vicious than even the enslavement of Africans in the Americas. See Kevin Bales, *Disposable People: New Slavery in the Global Economy* (Berkeley: University of California Press, 1999).

21. For the following, see Robert W. Venables, *American Indian History: Five Centuries of Conflict and Coexistence*, vol. 2 (Santa Fe: Clear Light Publishers, 2004), 361–81.

22. See, for example, the discussions in *Debating Empire*, ed. Gopal Balakrishnan (London: Verso, 2003). While Hardt and Negri, *Empire*, emphasize the dispersion of power, a few years later, in *Multitude: War and Democracy in the Age of Empire* (New York: Penguin Press, 2004), they observe that war has become part of a "permanent social relation" (12). "Security [the term preferred by the Bush administration to the older notion of defense] requires rather actively and constantly *shaping the environment through military and/or police activity*" (20, emphasis in original). Ellen Meiksins Wood, "A Manifesto for Global Capitalism?" in *Debating Empire,* points out the continued importance of top-down political power: "However much class domination has shifted to the 'economy,' capital would be very uneasy if extra-economic coercive powers were in the hands of a truly democratic state" (80). David Harvey, *The New Imperialism* (Oxford: Oxford University Press, 2003) sums it up: "The US engages in both coercive and hegemonic practices simultaneously, though the balance between these two facets in the exercise of power may shift from one period to another and from one administration to another" (40).

23. This figure is claimed in a 1996 class action lawsuit by Eloise Cobell against the U.S. Department of the Interior. Reported on PBS by the *Newshour with Jim Lehrer*, September 17, 2002 (on the Web: http://www.pbs.org/newshour/extra/features/jan-june02/indian_land.html; accessed June 14, 2006).

24. Jonathan Schell, *The Unconquerable World: Power, Nonviolence, and the Will of the People* (New York: Metropolitan Books, 2003), 231.

25. Vine Deloria, Jr., *For This Land: Writings on Religion in America* (New York: Routledge, 1999), 48.

26. Hannah Arendt, *On Violence* (New York: Harcourt, Brace & World, 1970), 42, 52. "Power and violence are opposites; where the one rules absolutely, the other is absent," she writes (56). Note, however, that "no government exclusively based on the means of violence has ever existed," even the slave owners needed to construct a power base (50). Nevertheless, there are instances when "utterly impotent regimes" were in existence for a long time because there was no challenge (49).

27. Schell, *Unconquerable World*, 387.

28. Quoted in Churchill, *Struggle*, 371.

29. Ibid., 370. Churchill argues that one of the distinguishing marks between Indian and Western civilization is that while the West needs to dominate everything, for Indians not even nature is an enemy to be overcome.

30. For a more detailed analysis of these matters see Joerg Rieger, *Remember the Poor: The Challenge to Theology in the Twenty-First Century* (Harrisburg, Pa.: Trinity Press International, 1998), chapter 3, with references to Jacques Lacan and Walter Benjamin. See also Joerg Rieger, ed., *Opting for the Margins: Postmodernity and Liberation in Christian Theology*, American Academy of Religion, Reflection and Theory in the Study of Religion (Oxford: Oxford University Press, 2003), 181–85.

31. I deal with the question of a reversal of power in more detail in *Opting for the Margins*, 185ff.

32. Deloria, *For This Land*, 101.

33. Even Gayatri Chakravorti Spivak has lately agreed that there are ways in which the subaltern can indeed speak. See her book *A Critique of Postcolonial Reason: Toward a History of the Vanishing Present* (Cambridge, Mass.: Harvard University Press, 1999), 306–11.

34. For the reference to Engels see Hannah Arendt, *On Violence*, 11–12.

35. Relationality also finds expression in reciprocity. George E. Tinker, in *Spirit and Resistance: Political Theology and American Indian Liberation* (Minneapolis: Fortress Press, 2004), 19–20, 108–9, points out that even necessary violence, such as hunting or harvesting, needs the spirit of reciprocity. Those who hunt and harvest need to prepare themselves spiritually, asking permission from the animals and crops and giving thanks. An egalitarian balance includes all of nature. For more on the limits of life, see Tinker, *Spirit*, 20.

36. Deloria, *For This Land*, 263; Deloria adds that these insights are not the exclusive property of Native tribal traditions.

37. Ibid., 282: "Tribal religions were almost entirely focused on the group. The individual may have done the sun dance or vision quest but the traditional motivation was always to sacrifice for the benefit of the people."

38. Churchill, in *Struggle*, 19–24, demonstrates the geographical and political feasibility of Native American nations by drawing up a comparison to other small nations; the Navajos, for instance, own more land than some of the smaller European nations like Denmark, Switzerland, and the Netherlands; the Lakota Nation owns land that includes the one hundred most mineral-rich square miles of the earth. Nevertheless, he also makes clear that claims to the land would not lead to dispossession and eviction of individual non-Indian landholders; the thrust is to recover public land of state parks, forests, grasslands, military reservations, and sometimes corporate holdings. See ibid., 382ff.

39. Churchill, *Struggle*, 390.

40. Tinker, *Spirit and Resistance*, 14. Tinker finds a problem with Latin American liberation theology where "small but culturally integrous communities stand to be swallowed up by the vision of a classless society, an international workers' movement, or a burgeoning majority of Third World urban poor" (104). Unfortunately, his examples are from decades-old texts and do not take into account more recent developments. Nevertheless, it is true that the various liberation theologies will need to enter into a more sustained conversation with Native American traditions. Deloria, in *For This Land* (115) also calls for collaboration even though he had initially been highly critical of liberation theology because he perceived it as an effort of white liberal America to take over the particular struggles of liberation. See ibid., 100–107.

41. Tinker, in *Spirit* (15), quotes a letter by General William T. Sherman from the 1860s that the Indians do not know greed and thus do not understand the value of private ownership and property, an important pillar of civilization. Tinker argues that the Indian people certainly knew greed but had better mechanisms for dealing with it, for instance, by emphasizing the community before the individual—something that was often challenged by the missionaries who resented the fact that Native Americans would give away wealth freely. Tinker reports that in his own tribe of the Osage Nation people would not be considered for ruling elders unless they had given away all their belongings at least four times (*Spirit*, 19).

42. Ibid., 107. Here, Tinker points out the more subtle levels of this concern for the land, which is part of ceremonies, symbols, architecture, and the symbolic order of every tribe.

43. These issues are among others spelled out by Steven Charleston, "From Medicine Man to Marx," in *Native American Religious Identity: Unforgotten Gods*, ed. Jace Weaver (Maryknoll, N.Y.: Orbis, 1998), 168. Charleston challenges his Native American brothers and sisters to go beyond a recuperation of the Native traditions in their esoteric forms and consider economic implications.

44. Tinker, *Spirit*, 113.

45. The power of the king is challenged more strongly in earlier times, particularly in the time during and after the reign of Kings David and Solomon, until the division of Israel. See Crüsemann, *Widerstand*, 123–24.

46. See, for example, Tinker, *Spirit*, 55–78, and the more detailed reflections of Deloria, *For This Land*, 261–68.

47. This is the point of Tinker in *Missionary Conquest: The Gospel and Native American Cultural Genocide* (Minneapolis: Fortress Press, 1993); see also Tinker, *Spirit*, 103; even a Las Casas is no exception.

48. Tinker, *Spirit*, 26–27: "The liberation of euro-american peoples must be rooted in confession and repentance with respect to their relationship with the native peoples of this continent." Deloria, *For This Land*, 47: "We have traditionally skirted the question of evil in the world by observing, first, the needless suffering of people and jumping almost immediately to the question of how god can allow such things to happen." We should be asking, "why do men do evil things?"

49. Churchill, *Struggle*, 26, shows how restoring both land and independent nationhood to Native Americans amounts to the liberation of all, due to the implied challenge of economic, political, and military power.

50. Vine Deloria, Jr., *God Is Red: A Native View of Religion* (Golden, Colo.: Fulcrum Publishing, 1994), 284.

5. FROM METAPHORS AND MODELS TO MAPS

1. *New Oxford Dictionary of English*, s.v. "archipelago." The words of the definition have been formed as an archipelago of meaning—island by island—within the flow of the page.

2. Sallie McFague, *Models of God: Theology for an Ecological, Nuclear Age* (Philadelphia: Fortress Press, 1987), 38.

3. Mary Parker Buckles, *Margins: A Naturalist Meets Long Island Sound* (New York: North Point, 1997), xiii.

4. This summary is based on her presentation of our "new sensibility" and metaphorical theology in *Models of God*, 3–57.

5. In *Models of God*, McFague claims that a model is a metaphor with "staying power," such as God the Father (34).

6. McFague, *Models of God*, 40.

7. Sallie McFague, *Super, Natural Christians: How We Should Love Nature* (Minneapolis: Fortress Press, 1997), 94–95.

8. Rose Farrington, "Childhood Memories," in *Recollections from a Shoreline: North Beach Historical Society*, ed. Helen Weller (Perth, Western Australia: The Nine Club, 1980), 117. Emphasis added.

9. Annie Dillard, *Holy the Firm* (New York: Harper & Row, 1977), 23.

10. Rachel Carson's first essay, originally entitled "The World of Waters," was written that "we might shed our human perceptions of length and breadth and time and place, and enter vicariously into a universe of all-pervading water." See *Lost Woods: The Discovered Writing of Rachel Carson*, ed. Linda Lear (Boston: Beacon Press, 1998), 4. For Carson's environmental ontology, see Nancy M. Victorin-Vangerud, "Wisdom for Our Own Good: Rachel Carson's Oceanic Vision," *Seachanges: Journal of Women Scholars of Religion and Theology* 3 (2003), http://www.wsrt.com.au. The image "sea-change" alludes to the "rich and strange" transformations of Shakespeare's characters in *The Tempest*, Act 1, Scene II, lines 399–407.

11. Sheila Greeve Davaney, "Mapping Theologies: An Historicist Guide to Contemporary Theology," in *Changing Conversations: Religious Reflection and Cultural Analysis*, ed. Dwight N. Hopkins and Sheila Greeve Davaney (New York: Routledge, 1996), 26.

12. Tim Winton, *Land's Edge* (Sydney: Picador, 1993), 10.

13. In "Mapping Theologies," Davaney presents "an historicist guide" to "redraw some of the boundaries" and "add a few new landmarks" to the contemporary "theological landscape" (26).

14. McFague develops the concept of an "imaginative picture," based on Dennis Nineham's evaluation that "at the level of the imagination . . . contemporary Christianity is most weak," in *The Myth of God Incarnate*, ed. John Hick (Philadelphia: Westminster, 1977), 201–2, quoted in *Models of God*, 31. I am inspired by Ursula Le Guin, who drew the archipelagic map of Earthsea for the first book of her trilogy, *A Wizard of Earthsea* (Berkeley: Parnassus, 1968). In *Tales from Earthsea* (London: Orion, 2001), Le Guin redrew the map, after she "happily discovered a very old one in the Archives in Havnor" (xiii). She muses, "Imagination like all living things lives now, and it lives on true change . . . I lose my way on islands I thought I knew by heart" (xiv, xv).

15. In "Thinking Like a Mountain," Aldo Leopold challenged humans to become biotic citizens rather than conquerors of the land-community. See *A Sand County Almanac* (1949; repr., London: Oxford University Press, 1968), 129–33.

16. Jay B. McDaniel, *Earth, Sky, Gods, and Mortals: Developing an Ecological Spirituality* (Mystic, Conn.: Twenty-Third Publications, 1990), 38.

17. In the novel, *Dirt Music* (Sydney: Picador, 2001), Tim Winton tells the story of a wounded man, Luther Fox, who experiences a seascape of holy transformation (352, 354).

18. Geoffrey Blainey, *The Tyranny of Distance: How Distance Shaped Australia's History* (1968, repr., Sydney: Macmillian, 2001).

19. A. Grenfell Price, *Island Continent: Aspects of the Historical Geography of Australia and Its Territories* (Sydney: Angus and Robertson, 1972), 33–51.

20. "Thought experiment" is key to Sallie McFague's metaphorical theology as a playful and heuristic venture. See *Models of God*, 31.

21. Epeli Hau'ofa, "Our Sea of Islands," in *A New Oceania: Rediscovering Our Sea of Islands*, ed. Eric Waddell, Vijay Naidu, and Epeli Hau'ofa (Suva, Fiji: University of the South Pacific, 1993), 139.

22. McFague, *Models of God*, 10. See also McFague, *The Body of God: An Ecological Theology* (Minneapolis: Fortress Press, 1993), 15. In *Life Abundant: Rethinking Theology and Economy for a Planet in Peril* (Minneapolis: Fortress Press, 2001), McFague describes modernity's worldview: "Atomistic thinking, imagining the tiniest parts of reality as separate units colliding with each other in random ways but manipulable by human design, began to seep into the cultural consciousness" (78–79).

23. Liana Joy Christensen, *See the Islands* (Sydney: University of Technology, 2000), vi. The *New Oxford Dictionary of English* places the origin of the word *archipelago* in the early sixteenth century, "from Italian *arcipelago*, from Greek *arkhi-* 'chief' + *pelagos* 'sea'. The word was originally used as a proper name (the Archipelago Aegean Sea): the general sense arose because the Aegean Sea was notable for its large numbers of islands."

24. See my essays, "Sea-ing Spirit: Ecotheological Reflections on a Coastal Sense of Place," in *Architecture, Aesth/Ethics and Religion*, ed. Sigurd Bergmann (Frankfurt am Main, Germany: Verlag für interkulturelle Kommunikation, 2005), 159–86; "Sea-ing Faith, Fathoming Faith: Ecotheology in a World of Waters," in *Ecology and Spirituality: A Dialogue among Human Beings, the Land and the Sea*, ed. Chen Nan-Jou (Tainan, Taiwan: Ji-Kong Press, 2003), 131–66; "Sea-ing Faith, Fathoming Faith: Reflections on a Coastal Sense of Place,"*Eremos: Exploring Spirituality in Australia*, no. 79 (May 2002): 17–21; and "'The Sea Is Our Life!' Cross-Cultural Reflections on a Coastal Sense of Place," *In God's Image: Journal of Asian Women's Resource Centre for Culture and Theology* 20, no. 4 (December 2001): 34–38.

25. In *The Body of God*, McFague contrasts a modern, mechanical worldview with a postmodern, organic one: "Everything that exists—from the most distant galaxies to the tiniest fragment of life—has a common beginning and a common history: at some level and in a remote

or intimate way, everything is related to everything else. We are distant relatives to the stars and kissing cousins with the oceans, plants, and other creatures on earth" (27).

26. "World-traveling" is Maria C. Lugones's postcolonial image of cross-cultural and cross-racial learning based on love, rather than arrogance, assimilation, or conquest. See "Playfulness, 'World'-Traveling, and Loving Perception," *Hypatia* 2, no. 2 (1987): 3–19. For Lugones, "world-traveling" is an open, uncertain, imaginative, and surprising practice of seeing the other and oneself according to the worldview of the other.

27. Mary Yarmirr, from *Croker Island,* as cited in Nonie Sharp, *Saltwater People: The Waves of Memory* (Crows Nest, New South Wales: Allen & Unwin, 2002), 27. In a rejection of the *terra nullius* map, the Australian High Court recognized native title to sea country claimed by the Croker Islanders in Yarmirr v. Northern Territory on September 18, 2001.

28. Sharp, *Saltwater People*, xiii. Sharp claims that while seascapes have been part of the Western cultural tradition, artists (as observers) have portrayed them with a sublime aesthetic. But for saltwater people, the sights, sounds, and flows of the sea are animated with memory, ancestors, and daily communication. "Cross-cultural explorations of seascapes are only beginning. There is a need to reshape and expand our understanding of seascape, and to locate the traditions of people whose lives speak the movement, the sounds, the vibrancy and strength, the cross-currents of the sea" (55).

29. Raging storms, drownings, invaders, and colonialists—these come by the sea with sorrow, and are held in the seascapes of memory. See Sharp, *Saltwater People*, 82–84.

30. Ibid., 92–120.

31. Ibid., 97.

32. Lanani Marika, *Saltwater: Yirrkala Bark Paintings of Sea Country, Recognizing Indigenous Sea Rights* (Yirrkala, Northern Territories: Buku-Larrngay Mulka Centre, 1999), 19.

33. Hau'ofa, "Our Sea of Islands," 10–11.

34. Ibid., 5, hereafter cited in text.

35. Hau'ofa, "A Beginning,"*A New Oceania*, 131.

36. Ibid., 139.

37. J. B. Harley, "Deconstructing the Map," in *Writing Worlds: Discourse, Text, and Metaphor in the Representation of Landscape*, ed. Trevor Barnes and James Duncan (London: Routledge, 1992), 238.

38. William Wohlforth, "The Stability of a Unipolar World," *International Security* 21, no. 1 (Summer 1999): 6, 24, quoted by Gary M. Simpson, as indicative of the U.S. "neoconservative empire," in "Hope in the Face of Empire: Failed Patriotism, Civil International Publicity, and Patriotic Peacebuilding," *Word and World: Theology for Christian Ministry* 25, no. 2 (Spring 2005): 131.

39. Mary Parker Buckles, *Margins*, 270.

40. Catherine Keller, *From a Broken Web: Separation, Sexism, and Self* (Boston; Beacon Press, 1986),105.

41. Attributed to St. Columba, in Ray Simpson, *A Holy Island Prayer Book* (Norwich, England: Canterbury, 2002), 32

42. Catherine Keller, *Face of the Deep: A Theology of Becoming* (London: Routledge, 2002), 230. I am indebted to Keller's work in helping me construct theology in an archipelagic context. See Nancy M. Victorin-Vangerud, "Thinking like an Archipelago: Beyond Tehomophobic Theology," *Pacifica: Australian Theological Studies* 16, no. 2 (June 2003): 153–72.

43. In *Red: Passion and Patience in the Desert*, Terry Tempest Williams begins her essay "America's Redrock Wilderness" with the following declaration: "Wilderness is not a belief. It is a place" (61). She then lists place after place in the desertlands of Utah—canyons, mountains, gulches, hollows, etc. (61–69). In Utah, "We know these places by name" (61). I am grateful

to Nancy Menning for her paper, "Love as Complacency: A Thomistic Interpretation of Terry Tempest Williams' *Leap*," (Midwest AAR/SBL Meeting, Luther Seminary, St. Paul, Minnesota, April 1, 2005).

44. George Seddon, *Landprints: Reflections on Place and Landscape* (Cambridge: Cambridge University, 1997), 111.

45. John Inge, *A Christian Theology of Place* (Hampshire, England: Ashgate, 2003), ix.

46. Ibid., 32.

47. Various examples include: Yi-Fu Tuan, *Topophilia: A Study of Environmental Perception, Attitudes, and Values* (Eaglewood Cliffs, N.J.: Prentice Hall, 1974); Gillian Rose, *Feminism and Geography: The Limits of Geographical Knowledge* (Cambridge: Polity, 1993); Simon Schama, *Landscape and Memory* (New York: Alfred A. Knopf, 1995); Keith H. Basso, *Wisdom Sits in Places: Landscape and Language among the Western Apache* (Albuquerque: University of New Mexico Press, 1996); Edward Casey, *The Fate of Place: A Philosophical History* (Berkeley: University of California Press, 1997); Doreen Massey, John Allen, and Philip Sarre, ed., *Human Geography Today* (Cambridge: Polity, 1999); Robert M. Hamma, *Landscapes of the Soul: A Spirituality of Place* (Notre Dame, Ind.: Ave Maria, 1999); and Philip Sheldrake, *Spaces for the Sacred: Place, Memory, and Identity* (London: SCM, 2001). Examples of constructive theologians drawing on place: Ivone Gebara, *Longing for Running Water: Ecofeminism and Liberation* (Minneapolis: Fortress Press, 1999); Roald Kristiansen, "Arctic Ecotheology," *Ecotheology* 9 (July 2000): 8–26; Denis Edwards, ed., *Earth Revealing, Earth Healing: Ecotheology and Christian Tradition* (Collegeville, Minn.: Liturgical Press, 2001); Steven Bouma-Prediger, *For the Beauty of the Earth: A Christian Vision of Creation Care* (Grand Rapids, Mich.: Baker Academic, 2001); and George E. Tinker, *Spirit and Resistance: Political Theology and American Indian Liberation* (Minneapolis: Fortress Press, 2004).

48. Sigurd Bergmann, *God in Context: A Survey of Contextual Theology* (Hants, England: Ashgate, 2003), 45, 57, 70.

49. See Tony Kelly, *A New Imagining: Towards an Australian Spirituality* (Melbourne, Victoria: CollinsDove, 1990); G. Ferguson and J. Chryssavgis, ed., *The Desert Is Alive: Dimensions of Australian Spirituality* (Melbourne, Victoria: Joint Board of Christian Education, 1990); Anne Pattel-Gray, ed., *Aboriginal Spirituality: Past, Present, Future* (Blackburn, Victoria: HarperCollins, 1996); Rainbow Spirit Elders, *Rainbow Spirit Theology: Towards an Australian Aboriginal Theology* (Blackburn, Victoria: HarperCollins, 1997); Norman C. Habel, *Reconciliation: Searching for Australia's Soul* (Sydney: HarperCollins, 1999); and Peter Malone, ed., *Developing an Australian Theology* (Strathfield, New South Wales: 1999).

50. Geoffrey R. Lilburne, *A Sense of Place: A Christian Theology of the Land* (Nashville, Tenn.: Abingdon, 1989), 71.

51. See David Tacey, *Edge of the Sacred: Transformation in Australia* (Blackburn, Victoria: HarperCollins, 1995), and *Re-enchantment: The New Australian Spirituality* (Sydney: HarperCollins, 2000).

52. Leone Huntsman, *Sand in Our Souls: The Beach in Australian History* (Melbourne, Victoria: Melbourne University Press, 2001). She explains, "It seems to me that the place of the beach in Australian life is too prominent, our attachment to it too deep, for its history to remain unrecorded and its deeper significance to be ignored and unexamined"(5).

53. Frances Bonner, Susan McKay, and Alan McKee, "On the Beach," *Continuum: Journal of Media & Cultural Studies* 15, no. 3 (2001): 269.

54. Meaghan Morris, "On the Beach," in *Cultural Studies*, ed. Lawrence Grossberg, Cary Nelson, and Paula A. Treichler (New York: Routledge, 1992), 458.

55. David Malouf, *A Spirit of Play: The Making of Australian Consciousness* (Sydney: ABC Books, 1998), 31–32.

56. Margaret Somerville, *Body/Landscape Journals* (North Melbourne, Victoria: Spinifex, 1999), 166. I am very grateful to Brenda Roy and her Murdoch University honours project on Somerville's work.

57. Early explorations of "sacred edge" mapping can be found in Nancy M. Victorin-Vangerud, "The Sacred Edge: Seascape as Spiritual Resource for an Australian Eco-eschatology," *Ecotheology* 6 (July 2001 & January 2002): 167–85; and "The Sacred Edge: Women, Sea, and Spirit," *SeaChanges: Journal of Women Scholars of Religion and Theology* 1 (2001): 1–28, http://www.wsrt.com.au (accessed June 14, 2006).

58. Davaney, "Mapping Theologies," 37.

59. These interviews are part of my research project, "Learning the Language of the Sea," begun in 2001–2002 through a Murdoch University Small Research Grant, while I was on faculty.

60. Tim Winton, *Land's Edge*, 36, 85.

61. Karen Baker-Fletcher, *Sisters of Dust, Sisters of Spirit: Womanist Wordings on God and Creation* (Minneapolis: Fortress Press, 1998), 23.

62. Ibid., 25.

63. McFague, *Models of God*, 81.

64. See ibid., 80–81; and Gordon D. Kaufman, *God—Mystery—Diversity: Christian Theology in a Pluralistic* World (Minneapolis: Fortress Press, 1996), 100–101.

65. Veronica Strang, *The Meaning of Water* (Oxford: Berg, 2004), 250, 251, 122.

66. Gill Valentine plays with Edward Said's concept of an "imaginative geography," which he introduced in *Orientalism: Western Conceptions of the Orient* (Harmondsworth, England: Penguin, 1978), 54–55. See Valentine, "Imagined Geographies: Geographical Knowledges of Self and Other in Everyday Life," in *Human Geography Today*, 58.

67. Tim Winton, *The Deep* (Fremantle, Western Australia: Sandcastle Books, 1998).

68. Karl Rahner, *Foundations of Christian Faith* (New York: Seabury, 1978), 22, quoted in Kaufmann, *God, Mystery, Diversity*, 96. Translation slightly altered by Kaufmann.

69. Dillard, *Holy the Firm*, 21.

6. THE FLESH OF GOD

1. Charles Hartshorne, *Omnipotence and Other Theological Mistakes* (Albany: State University of New York, 1984), 53ff.

2. The world as "body of God" was already launched as a metaphor in her *Models of God: Theology for an Ecological, Nuclear Age* (Philadelphia: Fortress Press, 1987) before being systematically unfolded in *The Body of God: An Ecological Theology* (Minneapolis: Fortress Press, 1993).

3. Catherine Keller, Michael Nausner, Mayra Rivera, eds., introduction to *Postcolonial Theologies: Divinity and Empire* (St. Louis, Mo.: Chalice Press, 2004).

4. Stuart Kauffman is a leading thinker on chaos and complexity in biology and other sciences. See his book, *At Home in the Universe: The Search for Laws of Self-organization and Complexity* (New York: Oxford University Press, 1995), 10.

5. Cf. Stuart Kauffman, *Investigations* (Oxford: Oxford University Press, 2002).

6. The phrase "edge of chaos" has wide currency across the sciences, denoting the phase-transition in which complexity emerges, from a far-from-equilibrium condition that is neither too orderly nor too chaotic. Cf. M. Mitchell Waldrop, *Complexity: The Emerging Science at the Edge of Order and Chaos* (New York: Touchstone, 1992); John Gribbin, *Deep Simplicity: Chaos, Complexity and the Emergence of Life* (London: Penguin, 2004). See also my theological development of this metaphor in *Face of the Deep: A Theology of Becoming* (London: Routledge, 2002).

7. Sallie McFague, *Life Abundant: Rethinking Theology and Economy for a Planet in Peril* (Minneapolis: Fortress Press, 2001), 141

8. Ibid.

9. McFague, *Body of God,* 144.

10. Ibid., 145.

11. In this, McFague's work is close to that of Elizabeth Johnson on one side, Jürgen Molt-mann on the other, in the trinitiarian endeavor to bring the Spirit into its/her own, for which much great twentieth-century work has prepared the way.

12. McFague, *Body of God,* 149.

13. I will elaborate on this idea in my forthcoming "Talking Dirty: Ground Versus Foun-dation," in *Ecospirit,* ed. Catherine Keller and Laurel Kearns (New York: Fordham University Press), 2007.

14. McFague, *Body of God,* 20

15. Ibid., 170

16. "Thus all societies require interplay with their environment; and in the case of liv-ing societies this interplay takes the form of robbery. . . . It is at this point that with life morals become acute. The robber requires justification." Alfred North Whitehead, *Process and Reality: An Essay in Cosmology,* ed. David R. Griffin and Donald W. Sherburne (New York: The Free Press, 1929), 105.

17. See Waldorp, *Complexity,* and Gribbin, *Deep Simplicity.*

18. Graham Ward and McFague continue this anti-Spinozism. Spinoza might have much more to reward a careful Christian reading than the stereotype of "pantheism" suggests, but it is not the task of this meditation to sift the real Spinoza, a Jewish philosopher asking impossibly lonely questions at the ferociously anti-Semitic beginning of modernity, from the straw man of pantheism. See Graham Ward, *True Religion* (Oxford: Oxford University Press, 2003), 87–88.

19. See McFague on Augustine in *Life Abundant,* 164; also, similarly, see Moltmann on Augustine, not coincidentally a climactic moment of *The Spirit of Life: A Universal Afirmation* (Minneapolis: Fortress Press, 1992), 98.

20. See, for example, the Cornwall Declaration, available at http://www.acton.org/ppolicy/environment/cornwall.html (accessed June 12, 2006).

21. McFague, *The Body of God,* 143.

22. From Nicholas of Cusa, "De Docta Ignorantia," cited in Keller, *Face of the Deep,* 206.

23. See Boston Women's Health Book Collective, *Our Bodies, Ourselves: A New Edition for a New Era* (Boston: Touchstone, 2005).

24. John Gribbin, *Deep Simplicity: Bringing Order to Chaos and Complexity* (New York: Random House, 2004), 109.

25. Ibid.

26. I would not argue, as some leading thinkers in science and religion are tempted to do, that divine agency should be located within these indeterminacies, as though to be squeezed into the openings of the open system: that would mean just another "God of the gaps." See John C. Polkinghorne, *Exploring Reality: Intertwining Science and Religion* (New Haven, Conn.: Yale University Press, 2006).

27. See Catherine Keller, "Salvation Flows: Eschatology for a Feminist Wesleyanism," *Quar-terly Review* 4 (2003).

28. See McFague, *Body of God,* 150, 162–70.

29. See my "Politics of Love," with Mario Costa and Anna Mercedes, in Peter Heltzel, ed., *Empire and Evangelicalism* (Oxford: Oxford University Press, 2007).

30. See Catherine Keller, *Face of the Deep: A Theology of Becoming* (New York: Routledge, 2003), 124–40.

7. THE HUMAN NICHE IN EARTH'S ECOLOGICAL ORDER

1. For my view of the utter dependence of the entire universe, and human existence in particular, on the divine creativity, see *In the beginning . . . Creativity* (Minneapolis: Fortress Press, 2004).

2. *The Interpretation of Cultures* (New York: Basic Books, 1973), 67. The sociobiologists C. J. Lumsden and E. O. Wilson, with their concept of "gene-culture coevolution," appear to concur with this judgment; see *Promethean Fire: Reflections on the Origin of Mind* (Cambridge, Mass.: Harvard University Press, 1983).

3. Geertz, *Interpretation of Cultures,* 49.

4. See Terrence Deacon, *The Symbolic Species: The Co-evolution of Language and the Brain* (New York: Norton, 1997).

5. I argued this point in detail in my book, *In Face of Mystery: A Constructive Theology* (Cambridge, Mass.: Harvard University Press, 1993), see esp. pt. 2. See also *In the beginning . . . Creativity*, esp. pp. 82–86 and 93–100.

6. For a full discussion of human creativity, see *In the beginning . . . Creativity*, chap. 3.

7. The concept of "steps of faith" is developed and elaborated in *In Face of Mystery*, see esp. pp. 63f. and chaps. 17 and 29.

8. *Toward a New Philosophy of Biology* (Cambridge, Mass.: Harvard University Press, 1988), 435.

9. For further discussion of "serendipitous creativity" and of evolutionary and historical "trajectories," see *In Face of Mystery*, chaps. 19–20; and *In the beginning . . . Creativity*, chaps. 1–3. See also footnote 11, below.

8. For further elaboration, see *In the beginning . . . Creativity*, pp. 80–100.

9. According to the new theories of complexity that are now appearing, *complexity itself*—as mysterious as this may sound—is what brings forth new forms of being. It has been the gradual growth, over billions of years, of increasingly complex organizational patterns—first in galaxies and stars, and atoms and molecules—that eventually made possible the emergence of life. It was the increasing complexity of life which gradually brought into being the countless life-forms that have evolved, including those forms that have become conscious, thoughtful, imaginative, and responsible agents—humans. Creativity presents itself, thus, as somehow emerging—mysteriously, without explanation—between the order and the disorder, the "information" and the "noise" (to use the more technical terms in which these analyses are often expressed) always found in systems and structures. The womb within which new forms are created is this complex interactive intermix of order and disorder, sometimes coming to the very "edge of chaos," as it is sometimes put. (See *In the beginning . . . Creativity*, pp. 89–93, for a larger discussion of this mystery. My account there is based on Mark C. Taylor's recent book, *The Moment of Complexity: Emerging Network Culture* [Chicago: University of Chicago Press, 2001], especially chaps. 4–5; the quoted phrase is on p. 16. Taylor explores in detail some of the important recent literature dealing with these matters.)

10. A much more elaborate sketch of the ethic implied by the *biohistorical* character of human existence will be found in *In Face of Mystery*, chaps. 10–15. See also *In the beginning . . . Creativity*, esp. chap. 3 and the epilogue.

11. I have attempted to do precisely this in my recent books, *In the beginning . . . Creativity*, chaps. 1–3; *God—Mystery—Diversity: Christian Theology in a Pluralistic World* (Minneapolis: Fortress Press, 1996); and (as part of an overall constructive theology) *In Face of Mystery*, esp. pts. 3 and 4.

8. CRUM CREEK SPIRITUALITY

1. Henry David Thoreau, "Walking," in *The Norton Book of Nature Writing*, ed. Robert Finch and John Elder (New York: W. W. Norton, 1990), 183.

2. Sallie McFague, *The Body of God: An Ecological Theology* (Minneapolis: Fortress Press, 1993), 176.

3. Lew Welch, "Gentle Goddess," in *Earth Prayers: From around the World*, ed. Elizabeth Roberts and Elias Amidon (San Francisco: HarperSanFrancisco, 1991), 142.

4. As I perform a retrieval of the Spirit's *earthen* identity in this chapter, I also hope to recover the Spirit's *female* identity. As God's indwelling, corporeal presence within the created order, the Spirit is variously identified with feminine and maternal characteristics in the biblical witness. In the Bible the Spirit is envisioned as God's helping, nurturing, inspiring, and birthing presence in creation. The mother Spirit Bird in the opening creation song of Genesis, like a giant hen sitting on her cosmic nest egg, broods over the earth and brings all things into life and fruition. In turn, this same hovering Spirit Bird, as a dove that alights on Jesus as he comes up through the waters of his baptism, appears in all four of the Gospels to signal God's approval of Jesus' public work. In this chapter, I will take the liberty of referring to the Spirit as "she" in order to recapture something of the biblical understanding of God as feminine Spirit within the created order.

5. Plato, *Timaeus,* in *The Collected Dialogues of Plato*, ed. Edith Hamilton and Huntington Cairns (Princeton: Princeton University Press, 1961), 42–49, 89–92.

6. Peter Brown, *The Body and Society: Men, Women, and Sexual Renunciation in Early Christianity* (New York: Columbia University Press, 1988), 160–89.

7. Augustine, *The Confessions,* trans. Edward Bouverie Pusey, Great Books of the Western World, vol. 18 (Chicago: Encyclopedia Britannica, 1952), 43–61. Also see Peter Brown, *Augustine of Hippo* (Berkeley: University of California Press, 1969), 158–81, 340–97, and Elaine Pagels, *Adam, Eve, and the Serpent* (New York: Random House, 1988), 98–154.

8. See Sallie McFague, *Models of God: Theology for an Ecological, Nuclear Age* (Philadelphia: Fortress Press, 1987), 169–72.

9. McFague, *The Body of God*, 141–50.

10. Ibid.*,* 143.

11. The hope for a recovery of Christian love and passion for flesh and the body is to go back to the future, to retrieve the Bible's fecund earth symbols for God as the beginning of a new ecological Christianity. Deep strains within Christian spirituality are marked by indifference (or even hostility) to "this world" in favor of "the world to come." But not all Christian thinkers have suffered from this debilitating dualism. In the thirteenth century c.e., St. Francis of Assisi celebrated the four cardinal elements, along with human beings and animal beings, as members of the same cosmic family parented by a caring creator God. St. Francis's poetry is suffused with biophilic earth imagery. "Be praised my lord for Brother Wind and for the air and cloudy days/ Be praised my lord for Sister Water because she shows great use and humbleness in herself and preciousness and depth/Be praised my lord for Brother Fire through whom you light all nights upon the earth/Be praised my lord because our sister Mother Earth sustains and rules us and raises food to feed us" (St. Francis of Assisi, "Be Praised My Lord with All Your Creatures," in *Earth Prayers*, 226–27).

12. Hildegard of Bingen, *Scivias*, trans. Mother Columba Hart and Jane Bishop (New York: Paulist, 1979), 2.1: 150.

13. Ibid., 3.7.9: 418.

14. Elizabeth Dreyer, "An Advent of the Spirit: Medieval Mystics and Saints," in *Advents of the Spirit: An Introduction to the Current Study of Pneumatology*, ed. Bradford E. Hinze and D. Lyle Dabney (Marquette, Wisc.: Marquette University Press, 2001), 134.

15. I have drawn my knowledge about the Crum Creek watershed from Roger Latham, "The Crum Woods in Peril: Toward Reversing the Decline of an Irreplaceable Resource for Learning, Research, Recreation and Reflection," http://www.swarthmore.edu/NatSci/Biology/bio_professors/latham/crumwoods.html; "Crum Creek Watershed: A Protection Guide," Chester-Ridley-Crum Watersheds Association pamphlet; and "Crum Creek 1995," report by the Advanced

Research Biology Students of Conestoga High School, Pennsylvania, under the direction of Norman E. Marriner.

16. McFague, *Models of God*, 72.

17. McFague, *Body of God*, 149.

18. Ibid., 59–69.

19. John B. Cobb, Jr., "Protestant Theology and Deep Ecology," in *Deep Ecology and World Religions: New Essays on Sacred Ground*, ed. David Landhis Barnhill and Roger S. Gottlieb (Albany: State University of New York Press, 2001), 223. Other environmental theologians make a similar point. James A. Nash says that while "only the Creator is worthy of worship, all God's creatures are worthy of moral consideration" (*Loving Nature: Ecological Integrity and Christian Responsibility* [Nashville: Abingdon, 1991], 96).

20. McFague, *Body of God*, 209, 211.

9. THE GLOBALIZATION OF NOTHING AND CREATIO EX NIHILO

1. George Ritzer, *The Globalization of Nothing* (Thousand Oaks, Calif.: Pine Forge Press, 2004), 143.

2. William Schweiker, *Theological Ethics and Global Dynamics in the Time of Many Worlds* (Malden, Mass.: Blackwell, 2004), 39.

3. Sallie McFague, *Life Abundant: Rethinking Theology and Economy for a Planet in Peril* (Minneapolis: Fortress Press, 2001), 20.

4. James Weldon Johnson, from "The Creation," in *God's Trombones: Seven Negro Sermons in Verse* (1927; repr., New York: Penguin, 1976), 17.

5. To identify myself as an African American womanist Christian liberation ethicist is to embrace the term for a black feminist ("womanist") coined by Alice Walker, as a way of affirming my particular understanding of my self-identity and vocation. This also means that my ethical reflection is guided by the following assumptions: (*a*) authoritative ethical thinking recognizes its own biases and the biases that pervade the sociomoral context, (*b*) particularity, such as communal or social group identity, is critical, for it is not autonomous selves but communal selves or social groups who are moral actors, (*c*) morality and moral choices are embedded in a context, in a specific locale and time period, (*d*) historicity or a sense of time, of the relationship between the past, the present, and the future, is important, (*e*) we must affirm our embodiment, that we are human beings whose physical attributes and needs do matter as we form and interact in moral communities, and (*f*) to do womanist liberation thinking is to emphasize the relative character of the ethical; the ethical is always relative to specific, concrete circumstances.

6. Ritzer, *The Globalization of Nothing*, 3, hereafter cited in text.

7. *Encyclopedia of Social Theory*, ed. George Ritzer, s.v. "Globalization" (by Frank Lechner) (Thousand Oaks, Calif.: Sage Publications, 2006), quoted in Ritzer, *Globalization of Nothing*, 72.

8. Schweiker, *Theological Ethics*, xi–xii, hereafter cited in text.

9. McFague, *Life Abundant*, 89–93, hereafter cited in text.

10. "The Creation" was written by James Weldon Johnson, who was born during Reconstruction in 1871 and died in 1938. The poem is one of a collection of poems entitled *God's Trombones: Seven Negro Sermons in Verse* (New York: Viking, 1927). This collection was published late in Johnson's career and was adapted for stage several times.

11. *A Handbook of Theological Terms*, ed. Van A. Harvey, s.v. "creation" (New York: Macmillan, 1964), 62–64. Harvey notes that *creatio ex nihilo* has lost precise meaning today and is regarded as a mythological symbol for classical theological affirmations about creation.

12. Johnson, "The Creation," 17–18. I will allow Johnson's use of the male pronoun for God throughout this section of the essay, in which I explicate the poem.

13. *Exploring Poetry*, Gale. Gale Group, Inc., http://www.english.uiuc.edu/maps/poets/g_l/johnson/creation.htm (accessed May 27, 2005).

14. Johnson, "The Creation," 19.

15. Ibid., 20.

10. IT'S ABOUT TIME

1. Sallie McFague, *Life Abundant: Rethinking Theology and Economy for a Planet in Peril* (Minneapolis: Fortress Press, 2001).

2. In response to the attacks of September 11, President Bush repeatedly identified shopping, spending, and buying as signs of American normalcy—indications that American citizens would not give in to fear nor allow chaos to overtake them. Consumerism was viewed as both the antidote to fear and chaos and a key sign of the nation's resolve not to allow the attacks to dismantle its identity and core values.

3. Harvey Cox, "The Market as God: Living in the New Dispensation" *The Atlantic Monthly* (March 1999), 23.

4. Jeremy Carrette and Richard King, *Selling Spirituality: The Silent Takeover of Religion* (New York: Routledge, 2005), 179.

5. See Sallie McFague, *The Body of God: An Ecological Theology* (Minneapolis: Fortress Press, 1993).

6. McFague, *Life Abundant*, 105.

7. William Greider, *The Soul of Capitalism: Opening Paths to a Moral Economy* (New York: Simon & Schuster, 2003), 17.

8. Ibid., 12.

9. According to the American Academy of Child and Adolescent Psychology, "children in the United States watch an average of three to four hours of television a day. By the time of high school graduation, they will have spent more time watching television than they have in the classroom," *Facts for Families*, no. 54 (Washington, D.C.: AACAP, 2001), 1. According to the State Department, the average adult male spends 29 hours per week watching television while the average adult female spends 34 hours per week (http://www.state.sd.us/doh/Nutrition/TV.pdf; accesed Jun 14, 2006).

10. Wayne Muller, *Sabbath: Finding Rest, Renewal, and Delight in Our Busy Lives* (New York: Bantam Books, 1999), 2.

11. Sharon D. Welch writes thoughtfully about this dynamic. See her *Communities of Resistance and Solidarity: A Feminist Theology of Liberation* (Maryknoll, N.Y.: Orbis, 1985); *A Feminist Ethic of Risk* (Minneapolis: Fortress Press, 1990); *Sweet Dreams in America: Making Ethics and Spirituality Work* (New York: Routledge, 1999); and *After Empire: The Art and Ethos of Enduring Peace* (Minneapolis: Fortress Press, 2004).

12. Muller, *Sabbath,* 160.

13. Ibid., 2.

14. Ibid.

15. Ibid., 5.

16. Ibid.

17. Abraham Joshua Heschel, *The Sabbath: Its Meaning for Modern Man* (New York: Farrar, Straus, and Giroux, 1951), 10.

18. Muller, *Sabbath*, 6.

19. Ibid., 137, 8.

20. See his essay, "In the Beginning is the Listening," in this volume.

21. Slow Food is an internationally proliferating grass-roots movement discussed at length by Carl Honore in *In Praise of Slowness: How a Worldwide Movement Is Challenging the Cult of Speed* (San Francisco: HarperSanFrancisco, 2004).

22. Heschel, *The Sabbath*, 66.

23. Ibid., 68.

24. Greider, *The Soul of Capitalism*, 49.

25. Ibid., 52.

26. See Plato's *The Republic*, book II (http://www.classics.mit.edu/Plato/republic.3.ii.html), and Chapter 1 of Adam Smith's *An Inquiry into the Nature and Causes of the Wealth of Nations,* ed. Edwin Cannan (London: Methuen and Co., Ltd., 1904; first published 1776), available online at http://www.econlib.org/LIBRARY/Smith/smWN.html (accessed June 14, 2006).

27. Frederick Taylor, *The Principles of Scientific Management* (New York: Harper & Brothers, 1929), 5.

28. Ibid., 7

29. Richard Sennett, *The Corrosion of Character: The Personal Consequences of Work in the New Capitalism* (New York: W. W. Norton, 1998), 10.

30. Ibid., 24.

31. Ibid., 21.

32. For a fuller discussion of Ritzer, see Marcia Riggs's essay in this volume.

33. George Ritzer, *The Globalization of Nothing* (Thousand Oaks, Calif.: Pine Forge Press, 2004), 3.

34. Catherine Keller, *Face of the Deep: A Theology of Becoming* (London: Routledge, 2002).

35. Quoted in ibid., 4.

36. Ibid., 53.

37. Muller, *Sabbath*, 114.

38. Heschel, *The Sabbath*, 21.

39. Ibid., 22.

11. THE CHURCH AS A HOUSEHOLD OF LIFE ABUNDANT

1. Sallie McFague, *Life Abundant: Rethinking Theology and Economy for a Planet in Peril* (Minneapolis: Fortress Press, 2001), 199.

2. This overarching metaphor of the church appropriates McFague's work. Ibid.

3. Reinhold Niebuhr, cited in Robert McAfee Brown, *Gustavo Gutiérrez: An Introduction to Liberation Theology* (Maryknoll, N.Y.: Orbis Books, 1990), 85.

4. Ibid.

5. *Summa Contra Gentiles*, book 1, chap. 3 (http://www.nd.edu/~afreddos/courses/264/scgbk1chap1-9.htm). For McFague's comment on this matter, see *Super, Natural Christians: How We Should Love Nature* (Minneapolis: Fortress Press, 1997), 6.

6. Marjorie Hewitt Suchocki puts it this way: "Paradoxically, for God to be revealed to and through our condition is also for God to be hidden through the veil of our condition." See *God, Christ, Church: A Practical Guide to Process Theology*, rev. ed. (New York: Crossroad, 1989), 40.

7. It is not my intention to write more about globalization because there is an abundant literature on this topic, but to use it as a context for reimagining the church. Globalization has been defined in many ways, depending on the concerns and perspective of the one interpreting. In its more generic sense, globalization is about the increasing interconnections of our common life at the global level, which is also to say that our interconnections extend to specific localities. Through fast telecommunication and transportation, our sense of time and space, says Robert Schreiter, is both extended and compressed (*The New Catholicity: Theology between the Global and the Local* [Maryknoll, N.Y.: Orbis Books, 1997], 11). We are globalized to the point that the global is lived locally and the local is lived globally. The global is not simply "out there" but also "in here," wherever our location is. The slogan, "think globally and act locally" is not as simple as

it sounds because the lines crisscross. Even the terms "Third World" and "First World" are complex, for much of the Third World lives in the First World, and the First World lives in the Third World. Also, see Pamela Brubaker, *Globalization at What Price? Economic Change and Daily Life* (Cleveland, Ohio: The Pilgrim Press, 2001); Jeremy Brecher and Tim Costello, *Global Village or Global Pillage: Economic Reconstruction from the Bottom Up*, 2nd ed. (Cambridge, Mass.: South End Press, 1998); Teresa Brennan, *Globalization and Its Terrors: Daily Life in the West* (London and New York: Routledge, 2003); Steven Flusty, *De-Coca-Colonization: Making the Globe from the Inside Out* (New York: Routledge, 2004); Scott Sernau, *Bound: Living in the Globalized World* (Bloomfield, Conn.: Kumarian Press, 2000); Akbar Ahmed, ed., *Islam, Globalization, and Postmodernity* (London: Routledge, 1994); M. Featherstone, ed., *Global Culture: Nationalism, Globalization, and Modernity* (London: Sage Publications, 1990); Max Stackhouse with Peter Paris, *God and Globalization: Religion and the Powers of the Common Life* (Harrisburg, Pa.: Trinity Press International, 2000); Chris Arthur, *The Globalization of Communications: Some Religious Implications* (Geneva: WCC Publications; London: World Association for Christian Communication, 1998); Max Stackhouse, Tim Dearborn, and Scott Paeth, ed., *The Local Church in a Global Era: Reflections for a New Century* (Grand Rapids, Mich.: Wm. B. Eerdmans, 2000).

8. Globalization is multidimensional, covering such aspects, according to Arjun Appadurai, as technoscapes (technology), finanscapes (financial), mediascapes (media), ideoscapes (ideology), ethnoscapes (ethnic plurality and migration), and mediscapes (medical) as the universal consequences of the HIV/AIDS and, more recently, SARS epidemic continue to unfold and remind us (Meredith Fort, Mary Anne Mercer, and Oscar Gish, ed., *Sickness and Health: The Corporate Assault on Global Health* [Cambridge, Mass.: South End Press, 2004]). We need to add to the list ecoscapes (ecology) as we are confronted with serious ecological crises. Also, not to be forgotten is religioscapes (Diana Eck, *A New Religious America: How a "Christian Country" Has Become the World's Most Religiously Diverse Nation* [San Francisco: HarperSanFrancisco, 2001]); Helen Rose Ebaugh and Janet Saltzman Chafetz, *Religion and the New Immigrants* [Walnut Creek, Calif.: AltaMira Press, 2000]), especially the encounters among believers of various religions that are becoming more common in localities that were once relatively homogenous. See Arjun Appadurai, "Disjuncture and Difference in the Global Cultural Economy," in Featherstone, ed., *Global Culture*, cited by Anthony H. Richmond, *Global Apartheid: Refugees, Racism, and the New World Order* (Toronto: Oxford University Press, 1994), 32–33. Also, see Roland Robertson, "Globalization and the Future of 'Traditional Religion,'" in Stackhouse and Paris, *God and Globalization*, 53–68. Robertson argues for the multi-dimensional aspect of globalization.

9. Marcus Borg, *The Heart of Christianity: Rediscovering a Life of Faith* (San Francisco: HarperSanFrancisco, 2003), 141.

10. Schreiter, *The New Catholicity*, 82. While most of those who have fallen by the wayside are still concentrated in the global South, citizens in the more affluent global North have not been spared. Thirty years ago the gap in salary between the chief executive officer and the average workers in U.S. corporations was 30 to 1. It is about the same today in Japan and Germany. But the gap has widened dramatically in the U.S., which is now about 519 to 1. See Jim Wallis, "Changing the Wind: The Role of Prophetic Witness and Faith-Based Initiatives in Tackling Inequality," in *Globalization and the Good*, ed. Peter Heslam (Grand Rapids, Mich.: Wm. B. Eerdmans, 2004), 123.

11. Mohandas Gandhi, cited in Carolyn Pogue, ed., *Treasury of Celebrations: Create Celebrations that Reflect Your Values and Don't Cost the Earth* (Kelowna, B.C.: Northstone, 1996), 39. Modified.

12. Migration has been a permanent feature in human history, which is both positive and negative. Recently, however, we have witnessed disturbing patterns in large-scale movements of people that point to a profound new reality of global migration. More than the increasing

movement of people because of cross-border transactions and tourism, or even voluntary movement in pursuit of education or for family reasons, what is disturbing is the massive movement of inhabitants from the global South to more affluent countries of the global North in spite of the tightening of immigration laws and increased surveillance. More particularly alarming is the reality of massive "forced" displacement. This phenomenon has been triggered by the disastrous effects of globalization. See *Moment to Choose: Risking to Be with Uprooted People* (Geneva: WCC Publications, 1996), 9–11.

13. Ted Peters, *Sin: Radical Evil in Soul and Society* (Grand Rapids, Mich.: Wm. B. Eerdmans, 1994), 183. The rise of racist violence against newcomers or longtime resident minorities in countries like Germany and the United States is too well known to require detailed description. Xenophobia is rising steadily in the whole German society. See Stephen Castles, *Ethnicity and Globalization* (London; Thousand Oaks, Calif.: Sage Publications, 2000), 155–56.

In the United States, beyond outright racist violence against minorities, conservative groups and their corporate supporters have been successful in passing legislation that roll back years of affirmative action. Politicians have been able to rally huge support from the population by fanning the people's fears of racial "others." When scrutinized carefully, the California Proposition 209, says Young Lee Hertig, is nothing other than violence dressed in the rhetoric of equality and discrimination. Racist violence can be sophisticated enough to hijack the language of the civil rights movement. Young Lee Hertig, "The Korean Immigrant Church and Naked Public Square," in *Realizing the America of Our Hearts: Theological Voices of Asian Americans,* ed. Fumitaka Matsuoka and Eleazar S. Fernandez (St. Louis: Chalice Press, 2003), 131–146.

14. David Lochhead, *Shifting Realities: Information Technology and the Church* (Geneva: WCC Publications, 1997), 100.

15. Lester Kutz, *Gods in the Global Village: The World's Religions in Sociological Perspective* (Thousand Oaks, Calif.: Pine Forge Press, 1995), 213–14. In a situation where people attempt to redraw boundaries that once seemed safe, new forms of "heresies" are likely to be identified.

16. See Jon Berquist, ed., *Strike Terror No More: Theology, Ethics, and the New War* (St. Louis: Chalice Press, 2002); Lee Griffith, *The War on Terrorism and the Terror of God* (Grand Rapids, Mich.: Wm. B. Eerdmans, 2002); Mark Juergensmeyer, *Terror in the Mind of God: The Global Rise of Religious Violence* (Berkeley: University of California Press, 2000); Ulrich Duchrow and Franz J. Hinkelammert, *Property for People, Not for Profit* (Geneva: WCC Publications, 2004), particularly pages 109–39; Noam Chomsky, *Pirates and Emperors, Old and New: International Terrorism in the Real World* (Cambridge, Mass.: South End Press, 2002).

17. While the overall ecosystem is in danger, it has been in the poor neighborhoods and developing nations that ecological destruction is more acutely felt. Powerful nations have dumped, clandestinely or for some consideration of money and pressure, hazardous and toxic wastes on the poor. The struggling racial communities have discovered that there is a functional relationship between racism and the industry's assault on the environment. "As long as there are . . . minority areas to dump on," argues Leon White, "corporate America won't be serious about finding alternatives to the way toxic materials are produced and managed." See Leon White of the Commission for Racial Justice as cited by Charles Lee, "The Integrity of Justice: Evidence of Environmental Racism," *Sojourners* 19 (February–March 1990): 25. Also, see United Church of Christ Commission for Racial Justice, *Toxic Wastes and Race in the United States: A National Report on the Racial and Socio-Economic Characteristics of Communities with Hazardous Waste Sites* (New York: Public Data Access, Inc., 1987).

Even in the midst of the Cold War, West Germany continued to send its toxic wastes to East Germany, which was desperate for foreign exchange. This was a well-kept secret until it was exposed after the collapse of the Berlin Wall (Center for Investigative Reporting and Bill Moyers, *Global Dumping Ground: The International Traffic in Hazardous Waste* [Washington, D.C.: Seven

Locks Press, 1990], 97). Fifteen tons of incinerator ash from the United States were dumped by a Norwegian ship on Kassa Island off the coast of Guinea in West Africa. A toxic dumping scandal happened near the port town of KoKo, Nigeria, when 150 tons of PCBs (polychlorinated biphenyls) shipped from Italy were discovered and exposed (Art Meyer and Jocele Meyer, *Earth-Keepers: Environmental Perspectives on Hunger, Poverty, and Injustice* [Waterloo, Ont.; Scottdale, Pa.: Herald Press, 1991], 59). The islands and waters of the South Pacific have also become dumping sites for toxic wastes by powerful nations, with disastrous consequences to the health of the Pacific Islanders (Samuel Rayan, "Theological Perspective on the Environmental Crisis," in *Frontiers in Asian Theology: Emerging Trends,* ed. R. S. Sugirtharajah [Maryknoll, N.Y.: Orbis Books, 1994], 225). The global South, indigenous people around the world, and poor communities have been the target of "environmental terrorism" or "radioactive terrorism" by the elite and powerful nations. Eighty to ninety percent of uranium mining and milling in the United States, for example, has taken place in or adjacent to American Indian reservations, with serious consequences to the health of American Indians (Grace Thorpe, "Our Homes Are Not Dumps: Creating Nuclear-Free Zones," in *Defending Mother Earth: Native American Perspectives on Environmental Justice,* ed. Jace Weaver [Maryknoll, N.Y.: Orbis Books, 1996], 47–58).

18. Vandana Shiva, *Stolen Harvest: The Hijacking of the Global Food Supply* (Cambridge, Mass.: South End Press, 2000), 75.

19. Tom Sine, *Mustard Seed versus McWorld: Reinventing Life and Faith for the Future* (Grand Rapids, Mich.: Baker, 1999), 21.

20. Jay McDaniel, *Living from the Center: Spirituality in an Age of Consumerism* (St. Louis: Chalice Press, 2000), 41.

21. Just like any social institutions, the day-to-day life of congregations has been impacted by the ebb and flow of the market. The changes in economic landscape, particularly movements of industries and businesses from one place to another in search of "favorable investment climate" (fat tax break, no Social Security and insurance benefits, no labor unions, and less government control regarding environment) have affected the survival and viability of many local congregations.

The demise of family in the United States, particularly in the 1980s in which around 600,000 farm families lost their land, has created a crisis beyond economic terms (stress, alcoholism, abuse, depression, and suicide) that poses a challenge to ministry among rural churches. Meanwhile, places on the receiving side of the flow of migrant workers have challenged the church to redefine itself and its ministry. See Shannon Jung, et al., *Rural Ministry: The Shape of the Renewal to Come* (Nashville: Abingdon Press, 1998), 100, 114.

In the global South, many local congregations have become dependent on the global market for various reasons. With few local resources, many church members have left their families and gone abroad for work. Some have found well-paying jobs, but the majority are barely making it. Many women have found jobs as domestic helpers and as entertainers, which is often a euphemism for prostitution. Whatever money they save, they send it to their families back home. Many local congregations are dependent on these families for financial support. Family separation has generated new challenges for church ministry in these settings and in places where migrant workers are settling.

22. Keith Russell, *In Search of the Church: New Testament Images for Tomorrow's Congregations* (Bethesda, Md.: Alban Institute, 1994), 76.

23. George B. Thompson, Jr., *Treasures in Clay Jars: New Ways to Understand Your Church* (Cleveland: The Pilgrim Press, 2003), 91–97.

24. Clark Williamson and Ronald Allen, *The Vital Church: Teaching, Worship, Community, Service* (St. Louis: Chalice Press, 1998), 20.

25. C. S. Song speaks of the centrality of the reign of God in his various works, but especially in his book *Jesus and the Reign of God.* The vision of God's reign is, for Song, the all-encompassing

principle, lens, or foundation with which we need to evaluate everything that Jesus did and said. (*Jesus and the Reign of God* [Minneapolis: Fortress Press, 1993], 2).

26. Wallis, "Changing the Wind," 117.

27. See M. Douglas Meeks, *God the Economist: The Doctrine of God and Political Economy* (Minneapolis: Fortress Press, 1989).

28. See Charles Kimball, *When Religion Becomes Evil* (San Francisco: HarperSanFrancisco, 2002).

29. Schreiter, *The New Catholicity*, 16.

30. Richard Falk, cited in Konrad Raiser, *For a Culture of Life: Transforming Globalization and Violence* (Geneva, Switzerland: World Council of Churches, 2002), 38.

31. Marianne Sawicki, "Salt and Leaven: Resistances to Empire in the Street-Smart Paleochurch" in *The Church as Counterculture,* ed. Michael Budde and Robert Brimlow (Albany, N.Y.: State University of New York Press, 2000), 60.

32. New Testament scholars have shown us that Jesus' response to Pilate that his "[*basileia*] is not of this world" (John 18:36), which was a stance adopted by the Johannine community, conveys the nonconformist stance rather than a mark of escapism. Jesus' etiology ("not of this world"), notes Jerome Neyrey, conveys the stance of the Johannine community; Jesus' etiology symbolizes the community. As Jesus is alien from this world and, in fact, hated by this world, so too are the members of the Johannine community. See Jerome Neyrey, *An Ideology of Revolt: John's Christology in Social-Science Perspective* (Philadelphia: Fortress Press, 1988), 116. This work used the insights of cultural anthropologist Mary Douglas. Several New Testament scholars in recent years have made use of Douglas' insights and have found them useful. A more comprehensive exposition on this approach is done by Bruce J. Malina, *Christian Origins and Cultural Anthropology: Practical Models for Biblical Interpretation* (Atlanta: John Knox Press, 1986); Eleazar S. Fernandez, "My Kingship is Not of This World: Must We Abandon the Earth in Order to Go to Heaven?" *Tugón* 11, no. 3 (1991): 393–408.

33. Stanley Hauerwas and William Willimon offer a prophetic critique for a church that has become comfortable with the world in its over-excitement to be relevant to the world. In its attempt to be credible to the world, the liberal church has fallen into what Willimon and Hauerwas call "Constantinian thinking," that is, it has led "Christians to judge their ethical positions, not on the basis of what is faithful to our peculiar tradition, but rather on the basis of how much Christian ethics Caesar can be induced to swallow without choking. See *Resident Aliens: A Provocative Christian Assessment of Culture and Ministry for People Who Know That Something Is Wrong* (Nashville, Tenn.: Abingdon Press, 1989), 72.

34. William McKinney and Wade Clark Roof, *American Mainline Religion* (New Brunswick, N.J.: Rutgers University Press, 1987), 22.

35. Williamson and Allen, *The Vital Church*, 21.

36. See Marcus Borg, *Jesus, A New Vision: Spirit, Culture, and the Life of Discipleship* (San Francisco: Harper & Row, 1987), 142.

37. Saying no. 82, cited in John Fuellenbach, *Church: Community for the Kingdom* (Maryknoll, N.Y.: Orbis Books, 2002), 203.

38. Ibid. His image of the church as one with a burning center and open borders finds resonance in Martin Marty's image of the church as one with "magnetic center" and open edges. See Marty, *The Fire We Can Light* (Garden City, N.Y.: Doubleday & Co., 1975), 220.

39. Meeks, *God the Economist*, 29.

40. Franz Hinkelammert, "The Economic Roots of Idolatry: Entrepreneurial Metaphysics," in *The Idols of Death and the God of Life: A Theology,* ed. Pablo Richard et al. (Maryknoll, N.Y.: Orbis Books, 1983), 165.

41. Ibid., 166.

42. Harvey Cox, "Mammon and the Culture of the Market: A Socio-Theological Critique," in *Liberating Faith: Religious Voices for Justice, Peace, and Ecological Wisdom,* ed. Roger Gottlieb (Lanham, Md.: Rowman & Littlefield, 2003), 274–83.

43. Ibid., 278–79.

44. John Cobb Jr., "Economism or Planetism: The Coming Choice," *Earth Ethics 3* (Fall 1991), cited in McFague, *Super, Natural Christians,* 13. EATWOT (Ecumenical Association of Third World Theologians) members also see globalization as a "new religion." The god of the market is money as well as profit. Its high priests are GATT, WTO, IMF-World Bank; doctrines and dogmas such as import liberalization, deregulation, and so forth; temples are the supermarket; victims on the altar of sacrifice are the majority of the world—the marginalized poor. See Mary John Mananzan, "Globalization and the Perennial Questions of Justice," in *Liberating Faith,* 271.

45. Ernst Bloch, cited in José Míguez Bonino, *Room to Be People: An Interpretation of the Message of the Bible in Today's World,* trans. Vickie Leach (Philadelphia: Fortress Press, 1979), 9–25.

46. See Walter Wink, *Unmasking the Powers: The Invisible Forces That Determine Human Existence* (Philadelphia: Fortress Press, 1986). Wink provides an extensive account of exorcism and its relevance to contemporary issues from a theological angle. "Exorcism in its New Testament context," notes Wink, "is the act of deliverance of a person or institution or society from its bondage to evil, and its restoration to the wholeness intrinsic to its creation." The evil condition is not only purged, but it is going to be replaced with a new way of life. In other words, it means liberation of those who have been possessed by the powers of death and their restoration to a liberated life. Wink points to Jesus' act of cleansing the temple (Mark 11:11, 15-19) as the paradigmatic act of collective exorcism in the New Testament.

47. Meeks, *God the Economist,* 45.

48. C. S. Song, *Jesus, The Crucified People* (Minneapolis: Fortress Press, 1990), 200.

49. John Dominic Crossan, *Jesus: A Revolutionary Biography* (San Francisco: HarperSanFrancisco, 1994), 179–81.

50. McFague, *Life Abundant,* 174–75.

51. McFague, *The Body of God,* 168–69; Also, see her work *Models of God: Theology for an Ecological, Nuclear Age* (Philadelphia: Fortress Press, 1987), 45–57.

52. Song, *Jesus, The Crucified People,* 204.

53. Chuck Latrop, "In Search of a Roundtable," cited in Letty Russell, *Church in the Round: Feminist Interpretation of the Church* (Louisville: Westminster John Knox Press, 1993), 17.

54. "Welcome Table," in *An Advent Sourcebook,* ed. Thomas O'Gorman (Chicago: Liturgy Training Publications, 1988), 50.

55. Peter McLaren, *Revolutionary Multiculturalism: Pedagogies of Dissent for the New Millennium* (Boulder, Colo.: Westview Press, 1997), 197.

56. Roger Gottlieb, *A Spirituality of Resistance* (New York: Crossroad, 1999).

57. James Hudnut-Beumler, *Generous Saints: Congregations Rethinking Ethics and Money* (Bethesda, Md.: Alban Institute, 1999), 2.

58. Ibid., 1.

59. See my work, *Reimagining the Human: Theological Anthropology in Response to Systemic Evil,* particularly pp. 198–99. Also, see Charles Avila, *Ownership: Early Christian Teaching* (Maryknoll, N.Y.: Orbis Books, 1983).

60. Paul Tillich, *The Courage to Be* (New Haven, Conn.: Yale University Press, 1952), 113–54.

61. Douglas John Hall, *Why Christian? For Those on the Edge of Faith* (Minneapolis: Fortress Press, 1998), 135.

62. Raimon Panikkar, *Cultural Disarmament: The Way to Peace* (Louisville: Westminster John Knox Press, 1995), 16.

63. R. B. J. Walker, *One World, Many Worlds: Struggles for a Just World Peace* (London: Zen Books Limited; Boulder, Colo.: Lynne Reinner Publishers, 1988), 169.

64. Loren B. Mead, *The Once and Future Church: Reinventing the Congregation for a New Mission Frontier* (Bethesda, Md.: The Alban Institute, 1991).

65. See Fernandez, *Reimagining the Human*, 25–27.

66. The principal meaning of the word "Islam" is "surrender" or "submission." "Muslim," a cognate word to "Islam," means one who submits to God. See Akbar S. Ahmed, *Islam Today: A Short Introduction to the Muslim World* (New York/London: I. B. Tauris Publishers, 1999), 17.

67. Thich Nhat Hanh, "The Fourteen Mindfulness Trainings of the Order of Interbeing," in *Liberating Faith*, 450.

68. Donald Messer, *A Conspiracy of Goodness: Contemporary Images of Christian Mission* (Nashville: Abingdon Press, 1992), 148.

69. Eleazar S. Fernandez, "Postcolonial Exorcism and Reconstruction: Filipino Americans' Search for Postcolonial Subjecthood," in *Realizing the America of Our Hearts*, 95.

70. Thich Nhat Hanh, *Creating True Peace: Ending Violence in Yourself, Your Family, Your Community, and the World* (New York: Free Press, 2003), 176.

71. Walker, *One World, Many Worlds*, 101.

72. Arundhati Roy, quoted in *Yes: A Journal of Positive Futures*, no. 29 (Spring 2004).

12. ARTISANS OF HOPE, ARTISANS OF WONDER

1. "One of the most famous lines in the culminating sections of one of his most famous dialogues announces that 'there is an old quarrel between philosophy and poetry' [Plato, *The Republic*, in *Plato in Twelve Volumes, Vols. 5 & 6*, trans. Paul Shorey (Cambridge, Mass.: Harvard University Press, 1969), 607b5–6]." Griswold goes on to note that "[n]one of this would matter much if superb poetry left us unmoved, or in any case as we were. Plato's critique depends on the assumption that poetry can and does shape the soul." *The Stanford Encyclopedia of Philosophy*, ed. Edward N. Zalta, s.v. "Plato on Rhetoric and Poetry" (by Charles Griswold), http://plato.stanford.edu/archives/sum2005/entries/plato-rhetoric/ (accessed summer 2005).

2. Representatives from the following organizations have been involved in these conversations in both New York and Washington, D.C.: Global Action to Prevent War; World Culture Organization; Psychologists for Social Responsibility; Search for Common Ground; Conscious Politics; Center for World Religions, Diplomacy, and Conflict Resolution; Institute for Conflict Analysis and Resolution; Friends Committee on National Legislation; Harvard Project on Negotiation; Center for International Conflict Resolution/Columbia University; National Coalition for Dialogue and Deliberation; and TomPaine.com.

3. Sallie McFague, *Models of God: Theology for an Ecological, Nuclear Age* (Philadelphia: Fortress Press, 1987), xii, 33.

4. Ibid., 35, 39.

5. Ibid., 39.

6. Sallie McFague, *Super, Natural Christians: How We Should Love Nature* (Minneapolis: Fortress Press, 1997), 96.

7. Ibid., J.

8. Ibid., 97.

9. Karen McCarthy Brown, "Making *Wanga*: A Haitian Response to an Infamous Case of Police Brutality" (Paine lecture, University of Missouri, Columbia, Mo., October 1999).

10. George Lakoff, *Moral Politics: How Liberals and Conservatives Think*, 2nd ed. (Chicago: University of Chicago Press, 2002), preface, chap. 2, chap. 5.

11. Ibid., 349–58.

12. "Photos allege abuse of Iraqis by British troops," *CNN.com,* Saturday, May 1, 2004, http://edition.cnn.com/2004/WORLD/meast/04/30/iraq.brit.prisoner.abuse/ (accessed June 14, 2006).

13. In May of 2005, Amnesty International asked for an independent investigation: "In Washington, William F. Schulz, executive director of Amnesty International USA, urged President Bush to press for a full investigation of what he called the "atrocious human rights violations at Abu Ghraib and other detention centers." Alan Cowell, "U.S. 'Thumbs its Nose' at Rights, Amnesty Says," *New York Times,* May 26, 2005, A8. In June 2005, some Republican members of the Senate, Lindsey Graham, John McCain, John Warner, and others, also asked for such an independent investigation. "Despite opposition from the White House, some Republicans have begun to join Congressional Democrats in calling for an independent commission to review accusations of abuse of prisoners by American forces in Guantanamo Bay, Cuba, and elsewhere." Douglas Jehl, "Some Republicans Seek Prison Abuse Panel," *New York Times,* June 22, 2005, A14. As of May 2006, no such independent investigations had been conducted.

14. Albert Bandura, "Moral Disengagement in the Perpetration of Inhumanities," *Personality and Social Psychology Review* 3 (Special Issue on Evil and Violence) (1999), 193–209. The quote by Gonzales is not noted by Bandura, but may be found in the transcript of the Amy Goodman radio show, "Gonzales Grilled on Role in Torture at Confirmation Hearing," January 7, 2005, http://www.democracynow.org/article.pl?sid=05/01/07/1621235 (accessed June 13, 2006).

15. On August 2, 2005, the Associated Press reported that 1,801 members of the U.S. military had died in the war in Iraq (Associated Press, "U.S. death toll passes 1,800," *Columbia Daily Tribune,* August 2, 2005). The number of civilian casualties has not been gathered by the United States. However, a research team at the Bloomberg School of Public Health at Johns Hopkins University estimates that 100,000 Iraqi civilians had been killed by October 2004. Elisabeth Rosenthal, "Study Puts Iraqi Deaths of Civilians at 100,000," *New York Times,* October 20, 2004.

16. John Tierney, "Republicans Outnumbered in Academia, Studies Find," *New York Times,* November 18, 2004, A19.

17. Adam Nagourney, "Dean Feisty and Unbowed, Stands by Words on DeLay," *New York Times*, May 23, 2005, A13.

18. Lakoff, chaps. 10, 11, and 13, pp. 201–4, 222–23.

19. The results of this research are described in the following essays: Suzanne Burgoyne, Karen Cockrell, Helen Neville, Peggy Placier, Sharon Welch, Meghan Davidson, Tamara Share, and Brock Fisher, in "Theatre of the Oppressed as an Instructional Practice: A Collaboration between Theatre and Education." *International Conference on the Scholarship of Teaching and Learning Proceedings 2001 and 2002*, ed. David Gosling and Vaneeta D'Andrea. (London: Educational Development Centre, City University, 2003).; See also Sharon D. Welch, "Ceremonies of Gratitude, Awakening, and Accountability: The Theory and Practice of Multicultural Education" in *To Do Our First Works Over,* ed. Jennifer Harvey, Karin A. Case, Robin Hawley Gorsline (Cleveland: Pilgrim Press, 2004), 249–80.

20. Vern Neufeld Redekop, *From Violence to Blessing: How an Understanding of Deep-rooted Conflict Can Open Paths to Reconciliation* (Ottawa: Novalis, Saint Paul University, 2002), 51.

21. Sallie McFague, *The Body of God: An Ecological Theology* (Minneapolis: Fortress Press, 1993), 197.

22. Ibid., 76.

23. McFague, *Models of God*, 117–18.

24. Ibid., 147.

25. Ibid., 148.

26. Ibid., 208.
27. Ibid., 206.
28. Ibid., 203.
29. Ibid., 204.
30. Ibid.
31. McFague, *The Body of God*, 210. Linda Holler also explores the significance of touch, of deep connection, for ethical perception and action, drawing on the experiences of people who are autistic, and on the insights of contemporary Buddhism. Linda Holler, *Erotic Morality: The Role of Touch in Moral Agency* (New Brunswick, N.J.: Rutgers University Press, 2002).
32. McFague, *Super, Natural Christians*, 99.
33. Ibid., 107.

EPILOGUE: HUMAN DIGNITY AND THE INTEGRITY OF CREATION

This essay was written as a lecture, which was delivered at "Reach Out 2004: Second Annual Outreach and Social Justice Conference," November 12-13, 2004, sponsored by Shaughnessy Heights United Church and the Vancouver School of Theology, Vancouver, BC.
1. Iris Murdoch, "The Sublime and the Good," *Chicago Review* 13 (Autumn 1959): 51.
2. John Woolman, *The Journal of John Woolman* (New York: Corinth Books, 1961), 8.
3. See Andrew Michael Flescher, *Heroes, Saints, and Ordinary Morality* (Washington, D.C.: Georgetown Univeristy Press, 2003).
4. *Opus Posthumous: Poems, Plays, Prose* (New York: Vintage, 1990), 163.
5. *The Disinherited Mind: Essays in Modern German Literature and Thought* (Cleveland: World, 1961), 211.
6. As quoted in Flescher, *Heroes,* 186.
7. *Emmanuel College Newsletter* (Toronto: Emmanuel College, Autumn 2004).
8. Gustavo Gutiérrez*A Theology of Liberation: History, Politics, and Salvation*, trans. Sister Caridad and John Eagleson (Maryknoll, N.Y.: Orbis Books, 1971), 201.
9. Dorothee Soelle, *The Silent Cry: Mysticism and Resistance* (Minneapolis: Fortress Press, 2001), 255.
10. Dorothy Day, *The Long Loneliness: The Autobiography of Dorothy Day* (New York: Curtis Books, 1952).
11. Flescher, *Heroes,* 316.
12. As quoted in ibid., 311.

Index